RUSSIAN EAST ARCTIC STUDIES

Proceedings of the International Scientific and Practice Conference
"Resource Economy in the Context of Modern Tendencies of Globalization"

HANKUK UNIVERSITY OF FOREIGN STUDIES
M.K. AMMOSOV NORTH-EASTERN FEDERAL UNIVERSITY

RUSSIAN EAST ARCTIC STUDIES

Proceedings of the International Scientific and Practice Conference

Prof. Bongchul Kim at HUFS
Prof. Larisa Pisareva at NEFU

Resource Economy in the Context of Modern Tendencies of Globalization

HU:iNE

CONTENTS

INTRODUCTION · 7

CHAPTER 1 CONTEMPORARY ISSUES OF RUSSIAN EAST ARCTIC SOCIAL DEVELOPMENT

PROSPECTS OF ENERGY SECURITY OF ARCTIC DISTRICTS OF THE SAKHA REPUBLIC (YAKUTIA) ON THE BASIS OF HYDROCARBON
Mariia Ivanovna Sleptsova 13

THE PRACTICE OF ETHNOLOGICAL EXAMINATION OF INVESTMENT PROJECTS OF THE INDUSTRIAL DEVELOPMENT OF THE TRADITIONAL NATURAL RESOURCE MANAGEMENT TERRITORIES IN THE ARCTIC DISTRICTS OF SAKHA REPUBLIC
Evdokia Innokentievna Burtseva, Anatoly Nickolaevich Sleptsov, Anna Nickolaevna Bysyina, Alla Semenovna Fedorova, Gavril Egorovich Dyachkovskij 31

UNIVERSITY CENTER FOR STRATEGIC PLANNING OF INTELLECTUAL ECONOMY
Afanasiy Afanasjevich Vinokurov, Roman Romanovich Nogovitsin 51

ARCTIC SPACE AS A METHOD OF PRESERVING ETHNIC SELF-IDENTIFICATION
Larisa Yurievna Pisareva 65

CONCEPTUAL MODEL OF THE DEVELOPMENT OF AUTONOMOUS LEARNING SKILLS AMONG YAKUT NATIVE STUDENTS
Uliana Semenovna Borisova, Galina. Mikhailovna Parnikova 85

THE USE OF LANGUAGES OF INDIGENOUS PEOPLES OF NORTH, SIBERIA AND FAR EAST IN SUBJECTS OF THE RUSSIAN FEDERATION IN ACTIVITIES OF PUBLIC AUTHORITIES AND LOCAL GOVERNMENTS
Ivan Vasilievich Yadreev 104

APPROACHES TO THE ACCELERATORS OF CREATOSPHERE IN THE REPUBLIC OF SAKHA (YAKUTIA)
Anna Viktorovna Mikhailova 128

CHAPTER 2 RESOURCE ECONOMY: ARCTIC DIMENTION

NEW APPROACHES TO COLD AS A NATURAL RESOURCE AND ECONOMIC CATEGORY
Andrey Revolievich Romanov, Roman Romanovich Nogovitsyn 157

UNIQUE HYDROCARBON POTENTIAL OF THE ECONOMY OF WESTERN YAKUTIA
Vyacheslav Stefanovich Sitnikov, Rosalia Fedorovna Sevostyanova, Mariia Ivanovna Sleptsova ······ 175

THE FORMATION OF INFORMATION DATABASE TO ESTIMATE THE EFFICIENCY OF USING LAND RESOURCES OF YAKUTIA
Luiza Mikhailovna Byastinova ······ 192

EVALUATION OF CHANGES IN THE ARCTIC FORESTS OF YAKUTIA IN THE CONDITIONS OF GLOBALIZATION
Romanov Prokopiy Georgievich, Chakhov Dmitriy Konstantinivich, Lavrov Michail Frumentievich, Ammosova Sargylana Polikarpovna ······ 204

THE LEGAL STATUS OF THE WOOD BISON IN RUSSIA AND REPUBLIC SAKHA (YAKUTIA)
Anatoliy V. Chemezov, Roman Romanovich Nogovitsyn ······ 217

CHAPTER 3 ECONOMY AND LEGISLATION OF NORTHERN ENTERPRISE

THEORETICAL BASIS FOR THE ORGANIZATION OF INTERACTION OF CONSUMER COOPERATION WITH AGRICULTURAL PRODUCERS IN THE ARCTIC ZONE OF THE REPUBLIC OF SAKHA (YAKUTIA)
Vasiliy Dmitrievich Borisov, Tatiana Dmitrievna Borisova ······ 241

ORGANIZATIONAL AND ECONOMIC BASES OF ORGANIC MARKET IN ARCTIC TERRITORIES: ON THE EXAMPLE OF REPUBLIC OF SAKHA (YAKUTIA)
Nikolai Petrovich Vasilev, Larisa Ivanovna Danilova ······ 258

DEVELOPMENT OF TRADITIONAL NATURE MANAGEMENT IN THE CONDITIONS OF INDUSTRIAL DEVELOPMENT OF THE TERRITORIES OF THE OLENEK EVENKIY NATIONAL AREA
Maria Ivanovna Nikolaeva, Roman Romanovich Nogovytsyn ······ 279

ESTABLISHMENT OF NEW TRADE LAW SYSTEM: TO PROMOTE SUSTAINABILITY BETWEEN KOREA AND THE RUSSIAN ARCTIC
Bongchul Kim, Sunghwah Ko ······ 293

DEVELOPMENT OF THE DIGITAL ECONOMY IN THE ARCTIC REGIONS OF RUSSIA: RESOURCE POTENTIAL OF THE REPUBLIC OF SAKHA (YAKUTIA)
Galina Ratz, Sardana Gavrileva, Liudmila Gavrilieva ······ 308

INTRODUCTION

The Arctic Area, which has long been a place where human power cannot reach, has also been a place where mankind constantly challenged despite much the expense. These days, in response to the international political and economic situation of modern society, the Artic is drawing more attention of many than ever before. In particular, environmental changes, such as global warming, dramatically increased the likelihood of further development in the Arctic, and many neighboring countries are attempting to explore and develop the natural resources of the region.

The Arctic perspective is becoming not only a source to write a heroic story about pioneers that started the exploration of its recourses but a dynamic agenda for the discussion of issues connected to sustainability of the development of rich, remote and sparsely populated territories of the world. The deeper the mankind is penetrated into the Arctic the more unpredictable may be its consequences.

Russia, which is the country bordering the Arctic in closest proximity, has recently been actively working on several projects to develop new routes and underground resources, including oil and gas in the region. These processes have been facilitated by the globalization of the international economy, and the communities have been responsive to many relevant variables. In fact, the Russian Arctic community is experiencing a variety of changes due to the development and globalization of natural resources. These changes, however, have put people in the Arctic in the midst of problems that are difficult to tackle. In fact, the development and the influx of modern technology have sparked a change in the natural environment and traditional culture of the surrounding region, triggering a crisis in indigenous people way of survival. Therefore, the international community and the Russian Federation and local governments are looking for sustainable development methods to solve the problems of the Arctic Region.

The Republic of Sakha-Yakutia (North-East of Russia), which occupies the largest area in the Russian Federation and also belongs to the Arctic Region, has been facing these real problems. The local government of the Republic of Sakha is trying to solve these problems of the people of the region, and it is trying to thoroughly scrutinize the recent opportunities and crises at the same time. Researchers in the region also are striving to face the challenge of development with enormous underground resources, and they clearly recognize the burden of solving various problems related to them.

The Polar Research Center at Hankuk University of Foreign Studies (HUFS) has been continuously conducting research on the Arctic region of Russia with the support of the Korea Polar Research Institute. This book is an extension of the study, which includes the region's problems and academic proposals discussed by researchers at North-Eastern Federal University (NEFU) in the Republic of Sakha and researchers at the Center for Polar Studies in Korea. The miscellany of this book is the result of the joint event of NEFU and HUFS held as the International Scientific and Practical Conference, "Recourse Economy in the context of modern tendencies of globalization" that took place on the basis of the Institute of Economics and Finance at NEFU in March 2019.

The event has ended with the fruitful works done by the scholars of the region. Among more than 130 participants who uploaded their articles for the Conference there were some that dealt with the issues of developing of Arctic recourses as well as the analysis of enterprises working in the conditions of deficiencies of the North infrastructure. Therefore, discussions in this book include socio-cultural changes and conservation issues, which are mainly related to the economic development potential of the Arctic region, and suggest remedies and problem-solving measures using laws and systems.

A huge contribution of many has assisted the publication of this book. We would like to pay tributes to researchers from Korea and Russia who worked on the project by flying across Korea, Russia, and the Republic of Sakha. Also, the publication of this book would not have been possible without the efforts and support of the Knowledge Publishing Institute at HUFS. Finally, we would like to clearly note that all studies have been based on works of exchange between the two places, which began in the 1990s by Emeritus Prof. Ducksoo Kang, an emeritus professor at HUFS and professor at Northeast Federal University.

Prof. Bongchul Kim at HUFS

Prof. Larisa Pisareva at NEFU

This book was supported by the Polar Academic Program (PE20900) of Korea Polar Research Institute.

CHAPTER 1

CONTEMPORARY ISSUES OF RUSSIAN EAST ARCTIC SOCIAL DEVELOPMENT

PROSPECTS OF ENERGY SECURITY OF ARCTIC DISTRICTS OF THE SAKHA REPUBLIC (YAKUTIA) ON THE BASIS OF HYDROCARBON

Mariia Ivanovna Sleptsova
Candidate of Sciences in Techniques, Senior Researcher, Institute of Problems of Oil and Gas, Siberian Branch of Russian Academy of Sciences
msleptsova@mail.ru

Abstract.

The territory of the Republic of Sakha (Yakutia) is the richest resource base in the east of the Russian Federation. The subsoil resources concentrated here are of key importance in the development of the economy of the whole country. The long-term forecast of socio-economic development of the republic is based on the prevailing role of mineral-raw materials and fuel and energy complexes in the economy of the republic in the long term, its strengthening due to increased production and exports, primarily energy types of raw materials (oil, gas, coal), and development of transport and energy infrastructure.

One of the important tasks of modern Russia is the development of the Arctic, since it concentrates huge reserves of strategic resources. The assessment of the resource base of oil and gas of the Arctic shelf of Russia. Volumes of seismic exploration work, their density, the number of identified local objects in the considered territory in comparison with other seas of the Russian Arctic are given.

13 regions of the republic belong to the Arctic. They are characterized by the unity of

climatic, geocryological, hydrohydrographic and economic conditions. The climate is very severe, the duration of the heating period is 320-360 days a year. 68.16 thousand people live on 1620.6 square meters. m. The population density of 42.1 people per 1000 square meters. Km. The total volume of demand for oil products is 206.062 thousand tons.

In the Arctic regions of Yakutia, there are 155 heat supply facilities, of which with a capacity of up to 3 Gcal / hour are 52, from 3 to 20 Gcal / hour - 100 and from 20 to 100 Gcal / hour - 3. Out of the 155 heat supply facilities, 83 work on solid fuel and 72 liquid.

The most likely way to optimize the technical and energy balance in the Arctic regions of the Republic of Sakha (Yakutia) in the coming years may be related to the development of local sources of hydrocarbon raw materials. The features of the geological structure, oil and gas conditions, a preliminary assessment of the hydrocarbon potential and the degree of geological and geophysical knowledge are considered.

In the eastern group of the arctic regions of the Republic of Sakha (Yakutia], the prospects for oil and gas potential are associated only with certain territories, including the large intermountain Indigiro-Zyryansky deflection, as well as with a number of depressions opened in the direction of the East Siberian Sea shelf (Tastakhdeflection, Ust-Yanskaya and Nizhnekolymsky depressions).

The heat and power problem of the arctic districts can be solved by developing local sources of hydrocarbon resources.

The development project of a small field with the aim of supplying petroleum products to the needs of heat supply to the northern regions of the republic will pay for itself taking into account all costs on the horizon of 10-15 years. The state in this case will save up to half of the budget funds spent. The prospecting and discovery of projected hydrocarbon deposits in the immediate vicinity of potential consumers will significantly optimize the fuel and energy balances of the Arctic and northern regions of the Republic of Sakha (Yakutia).

Keywords: the Arctic, Republic of Sakha (Yakutia), hydrocarbons, energy supply, oil, gas, forecast resources

I. Introduction

According to the unique wealth of mineral resources and a wide variety of minerals, the Republic of Sakha (Yakutia) is generally recognized as the only region in Russia and one of the few territories in the world. The explored reserves of many minerals that play a leading role in the world economy (diamonds, gold, coal, oil, gas, etc.), in the process of their long-term development, provide a decent level of social and economic development of the republic and unlimited opportunities for its further growth. As a result, the mineral resource complex and information about it are deservedly a kind of business card of the republic.

The location of deposits of various types of minerals is controlled by modern geological conditions and processes of the paleogeological development of specific territories. Within the Republic of Sakha (Yakutia), according to these data, the eastern part of the Siberian Platform is allocated, covering the whole of Western Yakutia. In the east of the republic there are mainly mountain buildings of the Verkhoyansk-Kolyma folded system. Taking into account the conditions for the formation of minerals, which are the main energy carriers (oil, gas, coal, oil shale, etc.), their placement in the republic is quite naturally due to platform territories. At the same time, there are definite prospects with regard to the availability of these minerals in the east of Yakutia, where it is forecasted (oil, gas) in intermontane depressions and deflections.

Taking into account the presence in the Republic of Sakha (Yakutia) of a large raw hydrocarbon base for the oil and gas industry and huge reserves for further accelerated growth of proven reserves of oil and gas, as well as the republic's leading role in the implementation of federal oil and gas megaprojects, including the long-term planned filling of existing main oil pipelines with hydrocarbon raw materials Eastern Siberia-Pacific Ocean, and the only pipeline built The Power of Siberia, The Government of the Republic of Sakha (Yakutia) has repeatedly appealed to the Federal Agency for Subsoil Use (Rosnedra) with a request to significantly increase funding and significantly expand the geography of geological exploration in the country.

However, these measures relate mainly to the territory that is located in the location of the existing and projected oil and gas pipeline system, that is, in the central and southern regions of Western Yakutia. In other parts of the republic, work on these minerals has recently not been carried out at all or is performed occasionally in extremely insignificant amounts.

The above data is directly reflected in the formation and implementation of fuel and energy balances in various regions of Yakutia. In particular, only in the southwestern and central and southern energy districts of the republic local sources of energy carriers (oil, gas, coal) are currently used. In all other uluses, including in the arctic regions, mainly imported energy carriers (crude oil, diesel fuel, coal) are used to some extent.

The methodology of the study is based on a comprehensive synthesis and analysis of all available data from different years on the socio-economic situation of the Arctic regions of the Republic of Sakha (Yakutia). The theoretical and methodological basis of the study was the work of Russian scientists on the theoretical and practical problems of the heat and power balance of the republic. To obtain the results, methods of theoretical analysis of information sources, generalization and comparison of information on the issue under study were used. Comparative and statistical analyzes are carried out. Used tabular methods for presenting research results. The research information base was made up of materials from the Government of the Republic of Sakha (Yakutia).

II. Estimated hydrocarbon resources

2.1. Prospective hydrocarbon resources of the Russian Arctic

One of the important tasks of modern Russia is t he development of the Arctic, since it concentrates huge reserves of strategic resources. The most probable volumes of hydrocarbon (hydrocarbon) initial resources of the northeastern Arctic shelf of Russia are estimated in the following volumes: LaptevskayaOGF (oil and gas region): oil (extract) - 2.3 billion tons, free gas - 4.2 trillion m3; East Arctic OGF: oil (extract) - 6.0 billion tons, gas free - 4.7 trillion m3; Novosibirsk-ChukotkaOGF: oil (extract) - 0.7 billion tons, gas free - 1.1 trillion m3 (Table 1) [1].

Table 1. Initial resources of oil, gas, condensate of the Russian Arctic waters

Oil and gasprovinces(areas)	Oil, billion tons	Gas passing, billion m3	Gas free, trillion	Condensate, million tons
Laptevskaya	2.3	63.0	4.2	15.0
East Arctic	6.0	18.0	4.7	17.0
Novosibirsk-Chukot	0.7	19.0	1.1	8.0
Total	9.0	100.0	10.0	40.0

To assess the resource base of oil and gas in the Arctic shelf of Russia Eremin N.A., Kondratyuk A.T. and Eremin A.N. operate with the following indicators: the area of the shelf and the continental slope of Russia is 6.2 million km2; a shelf of at least 4 million km2, the continental slope and deepwater zones of 0.4–0.5 million km2 are promising for oil and gas, where 20 large marine oil and gas bearing provinces and basins have been identified, of which 10 are with proven oil and gas content [2].

According to their estimates, the initial geological resources of hydrocarbons on the Russian shelf amount to 136 billion tons of standard fuel, and the initial recoverable resources of hydrocarbons reach 100 billion tons of standard fuel, including: 13 billion tons of oil and 87 trillion tons. m3 of gas [2]. The largest sedimentary basins in the Arctic part of Russia include: East Barents, South Kara, Laptev, East Siberian and Chukotka. Perspective hydrocarbon resources of the Russian Arctic are given in Table 2.

The same authors in their work as an alternative assessment of promising hydrocarbon resources in the waters of the Arctic seas of Russia cite data from USGS (2008) [2], which

Table 2. Prospective hydrocarbon resources of the Russian Arctic

Sea	Oil, billion tons	Gas passing, billion m3	Gas free, trillion m3	Condensate, million tons	HC, t.o.e. *
Laptev	0.724	273.12	1.555	199.50	2392.82
East Siberian	0.016	6.71	0.173	14.75	175.52
Chukotka	0.391	111.22	0.510	58.20	947.96
Arctic Ocean (remaining)	0.187	60.80	0.226	29.11	447.22
Всего	1.318	451.85	2.464	301.56	3963.52

Note: * - t.o.e. – ton of oil equivalent

compared with the above volumes Kontorovich and others [1]; Eremin and others [2]) differ in times less in terms of oil and gas and, as for condensate, on the contrary, they are several times more.

The first quantitative assessment of the prospects for the oil and gas potential of the Indigiro-Zyrianskydeflection in the north-east of Yakutia was made by VNIGRI in 1972 [3]. The calculation was made by various methods with a focus mainly on gas resources. When using the volumetric statistical method, the predicted gas resources in the Lower Cretaceous sediment deflection are determined at 1.16–1.20 trillion. m3. Taking into account the conventionality of many parameters used, the authors of the calculation accepted the forecast resources of HCG (hydrocarbon gases) in the amount of 1.0 – 1.2 trillion m3 as a resulting estimate.

2.2. Forecast resources of hydrocarbons in the north-eastern regions of the Yakutia

In 1987, the calculation of the forecast resources of hydrocarbons in the north-eastern regions of the YASSR (Yakutsk Autonomous Soviet Socialist Republic), including the territory of the Zyryansk deflection, was carried out by the Yakutskgeofizika trust. The same methods were used as before. The results of this calculation (830–870 billion m3) are slightly lower than previous estimates. Along with the conventionality of the accepted analogies, with a little knowledge of the object of calculation itself, the differences indicated are probably due to the difference in the choice of promising intervals (reservoirs). In the first case, the section of the Lower Cretaceous sediments was considered in full, in the second - only the Silyap and Ozhoginsky formations (the Buorkemus formation was distinguished as a screen). In addition, the VNIGRI data covered the entire Momo-Zyryan basin, including the Zyryan deflection and the Momsk depression [3].

Within the limits of the Omulevsky uplift bordering the Indigiro-Zyryansk deflection from the south, the Omulevsky possible oil and gas bearing area is distinguished [7, p.5]. Using the Turukhano-Norilsk OGF as a standard, according to the geological analogy, the author fulfilled

Table 3. Resources of HC Omulevskgo possible OGF

№	Site name	Area, km2	CHC, mln. Tons
1	Uyarinsky	460	9.2
2	Iryudian	150	3.0
3	Supkaninsky	340	6.8
4	Urultunsky	520	10.4
4 plots in total		1,470	29.4
Total Omulevskoypossible OGF		95,000	72.5

the forecast of the initial HC resources for the 4 promising areas identified by him and for the POGF (possibly the oil and gas region) as a whole.The density of hydrocarbons of Turukhano-Norilsk OGF (14.5 t / km2), taking into account unfavorable factors established within the boundaries of the OmulPOGF: the widespread development of magmatism, a high degree of catagenetic transformation of sedimentary formations, intense disjunctive tectonics, the author reduced by three times. The results of counting HC resources are shown in Table 3 [4].

2.3. Geological and geophysical study

A brief overview of the study of the territory in question shows that in recent decades in Russia and abroad, more and more attention has been paid to the study of the Arctic oil and gas belt. At the same time, the geological and geophysical knowledge of the waters of the eastern Arctic seas (Laptev, East Siberian and Chukchi), to date, in particular by seismic exploration, is very low, and deep drilling has not yet been carried out here. The volumes of seismic exploration, its density, the number of identified local objects in the territory under consideration in comparison with the other seas of the Russian Arctic can be given in Table 4 [5, 6].

Table 4. Geological and geophysical study of the waters of the Arctic seas of Russia

The Russian Arctic Seas	Knowledge		Amount of local objects
	Seismic exploration (SE), thousand km	DensitySE, km / km2	
Laptev	52.91	0.08	40
East Siberian	24.44	0.03	10
Chukotka	19.51	0.06	23

III. Arctic heat supply

3.1 Population and the area in the Arctic

13 districts of the Republic belong to the Arctic and the North: Abyisky, Anabarsky, Allaikhovsky, Bulunsky, Verkhnekolymsky, Verkhoyansky, Zhigansky, Momsky, Nizhnekolymsky, Oleneksky, Srednekolymsky, Ust-Yansky, Eveno-Bytantaysky. Of these, 7 are completely beyond the Arctic Circle, and the territory of the other 6 districts crosses the Arctic Circle.

The above-mentioned northern territories of the SakhaRepublic(Yakutia) are characterized by the unity of climatic, geocryological, orohydrographic and economic conditions. They are featured either by similarity or unityby the existing infrastructure and developed transport schemes. They are characterized by the unity of the mineral resource base and conditions for geological exploration, including for prospecting and exploration of mineral deposits, as well as for companies' operations in the development of existing mining and oil and gas centers.

Given the above arguments, the unity of conditions for all thirteen north territories of the SakhaRepublic (Yakutia) is quite obvious for the formation and implementation of their fuel and energy balances.

The above data is directly reflected in the formation and implementation of fuel and energy balances in various regions of Yakutia. For example, only in the southwestern and central and southern energy districts of the Republic local sources of energy products (oil, gas, coal) are currently used. In all other uluses, including in the arctic regions, mainly imported energy products (crude oil, diesel fuel, coal) are used to some extent.

In the Arctic and northern districts, the climate is very harsh, the duration of the heating period is 320–360 days a year.

In the north-eastern part of Yakutia, 68.16 thousand people live in 1620.6 square meters. m, which is respectively 7.07% and 52.56% of the total population and the entire territory of the Republic. The population density is 42.1 people per 1000 sq. Km. km (Table 5) [7].

Table 5. Average annual resident population and the area of the uluses of the north-eastern part of the Sakha Republic(Yakutia) on 01/01/2018

Districts	Population		Area		Density, (pop/1000 km²)
	people	% of the total population	thousand square kilometers	% to total number	
The Sakha Republic(Yakutia)	964,430	100	3083.5	100	312.8
Abyisky	4,018	0.42	69.4	2.25	57.9
Anabarsky	3,567	0.37	55.6	1.80	64.2
Allaikhovsky	2,716	0.28	107.3	3.48	25.3
Bulunsky	8,339	0.86	235.1	7.62	35.5
Verkhnekolymsky	4,123	0.43	67.8	2.20	60.8
Verkhoyansky	11,352	1.18	137.4	4.46	82.6
Zhigansky	4,222	0.44	140.2	4.55	30.1
Momsky	4,073	0.42	101.8	3.30	40.0
Nizhnekolymsky	4,290	0.44	86.8	2.81	49.4
Oleneksky	4,072	0.42	318.1	10.32	12.8
Srednekolymsky	7,499	0.78	125.2	4.06	59.9
Ust-Yansky	7,075	0.73	120.3	3.90	58.8
Eveno-Bytantaysky	2,813	0.29	55.6	1.80	50.6
Total	68,159	7.07	1620.6	52.56	42.1

3.2. The volume of demand for petroleum products

The total demand for petroleum products in the 13 uluses (districts) under consideration is 206,062 thousand tons, including 16,039 thousand tons of motor gasoline, 170,402 thousand tons of diesel fuel, 16,357 tons of jet fuel and 3,264 tons of lubricants (Table 6) [8].

Delivery of fuel to consumers in the northern part of the Republic is associated with large financial costs, the magnitude of these costs is significantly influenced by the seasonality of transport links. The settlements, generally, are small and dispersed throughout the vast expanses of northern Yakutia. Fuel is burned in most cases in boiler stations with low efficiency.

3.3. Supply facilities in the Arctic of Yakutia

In all other uluses, including in the arctic regions, mainly imported energy carriers (crude oil, diesel fuel, coal) are used to some extent. Information on the distribution of operating boiler houses using different types of fuel in the arctic regions of the republic is presented below in Table 3.

Table 6. The volume of demand for petroleum products in the districts

Districts	Total ton	including:			
		gasoline	diesel fuel	jet fuel	lubricants
The Sakha Republic(Yakutia)	9,834	874	7,996	855	109
Abyisky	29,869	301	29,476	0	92
Anabarsky	6,703	783	4,694	1,128	98
Allaikhovsky	16,809	1,128	13,767	1,554	360
Bulunsky	16,007	1,437	12,774	1,561	235
Verkhnekolymsky	32,796	3,374	24,981	3,845	596
Verkhoyansky	8,322	833	6,870	515	104
Zhigansky	18,383	1,091	16,029	1,097	166
Momsky	13,749	1,217	11,168	1,051	313
Nizhnekolymsky	3,929	347	3,490	0	92
Oleneksky	15,380	2,360	9,381	3,361	278
Srednekolymsky	30,822	1,854	26,838	1,390	740
Ust-Yansky	3,459	440	2,938	0	81
Eveno-Bytantaysky	206,062	16,039	170,402	16,357	3,264

Table 7. The number of heat supply facilities in the north-eastern areas of the Sakha Republic(Yakutia) at the end of 2016

Districts	Total	of them with power Gcal / hour			of them running on fuel	
		to3	from 3 to 20	from 20 to 100	solid	liquid
Abyisky	14	7	7	-	11	3
Anabarsky	8	1	7			8
Allaikhovsky	10	3	7	-	-	10
Bulunsky	11	3	7	1	-	11
Verkhnekolymsky	12	1	11	-	12	-
Verkhoyansky	24	12	12	-	24	
Zhigansky	8	5	2	1	7	1
Momsky	13	5	8	-	4	9
Nizhnekolymsky	6	-	6	-	4	2
Oleneksky	17	6	11	-	-	17
Srednekolymsky	14	3	11	-	13	1
Ust-Yansky	9	2	6	1	5	4
Eveno-Bytantaysky	9	4	5	-	3	6
Total	155	52	100	3	83	72

In the Arctic and northern regions of Yakutia, there are 155 heat supply facilities, of which with a capacity of up to 3 Gcal / hour are 52, from 3 to 20 Gcal / hour - 100 and from 20 to 100 Gcal / hour - 3. Of the 155 heat supply facilities, 83 work on solid fuel and 72 liquid (Table 7) [9].

It is known that in the Arctic regions of Yakutia there are many necessary conditions for the use of renewable energy sources (hydropower, solar energy, wind energy, nuclear energy). However, in our opinion, due to the specificity of each of the listed types of energy and the peculiarity of the real conditions in the north of the republic, they can be of considerable practical interest and create some competition to used non-renewable energy sources only in the long run.

VI. Perspective for oil and gas in the Arctic

4.1. Similarity between the two largest depressions

In our opinion, the most likely way to optimize the thermopile in the arctic regions of the Republic of Sakha (Yakutia) in the coming years may be associated with the development of local sources of hydrocarbons. In this regard, taking into account the peculiarities of the geological structure, oil and gas conditions, a preliminary assessment of the hydrocarbon potential and the degree of geological and geophysical knowledge, it is advisable to separately consider the western and eastern groups of the arctic territories of the republic.

In the west, within the north-east of the Siberian Platform, the largest areas are Leno-AnabarskayaOGFs and adjacent adjacent parts of Anabar-Khatanga, Predverhoyansk and AnabarskayaOGFs. The results of the geological-geophysical and paleographic constructions carried out at the Institute of Oil and Gas Problems of the SB RAS indicate the presence on the territory of the northeast sector of the Siberian platform and its paleogeological continuation towards the modern Morelaptevsky shelf of the largest Ripheandepocentre with significant capacities of terrigenous-carbonate strata formed in marine conditions and containing elevated concentrations of dispersed organic matter.

The complex multi-tiered structure of the sedimentary cover was established, the sedimentation of which was carried out with a predominance of both rift (Riphean, Middle Paleozoic, Cenozoic) and predominantly platform (Vendian-Early Paleozoic, Upper Paleozoic-Mesozoic, Cenozoic) modes of tectonic development. The discrepancy between the structural plans of sedimentary complexes formed under various tectonic regimes is noted.

It was established that the Lena-Anabarsky regional deflection, traditionally distinguished as part of the Siberian platform at the northern end of the modern continental land, is part of a larger tectonic structure, which is located mainly on the shelf of the Laptev Sea and is delineated by us as the Olenek syneclise.

According to many indicators characterizing the structure and geological development of the largest tectonic structures, there is a very significant similarity of the newly isolated Olenek syneclise to the more studied Viluyhemisyneclysis located in the eastern edge of the Siberian platform on the western extension of the Verkhoyansk incoming angle.

Within the same Vilyui OGF, the industrial gas content of the Upper Permian, Lower Triassic and Lower Jurassic horizons has been established to date. In general, a fairly large resource base for the gas industry (up to 500 billion m3 of HCG) has been prepared at the fields of the Khapchagay and Tyung gas regions.

In addition, industrial oil-bearing capacity of more ancient Cambrian carbonate strata is predicted in the onboard parts of the Vilyui hemisyneclise. The abundance of such a forecast, along with the presence of the necessary regional conditions, is evidenced by the numerous abundant oil manifestations recorded during exploration of previously identified gas condensate fields, and beyond their limits in many individual wells.

This similarity between the two largest depressions, characterized by ancient founding and long-term inherited development, allows at the next stage of research to proceed to a separate forecast of the oil and gas potential of the territories of the Morelaptevsky shelf and the adjacent continental land. Moreover, these data indicate the possibility of a significant refinement of the quantitative assessment of the predicted here geological resources of the SW in the direction of its significant increase.

4.2. Oil and gas potential in the Arctic

In the geological study and preparation for the industrial development of hydrocarbon resources, projected in the depths of the Western Group of the Arctic territories of the Sakha Republic (Yakutia) and on the adjacent shelf of the Laptev Sea, an active role. Especially in recent years, plays the largest oil and gas company "Rosneft."

In the eastern group of the arctic regions of the Republic of Sakha (Yakutia], the prospects for oil and gas potential are associated only with certain territories, including the large intermountain Indigiro-Zyryansky deflection, as well as with a number of depressions opened in the direction of the East Siberian Sea shelf (Tastakhdeflection, Ust-Yanskaya and Nizhnekolymsky depressions) [10].

The hydrocarbon potential of the above-mentioned prospective areas is associated with Cenozoic (Paleogene) and Upper Mesozoic (Cretaceous) sandy-clayey sediments, the thickness of which reaches 2 km or more. All of them vary considerably in their degree of geological and geophysical knowledge. The Indigiro-Zyrian deflection is the most studied. In its western part, along with the universally carried out electrical survey MTS, medium-scale gravity prospecting and seismic exploration CDR-2Dwas performed.The boundaries of the deflection, which were previously determined from geological survey data, were clarified, the presence of thrusts in its southern part, on the border with Ilin-Tassky anticlinorium, was confirmed. A number of promising anticlinal traps has been identified. During drilling, gas shows are noted.

The Tastakh deflection has been studied by a network of regional profiles by electroprospecting, seismic exploration, and geochemical studies using a program of direct methods to search for hydrocarbon deposits. It also highlights several anticlinal traps that coincide with geochemical anomalies. They are considered as promising objects for setting up hydrocarbon prospecting. According to geological and geo-chemical data, mainly gas accumulations are predicted here [11].

V. Conclusion

The heat and power problem of the northern and arctic districtscan be solved by developing local sources of hydrocarbon resources.

Considering the issue of energy supply, it is theoretically possible to organize the supply of energy to consumers in several ways, depending on which fields and how they will be developed.

The discovery of large oil and gas condensate fields will attract large operating companies to the region, and part of the production can be directed to the needs of thermal power.

In the case of the discovery of a large oil or gas condensate field and the beginning of its industrial development, a production scheme is possible, when the required volume of oil is purchased from the operating company, processing and delivery to the final consumer is organized.

Small oil and gas fields are not as attractive in terms of investment as large ones. Small oil fields can be developed by an interested investor with a focus on meeting the domestic fuel needs of the northern regions.

Assuming that the oil production rate will be at the level of 60-80 tons / day, for producing 90-100 thousand tons of oil per year, 7 production wells, 3 wells for maintaining reservoir pressure, 1 observation well will be required. In general, the arrangement of the fishery will require:

- 10-15 wells;
- Oil treatment unit;
- Powe station;
- Reservoir Park;
- Office space, residential premises;
- In-field communications.

The cost of drilling wells in remote areas in the Arctic will be significantly more expensive than in developed oil and gas regions. Expert evaluation of drilling a single vertical production well will cost 400 million rubles. Field equipment and facilities will cost an additional 1.5 billion rubles. Total capital investment in the project will be at least 4.5-6.5 billion rubles. excluding exploration work and the cost of creating a logistics chain. The cost of oil production will be about 20 thousand rubles / ton.

The selling price for petroleum products will be balanced on the one hand by the interests of the investor, and on the other hand by the interests of the state. A certain compromise price on the one hand will lead to a project payback, and on the other hand to a budget benefit. With the selling price of petroleum products at 35 thousand / rub. per ton the revenue of the operator of the field will be 3.5 billion rubles, the operating profit of 1.6 billion rubles. Thus, the development project of a small field with the aim of supplying petroleum products to the needs of heat supply to the northern regions of the republic will pay for itself taking into account all costs on the horizon of 10-15 years. The state in this case will save up to half of the budget funds spent.

Summarizing a very brief overview of the geological and geophysical exploration of the northeastern regions of Yakutia and the adjacent shelf of the East Arctic seas, it should be recognized that with a very positive assessment of the prospects for oil and gas potential, these territories of Russia remain the least studied for oil and gas in the Arctic zone of the country. Based on the global trend and growing interest in the development of the Arctic, it can be predicted that in the near future the situation with the geological and geophysical study of the northern territories of Yakutia and the adjacent shelf of the Arctic seas will change significantly. The basis for such an optimistic conclusion is the recent results obtained by Rosneft in the Krasnoyarsk Territory, including the discovery of a new large Central Olginsky gas condensate field on the west coast of the Khatanga Bay, and overall plans for the priority work of this largest company in the Laptev Sea on Ust-Lensky, Ust-Oleneksky and other licensed areas.

The prospecting and discovery of projected hydrocarbon deposits in the immediate vicinity of potential consumers will significantly optimize the fuel and energy balances of the Arctic and northern regions of the Republic of Sakha (Yakutia). Also, the development of local sources of hydrocarbon resourceswill contribute to improving the environmental conditions, raising the socio-economic standard of living in the Arctic and northern regions and ensuring the economic and energy security of the Sakha Republic (Yakutia).

References

1. Конторович А.Э., Эпов М.И., Бурштейн Л.М., Каминский В.Д., Курчиков А.Р., Малышев Н.А., Прищепа О.М., Сафронов А.Ф., Ступакова А.В., Супруненко О.И. Геология, ресурсы углеводородов шельфов арктических морей России и перспективы их освоения // Геология и геофизика. - 2010. – Т.51. - № 1. - С. 7-17. (Kontorovich A.E., EpovM.I..BursteinL.M.and others.Geology and hydrocarbon resources of the continental shelf in Russian Arctic seas and the prospects of their development // Geology and Geophysics. - 2010. – V.51. - № 1. - P. 7-17).
2. Еремин Н.А., Кондратюк А.Т., Еремин А.Н. Ресурсная база нефти и газа арктического шельфа России. // Георесурсы. Геоэнергетика. Геополитика. – 2010. - №1. – С. 1-11. (Eremin N.A., Kondratyuk A.T., Eremin A.N. Resource base of oil and gas in the Arctic shelf of Russia // Georesources. Geoenergetics. Geopolitics. - 2010. - №1. - P. 1-11).
3. Чочиа Н.Г., Вольнов Д.А., Гольбрайх И.Г. и др. Структурно-тектонический анализ Зырянского прогиба // Тектоника и нефтегазоносность востока СССР: труды ВНИГРИ. – Л, 1972. - Вып. №309. - С. 118-132. (Chochia N.G.,Volnov D.A., Golbraich I.G. and others. Structural-tectonic analysis of the Zyryanskydeflection //Tectonics and oil-and-gas content of the east of the USSR: works of VNIGRI. - L, 1972. - Issue №309. - P. 118-132).
4. Мигурский Ф.А. Перспективы нефтегазоносности Омулевского поднятия: автореф. дисс… канд. геол.-мин. наук / Мигурский Ф.А. – Новосибирск, 2007. – 21 с. (Migursky F.A. Prospects of the oil and gas potential of the Omulevsky elevation: dis ... of PhD in Geology and Mineralogy: 25.00.12: defense of the thesis 10.05.2007: approved 15.12.2007. - Novosibirsk, 2007. - 132 p.)
5. Сенин Б.В., Леончик М.И. Современное состояние фонда подготовленных к бурению объектов на акваториях Российской Федерации. // Методические

проблемы геолого-разведочных и научно-исследовательских работ в области геологии нефти и газа: матер. всеросс. совещания ВНИГНИ. – Москва, 16-18 октября 2013 г. – М, 2013. - С. 4-7. (Senin B.V.,Leonchik M.I. The current state of the fund of objects prepared for drilling in the water areas of the Russian Federation // Materials of the All-Russian VNIGNI meeting "Methodological problems of geological exploration and scientific research in the field of oil and gas geology." - M: VNIGNI, 2013. - P. 4-7.)

6. Каминский В.Д., Супруненко О.И., Черных А.А. Стратегия изучения и освоения нефтегазоносных ресурсов континентального шельфа Российской Федерации. - Санкт-Петербург: ФГУП ВНИИОкеангеология, 2014. – С. 52-61. (Kaminsky V.D., Suprunenko O.I., Chernykh A.A. Strategy of exploration and development of oil and gas resources of the continental shelf of the Russian Federation. - St. Petersburg: FSUE VNIIOkeangeologiya, 2014. - P. 52-61).
7. Сайт Территориальный орган Федеральной службы государственной статистики по Республике Саха (Якутия) - URL: http://sakha.gks.ru/wps/wcm/connect/rosstat_ts/sakha/ru/statistics/population/ (дата обращения application20.03.2019) (Site of the Territorial Body of the Federal State Statistics Service for the RS (Y) - URL:- URL: http://sakha.gks.ru/wps/wcm/connect/rosstat_ts/sakha/ru/statistics/population/ (date of the application20.03.2019).
8. Соколов А.Н., Слепцова М.И. Об энергообеспечении арктических территорий Республики Саха (Якутия) на углеводородной // Российский экономический интернет журнал [электронный ресурс] – Режим доступа URL: http://www.e-rej.ru/upload/iblock/13e/13e4b5290c3fb6feefab203c28edb49a.pdf (Sokolov A.N., Sleptsova M.I. On the hydrocarbon-based energy supply of the Arctic territories of the Republic of Sakha (Yakutia) // Russian economic Internet magazine/ - 2016 [Electronic resource] URL: URL: http://www.e-кej.ru/upload/iblock/13e/13e4b5290c3fb6feefab203c28 edb49a.pdf (date of the application 20.03.2019).
9. Жилищно-коммунальное хозяйство Республики Саха (Якутия). 2016: Статистический сборник / Саха (Якутия) стат. - Якутск, 2017. - 90 с. (Housing and

communal services of the Republic of Sakha (Yakutia). 2016: Statistical collection / Sakha (Yakutia) stat. - Yakutsk, 2017. - 90 p.)

10. Ситников В. С., Спектор В.Б. Геолого-геофизические особенности строения и развития потенциально нефтегазоносных территорий Севера Якутии // Проблемы поиска, разведки и разработки нефтяных и газовых месторождений в Якутии: сборник научных трудов - Якутск: ЯНЦ СО РАН, 1993. - С. 93-101. (Sitnikov V.S., Spector V.B. Geological and geophysical features of the structure and development of potentially oil-and-gas bearing territories in the north of Yakutia / Problems of prospecting, exploration and development of oil and gas fields in Yakutia: collection of scienifific works - Yakutsk: RAS SB YSC, 1993. - P. 93-101.)

11. Аржаков Н.А., Оболкин А.П., Ситников В.С. Анализ геолого-геофизической изученности потенциально нефтегазоносных районов Северо-Восточной Якутии и прилегающего шельфа Восточно-Арктических морей // Нефтегазовая геология. Теория и практика. – 2017. - Т.12. - №4. (ArzhakovN.A.,Obolkin A.P., SitnikovV.S. Geological-geophysicalstudyofpotentially petroleum bearing areas of North-Eastern Yakutia and the approaching Eastern Artic offshore //Oil and Gas Geology. Theory and practice. - 2017. - V.12. - № 4.)

THE PRACTICE OF ETHNOLOGICAL EXAMINATION OF INVESTMENT PROJECTS OF THE INDUSTRIAL DEVELOPMENT OF THE TRADITIONAL NATURAL RESOURCE MANAGEMENT TERRITORIES IN THE ARCTIC DISTRICTS OF SAKHA REPUBLIC

Evdokia Innokentievna Burtseva
Doctor of Geography, Pprofessor, Institue of Economics and Finance, NEFU
burtseva1999@mail.ru

Anatoly Nickolaevich Sleptsov
Candidate of Sciences in Law, Head of Department, Faculty of Law, NEFU
uyandi@mail.ru

Anna Nickolaevna Bysyina
Leading expert, Center for Strategic Researches of the Republic of Sakha (Yakutia)
ian.89@mail.ru

Alla Semenovna Fedorova
Head of the Laboratory of Electronic Cartographic Systems, Institute of Natural Sciences, NEFU
Fedas78@mail.ru

Gavril Egorovich Dyachkovskij
Leading Engineer of the Laboratory of Electronic Cartographic Systems,
Institute of Natural Sciences, NEFU
gavril_egorovich@mail.ru

Abstract.

In the Sakha (Yakutia) Republic, hereinafter SR, the Arctic districts are the original habitat of indigenous peoples, who can conduct economic activities only in undisturbed or lightly disturbed lands. The diamond mining, gold mining, and coal mining industrial facilities are located In the Arctic districts. In the future, it is planned to revive the tin industry, develop oil and gas fields and develop the Tomtor Complex Rare-Earth Deposit. From this point of view, the problem of cooperation between industrial companies and indigenous peoples has particular relevance.

This article analyzes experience of ethnological expertise of investment projects of industrial development in territories of traditional natural resource use (TTNRU) of the Arctic zone of Yakutia. The purpose of the study is to identify the main problems in life activity of indigenous small-numbered peoples during the industrial development of the TTNRU and recommendations for their solution. The study was conducted using historical-geographical, analytical, synthetic, and statistical methods. As a result of 75-year-old technogenic press in the Arctic territory due to the activity of industrial facilities, an unfavorable ecological situation has developed. A condition in Lena, Yana, Anabar, Indigirka, Kolyma and Olenek river basins is estimated as 3-4 pollution classes (very polluted and dirty). The clearest indicator of quality of life is public health. Along with bioclimatic factors, a social environment, in which he lives, has an impact on the human health. Its main components are: real wages, food quality, housing conditions, a degree of the health care development, etc. The average wage in the Arctic regions in 2013 amounted to 39.9 thousand rubles, which is 14.3% lower than a level prevailing in the Republic (46.5 thousand rubles). An unemployment rate in most uluses exceeds the national average (7.4%). The most acute problems are underdevelopment of social infrastructure, disrepair and the accident rate of the social facilities. To assess dependence of a state of health on the social environment, statistical medical-demographic indicators of the Yakut Republican Medical-Information-Analytical Center of Yakutia for 1982-2011 were analyzed for tuberculosis. In a ranked series of tuberculosis vulnerability of a population, the Arctic and northern uluses occupy the high and elevated vulnerability levels in the Republic of Sakha (Yakutia) (hereinafter RS (Y)).

Keywords: Arctic, mining industry, ecology, small-numbered peoples, damage compensation, traditional natural resource management.

I. Introduction

The main branch of economy of small nations is domestic reindeer husbandry. The Arctic zone, in terms of the number of deer stocks, occupies the first place in the republic (the share of this indicator in the republic is 70%). Since the 1930s, mining has begun to develop in the Arctic. Here, coal, tin, gold, and diamonds were mined. Market relations, which began in 1991, led to crisis situations in the mining industries and many enterprises were liquidated. Today. Vostok Engineering LLC, PJSC ALROSA, Rosneft OJSC, Almazy Anabara OJSC, and Nizhne-Lenskoye OJSC operate in the Arctic zone. At the same time, the North, due to its high vulnerability, low assimilation and self-cleaning ability, and the spread of permafrost, has low resistance to technogenic influences. In 2010, the Law "On Ethnological Expertise in the Places of Traditional Residence and Traditional Economic Activities of Indigenous Minorities of the North of the Republic of Sakha (Yakutia)" was issued. During the ethnological examination, it turned out that most of the questions and comments from both experts and tribal communities related to the compensation section for losses of indigenous small peoples of the North (SIM), which are caused not only by the quality of work of the developers of the "Impact Assessment on the Ethnological Environment" (OECS) as part of the projects, but mainly by the imperfection of the existing methodological approaches to calculating the losses caused to associations of indigenous peoples. The practice of conducting an ethnological examination in the Arctic zone of the republic showed that the submitted OECS documents do not always comply with the requirements of the Law "On Ethnological Expertise ..." and the official methodology for calculating losses of the indigenous peoples. To compensate for the social harm of the indigenous peoples, it is necessary to conclude a tripartite agreement on cooperation and promote the sustainable development of indigenous peoples in the project area of influence between the project customer, the RS (Y) state authorities and authorized representatives of the indigenous peoples to improve and improve the quality of life of indigenous peoples in the form of money or other social events . In order to recalculate the normative indicators of loss assessment, as well as to clarify the extent of damage, both environmental and socio-economic, it is necessary to adopt the Ethnoecological Monitoring Program for surveys in the areas of industrial development of TTP ethnoecological monitoring every 5 years based on certain indicators.

Within the territory of the SR there are 13 districts are assigned to the arctic and northern zone of the Republic, with population of more than 70,000 people, of which 20,000 are the indigenous small-numbered peoples of the North (ISNPN). The basis of development of indigenous people is renewable natural resources: reindeer pastures, hunting areas, water and fish resources, medicinal and food plants. The basic sector of the economy of indigenous peoples is the traditional natural resource management – reindeer husbandry, fishery and hunting, gathering wild-growing plants. Indigenous peoples of the North can conduct economic activities only in undisturbed or lightly disturbed ecosystems, developing extensive territories and using the landscapes mastered by them in the most natural state, preserving the level of biological diversity and productivity of land [1].

The purpose of this study is to identify the main problems of life activity of indigenous small-numbered peoples of the North (ISNPN) during industrial development of traditional natural resource management territories (TNRMT) and recommendations for solving them.

In the arctic zone of SR are mining "Vostok inginiring" LLC, "ALROSA" JSC, "Rosneft" PJSC, "Almazy Anabara" OJSC, "Nizhne-Lenskoe" OJSC. At the same time the North with high vulnerability, low assimilation and self-cleaning capacity, distribution of permafrost has low stability to man-made impacts. For this reason, the industrial development of the arctic zone of the SR it is necessary to introduce tight legal and territorial restrictions.

II. Environment

2.1. Natural and economic zones

The Arctic - one of the last most extensive untouched regions in the world, and its role for ecological balance of the northern hemisphere is enormous. The Arctic acts as one of areas of

Table 1. Natural and economic zones of the Arctic districts of SR

№	Natural and economic zones by background industries	District
1	Harvesting and reindeer herding in Arctic tundra	Anabarsky, Allaikhovsky, Bulunsky, Nizhnekolymsky, Ust-Yansky
2	Harvesting and reindeer herding in North-Western north taiga	Zhigansky, Oleneksky
3	Reindeer herding and cattle breeding in North-Eastern taiga and lake	Abyysky, Verkhnekolymsky, Srednekolymsky
4	Reindeer herding and cattle and horse breeding in North-Eastern mountain taiga	Verkhoyansky, Momsky, Eveno-B ytantaysky

global atmospheric processes on the planet, the regulator of content of oxygen, methane, the region of a drain of many chemical compounds, etc.

The bases of the natural resource of the economic activities of the indigenous peoples are background (zonal) types of environmental management: agriculture, forestry, fur, fishing trade, etc. In the Arctic districts of the SR on the background industries can be identified 4 natural and economic zones (Table 1, Figure 1).

The changes of the natural environment of the Arctic zone as a result of the global warming and the accelerated industrial development have generally negative character for the traditional life activity of indigenous peoples. Today in all natural and economic zones the industrial enterprises of the mining industry are placed.

As a result of a 75-year technogenic press in the Arctic territory as a result of activity of industrial facilities there was an unfavorable ecological situation has developed. The consequences of the industrial development of the Arctic of last years are still the sources of environmental pollution:

1. Disturbed l ands of the mining industry;
2. Objects of the liquidated enterprises of tin and gold mining industry (tailing dumps).
3. Arctic coast: the thrown meteorological stations (Bulunsky and Nizhnekolymsky districts).
4. Arctic coast (Kotelny and Bolshoy Lyakhovsky Islands): airfield platforms of military unit of the Ministry of Defence of the Russian Federation.

To date, the most acute problem in environmental terms is pollution of surface waters. The condition in the rivers of the Lensky basin is assessed by pollution class 4 (dirty). In

Figure 1. Natural and economic zones of the Arctic districts of SR

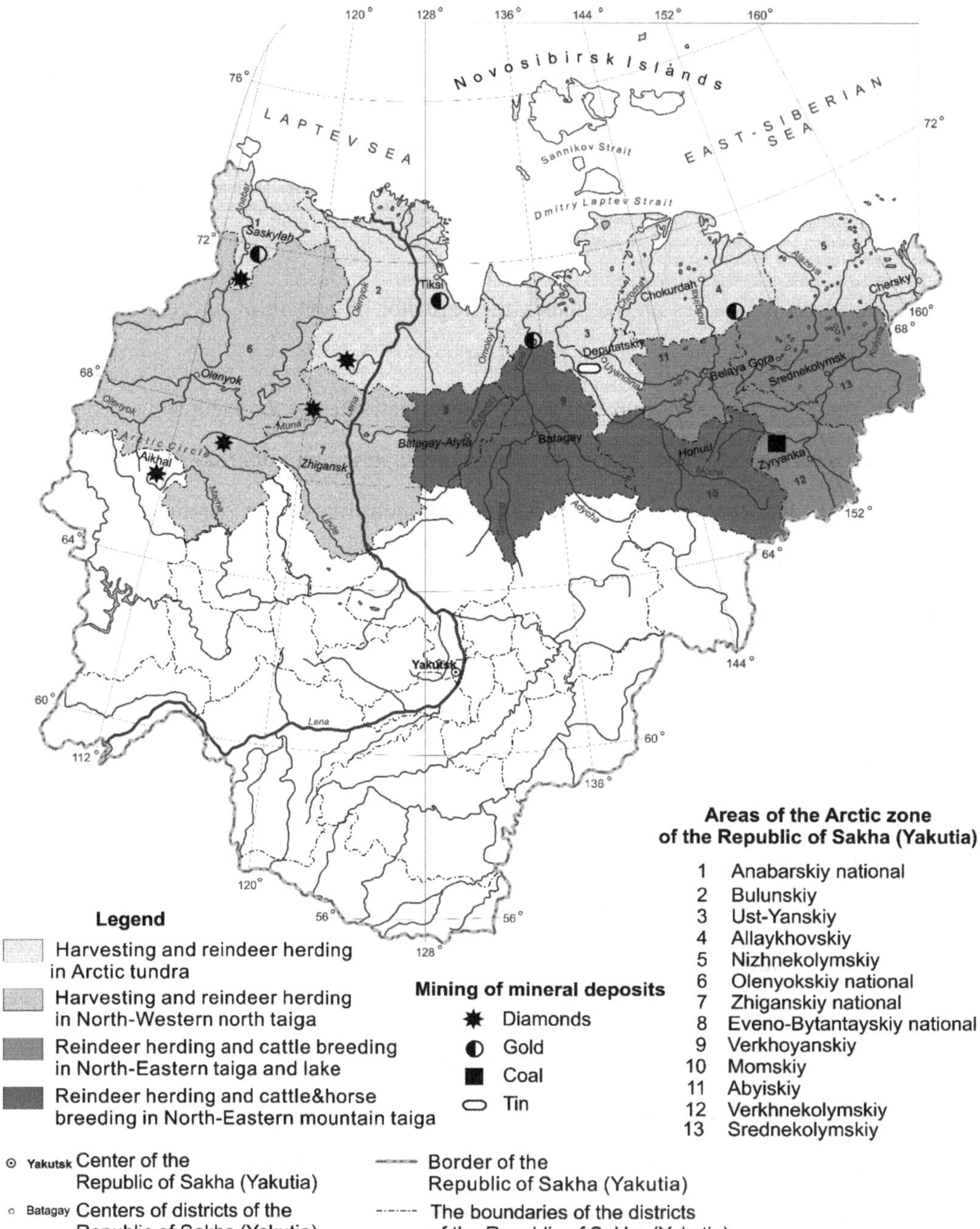

Source: https://www.mdpi.com/2079-9276/8/1/55/htm

2014 Neelov's gulf (Lena river delta) water quality was appraised 3 class of the "a" category ("polluted"). Amount of pollutants which considered in complex assessment increased to 6 from 14 ingredients and quality indicators. Critical indicators of pollution of waters were absent. The impurity was registered by compounds of manganese and copper in 100% of tests. According to the complex of the main pollutants, the waters of the river basin are classified as follows: Yana—"dirty"; Anabar at s. Saskylah—"very polluted"; Indigirka—"dirty"; Kolyma and Olenyok—"polluted" [2].

2.2. Social environment

The low density and the continuing migration outflow of the population, considerable distances between settlements, small population in most of them, high morbidity, reduced of the quality of educational and medical services are characterized the Arctic and northern territories of SR. The most accurate indicator of quality of life is health of the population. Along with bioclimatic factors the social environment in which he lives has an impact on human health. As its main components are considered: real wage, quality of food, living conditions, extent of development of health care, etc.

In 2013 the average salary on the Arctic districts was 39.9 thousand rubles, that it is 14.3% below than the level prevailing in the republic (46.5 thousand rubles). Unemployment rate exceeds a national average indicator (7.4%) in most of districts. The most burning issues are the backwardness of social infrastructure, dilapidation of buildings and accident rate of social objects [3].

For assessment of dependence of the state of health from the social environment, Republic Medico-Information and Analysis Center's statistical medico-demographic indicators about the tuberculosis, as to a socially important infectious disease, were analyzed during the period of 29 years (1982-2011).

In the ranked of a morbidity of the tuberculosis on increase of indicators: morbidities for the first time the revealed patients, the morbidities of staying on the registry patients and mortality, the Arctic and northern districts occupy the high and highest levels in the SR:

1. Eveno-Bytantaysky, Allaikhovsky, Anabarsky, Oleneksky (high level);

2. Momsky, Abyysky, Zhigansky (highest level).

In the ranked about increase of indicators of morbidity and mortality from the tuberculosis the last place in the republic there is Eveno-Bytantaysky district, where identification of patients is complicated by remoteness and low development of the social environment. In general the analysis of a morbidity of the population in the RS a socially important infectious disease – tuberculosis confirms the low level of the social environment of the Arctic and northern districts.

III. Northern reindeer breeding

3.1. Reindeer economy

The only branch of agriculture of the RS is Northern reindeer breeding where most of ISNPN are employed. The uniqueness of reindeer breeding is that it remains not only an industry, but also a way of life of families of reindeer breeders so far. Domestic deer feed indigenous people: give the main food product - meat; are used as the vehicle; production of winter clothes, footwear are also irreplaceable means for construction of the mobile dwelling [4].

The Arctic zone takes the first place in the republic by a quantity of a livestock of deer (share of this indicator in the republic - 70%). As of January 1, 2017, there are 110 households with the number of employees of 1.8 thousand people, who contain a livestock of deer in households of all categories 156,814 a livestock of deer, from them in the Arctic zone - 150,000. The maximum quantity of a livestock of deer was observed in the 1980, since 1990 in connection with the collapse of the USSR and reorganization of all economy of the Russian Federation there was a sharp reduction of number of deer: by 2-2.5 times. If in the 1980s in the SR the number of districts with a livestock of deer more than 1000 was 21 (Bulunsky district was on the first place: 40,755 heads), in 2016 those remained only 6 (on the first place - the Ust-Yansky district: 21,714 heads) (Figure 2).

The dynamics of the deer population over 2010 – 2016 shows positive changes in Abyysky, Nizhnekolymsky, Ust-Yansky districts. Negative values observed in: Allaikhovskiy (the complete destruction of livestock), Bulunsky, Verkhoyansky, Zhigansky, and other districts. In general on the Arctic zone except the first three listed districts negative dynamics of quantity of a livestock of deer (Table. 2) is observed.

The number of workers employed in reindeer breeding for 2006-2016 was reduced by 34.6% [5]. The highest number of reindeer breeders remains in large reindeer-breeding districts: Bulunsky, Momsky, Nizhnekolymsky, Eveno-Bytantaysky and Ust Yansky. In the industry the acute staff shortage is observed. Training for reindeer breeding is carried out in Nizhnekolymsky college of peoples of the North in the Chersky village of Nizhnekolymsky district.

Fixing of employees requires improvement of working and living conditions of workers of reindeer breeding, implementation of innovative technologies, increases in profitability of the industry.

Figure 2. Dynamics of the number of deer in districts there were more than 10 thousand deer

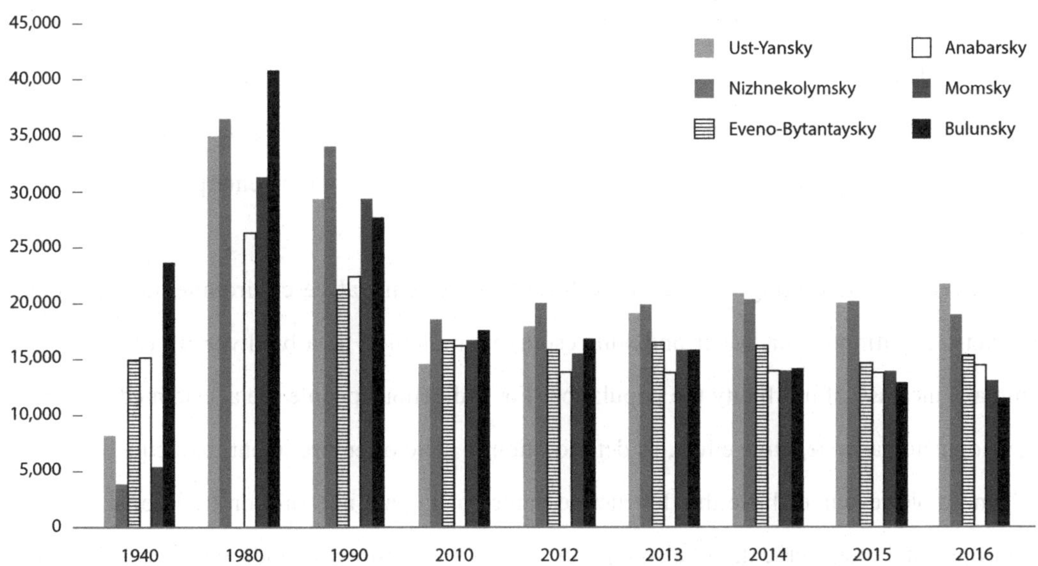

Table 2. Dynamics of the number of deer in all categories of farms of the SR for 2009-2016, for the beginning of the year number of reindeer

District	2009	2010	2011	2012	2013	2014	2015	2016
Ust-Yansky	12,852	14,657	16,832	17,918	19,217	20,903	20,117	21,714
Nizhnekolymsky	16,773	18,669	18,425	20,062	19,911	20,377	20,130	19,067
Eveno-Bytantaysky	16,132	16,763	17,426	15,880	16,639	16,182	14,648	15,371
Anabarsky	15,485	16,284	17,333	13,871	13,800	13,922	13,825	14,503
Momsky	16,224	16,800	16,838	15,581	15,901	13,904	14,009	13,186
Bulunsky	15,770	17,608	17,095	16,851	15,821	14,153	13,007	11,526
Oleneksky	4,694	4,794	4,946	4,915	5,901	5,463	4,864	4,187
Верхоянский	5,878	6,785	4,771	4,610	5,036	4,275	4,350	3,459
Zhigansky	6,164	6,603	6,701	6,004	6,322	5,228	4,004	3,081
Srednekolymsky	2,680	2,846	3,174	3,161	3,164	2,313	2,172	2,033
Verkhnekolymsky	1,157	1,057	1,085	1,178	1,122	1,203	1,121	1,016
Abyysky	358	424	460	453	524	626	703	446
Allaikhovsky	2,207	2,686	1,766	1,189	2,764	1,044	620	
Total on the Arctic zone	116,374	125,976	126,852	121,673	126,122	119,593	113,570	109,589
Total on the RS	190,125	200,825	200,280	194,903	191,070	177,431	165,270	156,011

3.2. The mining industry activities in the Arctic

The mining industry in the Arctic and the northern territories began to develop in 1930. There was coal, tin, gold and diamonds mining. Market relations, who began in 1991, led to the emergence of crises in almost all sectors of the mining industry of RS and many enterprises were liquidated.

Today in the districts of the arctic and northern zone there are objects of diamond, gold, coal and tin mining industries. The Table 3 had given the active mining enterprises in the arctic regions.

Activity of the mining industry is followed by huge negative environmental and social impacts: pollution of air, water and soil resources, reduction of a biodiversity of plants and animals, increase of morbidity the population. For indigenous people the accelerated industrial development has a negative effect, as deterioration in state of environment, reduction of stocks of renewable resources have the destructive nature of impact not only on traditional types of environmental management, but also on their mentality, culture and traditions. From this point

Table 3. Active mining enterprises in the arctic regions (1998–2015)

Industry	Enterprise	Start	Mining method	District
Diamond Mining	"Aikhal" Deposit	1998	Closed (underground)	Mirninsky
	"Almazy Anabara" OJSC	1998	Open (open-pit mine)	Anabarsky, Bulunsky, Zhigansky, Olenekskу
Gold Mining	"Arctic-Capital" Holding	2015	« »	Anabarsky, Allaikhovsky, Bulunsky, Ust-Yansky
Coal Mining	Zyryansky Coal Mine	1936	« »	Verkhnekolymsky
Tin Mining	"Tirekhtyakh" RIC	2015	« »	Ust-Yansky

of view, one of the burning issues for ISNPN there is a question of fair compensation of the natural and social damage caused by the industrial enterprises, to land users of the TNRMT.

IV. Ethnological Expertise

4.1. Ethnological expertise Law

In 2010, a law of the SR was passed: "On Ethnological Expertise in the Places of Traditional Residence and Traditional Economic Activities of the Peoples of the SR" [6]. The law still only, and also found support in Russian Federation, now taking into account the law RS federal normative legal acts are drafted.

The procedure of ethnological examination begins with a competitive tender for its implementation. The main documents submitted for ethnological expertise are (a) a draft of proposed economic and other activities; (b) an assessment of the impact of the projected activity on the original habitat and socio-cultural situation of small peoples (Foreign Economic Relations Department—FERD). The composition of the expert committee and the expert opinion are approved by the Government of the SR. [7]. To date, in the ethnological examination of SR, were reviewed 13 investment projects, including 5 projects in the arctic regions (Table 4).

In the course of ethnological expertise, it turned out that most of the questions and the comments from both experts and tribal communities concern the section of compensation for damages of the ISNPN, which are caused not only by the quality of work of OVES developers,

Table 4. Investment projects have investigated in the ethnological examination of SR in the arctic regions (2014-2017)

Investment project	District	Natural and economic activity zones in distribution on the industries	Date
Complex of geological and geophysical studies in the Arctic shelf	Anabarsky, Bulunsky	Harvesting and reindeer herding in Arctic tundra	2014
Mining of the diamond "Verkhne-Munskoe" field	Oleneksky	Harvesting and reindeer herding in North-Western north taiga	2016
Development of the diamond field on the Bolshaya Kuonamka and the Talakhtakh rivers	Oleneksky		2016
Mining on the rivers Malaya Kuonamka and Maspaky	Oleneksky		2016
Project and construction of the facility Concentrating factory on processing of gold-antimony ore of the field "Sentachan"	Verkhoyansky	Reindeer herding and cattle and horse breeding in North-Eastern mountain taiga	2017

but generally imperfection of the operating methodical approaches to calculation of the losses caused to associations of indigenous people.

4.2. Cases of ethnological expertise

Project "Complex geological and geophysical studies in the junction area of the Leno-Tunguska oil and gas province and the Laptevskaya potential oil and gas area." Developer of OVES: "Sever Project" LLC, Moscow.

The area of complex geological and geophysical works for the search for oil and gas deposits and their subsequent exploitation is located in the territory of the Bulunsky and Anabarsky Districts of the SR. The following will fall under the influence of geological and geophysical works in the territory of the Anabarsky Ulus 4 tribal communities and 2 municipal unitary enterprises. In the Bulunsky District - 1 municipal unitary enterprises and 1individual enterprises.

The main remarks of the expert in compensation of losses of ISNPN on the Anabarsky and Bulunsky districts:

- calculation of annual gross revenue from all types of crafts of the Anabarsky district (a tundra zone of the Arctic) is carried out according to the Aldansky and Olyokminsky districts (a medialtaiga zone of South Yakutia);
- types which do not meet in a tundra zone were included in the list of hunting animal

species and birds: a snow ram, manchurian deer, a roe, a musk deer, a squirrel, an elk, a lynx, a sable, columns, a glutton, columns, a wood-grouse, a hazel grouse who are characteristic of South Yakutia;

- the list of herbs is submitted by types which do not grow in a tundra zone: cranberry, cowberry, blueberry;
- market prices as for wild plants, and hunting types are underestimated;
- wrong establishment of income taking into account remoteness of a contour to point of realization: Aldan, Olekminsk, Hatystyr (medialtayga zone of South Yakutia).

The expert group of the Expert Commission of Ethnological Expertise offered:

- to supplement project documentation with data of characteristic of types of traditional economic activity, ethnocultural and socio-economic development of indigenous peoples of the Bulunsky district;
- to finish sections by calculations of compensation of losses of indigenous peoples according with the remarks;

The expert group of Commission of experts of ethnological expertise of Republic of Sakha (Yakutia) on a first stage of consideration of OVES drew the negative conclusion and recommended to finish the document. After correction of the main remarks the expert group took out the positive conclusion on materials of "Complex geologic-geophysical works in the field of a joint of Leno-Tungussky NGP and Laptevsky PNGO."

Technical project about mining of the "Verkhne-Munskoe" diamond field. Developer of OVES: "Sever Project" LLC, Moscow.

Territory of mining: the land plots used under infrastructure of 13 objects of the "Verkhne-Munskoe" field for construction and operation on the TNRMT of local value of the municipal unit "Oleneksky national district." The ground under construction and operation of the field was brought out of the inter-settlement territory which is a zone of absolute rest in the natural republican wildlife reserve of "Beke" according to the Order of the Government of the Russian Federation of April 8, 2011 [8]. In total the expert in compensation of losses of ISNPN gave 10 remarks, some of them are given here:

- the general comment specified insufficiently full use of initial materials: these tribal communities when calculating standard indicators according to gross revenue of households;
- for assessment of market prices of products of traditional environmental management the certified documents of tribal community of RKO "Amin" ("Amga") of the Aldansky district (a medialtayga zone of South Yakutia) which are used for Oleneksky district (a rare North taiga zone) led to the gross blunder as by types (existence of a snow ram, manchurian deer, cedar), and actual market prices of products of wild plants, hunting and fish resources;
- calculations of compensation of losses of ISNPN the price of products of reindeer breeding is underestimated by 3 times: venison - 100 rub/kg., and according to materials of OVES - 300 rub/kg. Also the deer capacity of pastures on the basis of which the products are calculated is underestimated in calculations: 4.3 deer a day on a hectare, and in appendix 4 of OVES - 15.1 deer a day on a hectare.
- the coefficient of decline of quality of pastures in annexes 10 and 13 of OVES makes in the first zone of influence 1.0, in the 2nd - 0.5. According to the Methodology, the 2nd zone is equated to withdrawal that is it has to calculate with coefficient 1.0 (100%). In annex 16 – in the 1st zone the coefficient of decline in quality makes 0.8, in the 2nd – 0.5, that is in the first zone decline in quality of pastures is underestimated by 20%, in the second - by 50%.

Taking into account the listed remarks, a global ecological and biospheric role of the Arctic in maintenance of balance of the nature of the Northern hemisphere, high vulnerability of natural complexes to technogenic impact and existence of especially protected natural territories and also possible mining of diamonds with the increased environmental risk, the expert recommends to finish sections by calculations of compensation of losses. The commission of experts at the 1st stage of consideration of the document drew the negative conclusion and recommended to finish the presented materials of OVES. After correction of the main remarks of OVES as a part of the project documentation The engineering design of working off of the "Verkhne Munskoe" field the commission of experts took out the positive conclusion.

Technical project of the development of the diamond field on the Bolshaya Kuonamka and the Talakhtakh rivers. Developer of OVES: Interregional center of the environmental audit and consulting LLC, Moscow.

One of positive results of work is geobotanical inspection of the current state of efficiency of cervine pastures in 2015. It is the first work which at the 1st stage passed the ethnological examination. In total the expert in compensation of losses of ISNPN gave 10 remarks, some of them are given here:

- work is performed as the scientific report, but not as OVES as a part of the Project. In the report there are a lot of excess descriptions of scientific character, at the same time concrete data on an object of a research and justifications of application of these or those approaches to assessment of losses of ISNPN are not sufficient;
- the cost of products of a domestic and wild deer has to be determined by market, but not book value and is underestimated by 1.5-1.7 times, the damage to hunting animal species is also underestimated;
- for calculations of losses to fishing trade fish price according to poll of the population of the settlement of Zhilinda is used and averages 90 rub/kg that it is also underestimated.

Taking into account the listed remarks and their subsequent specification during ethnological monitoring of the TNRMT, the presented materials of OVES for ethnological examination on the prospective area of Bolshaya Kuonamka and the Talakhtakh Rivers are assessed by commission of experts positively.

The project on production of search and estimated works on alluvial diamonds in basins of the rivers Malaya Kuonamka and Maspaky in 2015-2017. Developer of OVES: Interregional center of the environmental audit and consulting LLC, Moscow.

One of positive results of work is geobotanical inspection of the current state of efficiency of cervine pastures in 2015. The main remarks to OVES in general are identical with comments on the project of development of the loose diamond field on the prospective area of river Malaya Kuonamka. Experts made 11 remarks of the general character and 6 remarks according to ISNPN losses by the all 4th types of traditional environmental management (reindeer breeding, hunting and fishing crafts, collecting). All remarks are generally identical with the remarks of experts of the object of Bolshaya Kuonamka, which are not corrected according to the recommendations of experts, so the Expert Commission drew the negative conclusion at the 1st stage of examination.

In the processed OVES option of a remark of experts are generally corrected, the total amount of work was reduced (unnecessary scientific reasoning are excluded), despite the addition of 2 new sections.

It is very remarkable that "Almazy Anabara" OJSC and "Nizhne-Lenskoe" OJSC had socially oriented business in 8 districts where their activities is conducted. Contracts about cooperation in socio-economic development were signed with five districts (in the territory of which extraction of diamonds is conducted), the social and economic help to these districts is rendered on the sum of 1 431.4 million rub. The annual damage caused to the land user (the Oleneksky district) as a result of mountain and mining works of "Almazy Anabara" OJSC in basins of the rivers of Malaya Kuonamka with inflow of Maspaky, is estimated at 10.181 million rub in the prices of 2015.

Commission of experts of ethnological expertise for the processed version of the OVES about the project for production of search and estimated works on alluvial diamonds in basins of the rivers Malaya Kuonamka and Maspaky took out the positive conclusion.

Project and construction of the facility "Concentrating factory on processing of gold-antimony ore of the field "Sentachan." Developer of FERD: "Sever Project" LLC, Moscow."

The land plot under concentrating factory of the Sentachan field is on the TNRMT of local Tabalakhsky value of the Verkhoyansky district.

In general work is made not correctly and does not answer the official document OVES as a part of the project: a descriptive part of a method of calculation of losses of ISNPN occupies the most part of the report, results of assessment of losses of ISNPN – smaller, completely there is not at all calculation of the losses caused to the local TNRMT of Tabalakhsky of the Verkhoyansky district. In total, the damage compensation expert gave 8 remarks, according of the other sections of OVES - more than 10 remarks. Here are only a part of remarks of the damage compensation expert:

1. Calculation of additional products (camus, horns, an offal, a skin, horns, punts) is made on the basis of percent of the their cost to meat and taken at the level of 50%, currently additional products are sold individually, therefore approach of reduction of the cost of additional products to meat does not work today.
2. In the economic and geobotanical map according to the legend, the capacity of reindeer pastures is averages 4.8 deer/hectare (calculation of the expert), it is necessary to give a formula that the capacity of reindeer for definition of gross revenue, equal 2.4 is calculated
3. On p.26 it is told that in explications (annex 3) of land grounds are given characteristics on existence of reindeer pastures and also calculation for an economic stock of wild plants. Also there have to be sheets of capacity of pastures, but annex 3 is absent, there are also no annexes 4-8.
4. Text of calculation of damage of Municipality of «Tabalakhsky district» is given in annex 9-20, but there are absent.
5. The material damage to property of tribal communities is not assessed. In the work there is no data about hunting winter quarters, transitional and temporary small huts. If in a zone of influence of industrial facilities economic objects of tribal community get, then they must be marked on the map and for them calculations of damage are carried out.

Taking into account comments, experts at the 1st stage of consideration of the document drew the negative conclusion and recommended to finish OVES. After correction of the main remarks of experts, commission at the 2nd stage of consideration OVES took out the positive conclusion on the provided documents with the recommendation to solve the remarks listed in the conclusion during ethnological monitoring, on which the extent of the missed benefit of land users depends.

Practice of conducting ethnological examination in the Arctic zone of the republic showed that the submitted documents OVES not always conform to requirements of the Law "About Ethnological Examination …" and an official method of calculation of losses of ISNPN [9].

V. Conclusion

1. Practice of ethnological examination showed that the main remarks of experts are caused by insufficient knowledge of OVES developers of an object of a research: confusion in names of administrative regions, bad awareness on the TNRMT biological resources on administrative regions: types of a taiga zone etc. are given in a tundra zone ("Sever project" LLC).

2. In order to compensate for the social damage of indigenous people, to conclude tripartite Agreement on Cooperation and Promote Sustainable Development of ISNPN in the Project's Area of Influence Between the Project Customer, SR Government Authorities and Authorized Representatives of the Indigenous Minorities to improve and improve the quality of life of indigenous peoples in the form of cash or other social activities.

3. To recalculation of standard indicators of assessment of losses and also to specification of the extent of damage, both ecological, and social and economic it is necessary to adopt the Program of ethno and eco environmental monitoring in districts of industrial development of the TNRMT every 5 years based of certain indicators.

References

1. Бурцева Е.И. Компенсация убытков, причиненных объединениям коренных малочисленных народов, в условиях промышленного освоения территорий

// Экономика природопользования. – 2018. - № 2. Стр. 23-38. (Burtseva, E.I. Compensation of losses caused to associations of indigenous small-numbered peoples in conditions of industrial development of territories. Econ. Nat. Manag. 2018, 118, 24–38).

2. Государственный доклад о состоянии и охране окружающей среды Республики Саха (Якутия) в 2014 году / Правительство Респ. Саха (Якутия), М-во охраны природы Респ. Саха (Якутия). – http://old.sakha.gov.ru/min-ohrany-prirody. (Government Report about the State and Environmental Protection of the Republic of Sakha (Yakutia) in 2014 / Government Rep. Sakha (Yakutia), the Ministry of Nature Protection Rep. Sakha (Yakutia). – http://old.sakha.gov.ru/min-ohrany-prirody)
3. Постановление Правительства Республики Саха (Якутия) О комплексной программе Республики Саха (Якутия) «Социально-экономическое развитие арктических и северных районов республики Саха (Якутия) на 2014-2017 годы и на период до 2020 года». От 15.08.2014 №251 (в редакции постановления Правительства Республики Саха (Якутия от 25.01.2016 N 12). (Government Decree of the SR on the Integrated Program "Socio-Economic Development of the Arctic and Northern Districts for 2014–2017 and for the Period up to 2020" dated 15.08.2014. No.251 (red. 3. Government Decree of the SR dated 25.01.2016. No.12).
4. Донской Ф.С. Коренные малочисленные народы Севера, Сибири и Дальнего Востока во второй половине XX века. Т.2. Якутск, 2004. 320 с. (Donskoy F.S. Indigenous ethnic groups of the North, Siberia and the Far East in the second half of the 20th century. T.2. Yakutsk, 2004. 320)
5. Статистический ежегодник Республики Саха (Якутия): стат. Сб. /Федерал. служба гос. статистики по Респ. Саха (Якутия). Якутск, 2010. 704 с. (Statistical book of the Republic of Sakha (Yakutia)/Federal state service of statistics on the Republic of Sakha (Yakutia). Yakutsk, 2010. P.704).
6. Закон РС (Я) «Об этнологической экспертизе в местах традиционного проживания и традиционной хозяйственной деятельности коренных малочисленных народов Севера Республики Саха (Якутия)» от 14.04.2010 г. 820-З № 537-IV. (Law of the Sakha

(Yakutia) Republic "On Ethnological Expertise in Places of Traditional Residence and Traditional Economic Activities of Indigenous Peoples of the North of Sakha (Yakutia) Republic" dated 04.14.2010. 820-3 No. 537-IV).

7. Burtseva Evdokia, Bysyina Anna. Damage Compensation for Indigenous Peoples in the Conditions of Industrial Development of Territories on the Example of the Arctic Zone of the Sakha Republic // Resources - 2019. – vol. 8 - Number 55.
8. Распоряжение Правительства РФ от 8 апреля 2011 г. «О предоставлении закрытому акционерному обществу Акционерная компания "АЛРОСА" права пользования участком недр для разведки и добычи алмазов на территории Оленекского улуса». [Электронный ресурс] - 2014. Режим доступа: http://trud-ost.ru/?p=281676 -дата обращения 10.01.2017 (Order of the Government of the Russian Federation of April 8, 2011. "About granting to ALROSA JSC closed joint stock company the right of use of the subsoil plot for exploration and production of diamonds in the territory of the Oleneksky district." [An electronic resource] - 2014. Access mode: http://trud-ost.ru/?p=281676).
9. Методика исчисления размера убытков, причиненных объединениям коренных малочисленных народов Севера, Сибири и Дальнего Востока Российской Федерации в результате хозяйственной и иной деятельности в местах традиционного проживания и традиционной хозяйственной деятельности коренных малочисленных народов Российской Федерации. Утверждена Приказом Министерства регионального развития РФ от 09.12.2009 г. № 565 (Method of Calculating the Amount of Damages Caused to Associations of Small-Numbered Indigenous Peoples of the North, Siberia and the Far East of the Russian Federation as a Result of Economic and Other Activities in the Places of Traditional Residence and Traditional Economic Activities of Small Indigenous Peoples of the Russian Federation. Approved by the Order of the Ministry of Regional Development of the Russian Federation dated 9 December 2009 No. 565.)

UNIVERSITY CENTER FOR STRATEGIC PLANNING OF INTELLECTUAL ECONOMY

Afanasiy Afanasjevich Vinokurov
Candidate of Sciences in Techniques, Director of the Center of Intellectual Property,
North-Eastern Federal University named after M.K.Ammosov
xitvaa@yandex.ru

Roman Romanovich Nogovitsin
Doctor of Economics, Head of the Chair of Economy and Territorial Development
Institute of Economics and Finance,
North-Eastern Federal University named after M.K.Ammosov
mggo04@mail.ru

Abstract.

New tasks have been set for future periods to improve the intellectual property management system, which is able to create in-demand innovations for the goods and services market, based on the support of «intellectual economy» processes as the final stage of the innovation chain of science and technology. Plan for improving the system on the example of the North-Eastern Federal University after named M.K. Ammosov (Yakutsk) in order to form a new intra-university economy based on knowledge and focused on meeting the needs, ensuring sustainable development and social partnership for the university, is aimed at fulfilling the tasks of infrastructure support and achieving leading positions in the field of intellectual activity. The proposed platform of the university's intellectual economy is a highly effective mechanism for the development of tools for the commercialization of intellectual rights, taking into account the quantitative and qualitative composition of transactions and their profitability. At the same time, there is a clear idea of the state of affairs and the university's place in the intellectual property market. The aim of the project is to improve the university intellectual property management system.

Keywords: Intellectual property, management of intellectual property, effectiveness of intellectual activity, intellectual economy.

I. Introduction

In one of the last Messages to the Federal Assembly, President of Russia V.V. Putin noted that an enormous technological potential is accumulating in the world today, which makes it possible to make a real breakthrough in improving the quality of life of people, in modernizing the economy, infrastructure and public administration, and the efficiency of using this opportunity of the technological revolution depends on each participant in the process, and noted that we are talking about a convenient infrastructure, comfortable tax regimes, protection of intellectual property, technical regulation and venture financing [1].

II. Analysis of the current state of the state policy of intellectual property

2.1. Patenting activity in Russia

The Russian Federation is a party to international treaties operating under the auspices of the World Intellectual Property Organization (WIPO, Geneva), as well as a member of the Eurasian Patent Organization (EAPO). The legislation of the Russian Federation allows domestic and foreign entities to provide reliable protection and effective use of the results of intellectual activity, to obtain additional profit, competitive advantages and ensures a stable and

Table 1. Dynamics of filing applications for the grant of patents of Russia for inventions

Indicators	2013	2014	2015	2016	2017	2018
Applications submitted to Rospatent, in total, of them:	44,914	40,308	45,517	41,587	36,454	37,957
Russian applicants	28,765	24,072	29,269	26,795	22,777	24,926

secure presence of goods and services in the domestic and foreign markets.

It is known from the annual report of the Federal Service for Intellectual Property (Rospatent, www.rupto.ru) [2] that in the country about 35-40 thousand applications for patenting inventions are filed annually (see Table 1), moreover, from Russian applicants about 25 thousand applications.

At the same time, Moscow and St. Petersburg, Ivanovo, Moscow, Tomsk, Kursk, Kaluga, Voronezh, Novosibirsk regions and the Republic of Tatarstan were identified as leaders in inventive activity among the regions of Russia. The average index of the coefficient of inventive activity of the leading regions, defined as the number of applications for inventions filed by Russian applicants per 10,000 people in the region, was 0.92.

Table 2. The coefficient of inventive activity in the regions of the Far Eastern Federal District of Russia

	2009	2010	2011	2012	2013	2014	2015	2016	2017	2018
Far Eastern Federal District	0.97	1.18	1.24	1.35	1.42	1.35	1.4	1.3	1.02	0.77
The Republic of Sakha (Yakutia)	0.87	0.94	1.14	1.07	1.15	1.28	1.1	1.05	0.95	1.12
Kamchatka Krai	0.34	0.40	0.73	0.56	0.74	0.79	0.32	0.6	0.41	0.29
Primorsky Krai	1.21	1.34	1.40	1.53	1.47	1.46	1.45	1.34	1.19	1.10
Khabarovsk region	1.10	1.60	1.64	2.13	1.87	1.88	1.87	1.68	1.25	1.08
Amur region	1.37	1.61	1.47	1.47	1.94	1.57	2.07	1.75	1.22	0.98
Magadan Region	0.42	0.68	0.87	0.66	0.59	0.61	1.09	1.1	0.82	0.49
Sakhalin region	0.17	0.25	0.31	0.22	0.18	0.12	0.39	0.39	0.14	0.16
Jewish Autonomous Region	0.05	0.10	0.00	0.17	0.34	0.77	1.26	1.64	0.85	0.56
Chukotka	0.00	0.00	0.00	0.00	0.00	0.00	0.00	0.20	0.00	0.00
The Republic of Buryatia										0.38
Transbaikal region										0.21
Middle circle	0.62	0.77	0.84	0.87	0.96	0.94	1.06	1.08	0.76	0.58

The coefficient of inventive activity in the Republic of Sakha (Yakutia) over the past 5 years has averaged 1.18 (see Table 2), while 1/4 of them are applications from the M.K. Ammosov North-Eastern Federal University (NEFU). At the end of 2018, Yakutia became the leader in terms of this indicator among the regions of the Far Eastern Federal District.

2.2. Patenting in the Republic of Sakha (Yakutia)

Analysis of staffing of patent services of organizations of the scientific and educational sector of the republic shows that the average age of specialists is at least 55 years old, and, moreover, targeted professional training of new personnel is practically not conducted. No specialist in the status of patent attorney of the Russian Federation is certified and registered from the republic.

With a view to enhancing inventive activity, the department plans to solve, among other things, the task of including indicators characterizing the increase in the effectiveness of scientific research in the system of target indicators of state programs involving the implementation of research, scientific and technical programs and projects. In addition, changes will be made to the legislation on service inventions in order to increase the creative activity of workers and develop systems of professional standards for all activities in the field of intellectual property.

At the same time, the following documents were identified as strategic planning documents:

- An action plan for the implementation of the Strategy for the Scientific and Technological Development of the Russian Federation for 2017–2019, approved by Decree of the Government of the Russian Federation dated June 24, 2017 No. 1325-p [3];
- Action plans for the areas of the Digital Economy of the Russian Federation program, approved by Decree of the Government of the Russian Federation of July 28, 2017 No. 1632-p [4];
- The plan of activities aimed at stimulating the innovation development of the Russian Federation for 2017–2018, approved by Decree of the Government of the Russian Federation of August 25, 2017 No. 1817-p [5], etc.

III. The role of higher education in the formation of a regional intellectual property market

3.1. Intellectual property infrastructure

In the period of university transformation in order to enhance its impact on the socio-economic development of territories associated with the transition of the state economy to an innovative development path, the ability of the university to create and implement large-scale innovations for the goods and services market becomes a priority. This ability can only be based on knowledge, in which intellectual property is the determining factor for entering the market.

Back in 2012, the Technology and Innovation Support Center (TISC) was established on the basis of the NEFU in Russia according to the international project of Rospatent and WIPO (www.wipo.int).

This event was promoted by the existing foundation of the university in the field of intellectual property management, in particular, in 2011, the university created a unique in the Northeast region of the country information resource of patent and information funds of Russia and the leading countries of the world, based on information resources of Rospatent, the Eurasian Patent Office , European Patent Office, etc. The total amount of information files is more than 2.5 TB. With the creation of TISCs, the university received opportunities for training specialists and popularizing knowledge in the field of intellectual property for a wide mass of users.

The network of TISC NEFU includes, in addition to the head, a newly created center of the 2nd level on the basis of the National Library of the Republic of Sakha (Yakutia) and centers in Neryungri and Mirny, on the basis of the university branches, thereby the university together with Rospatent and WIPO created all the conditions for information support and consulting support for the innovation movement in all major cities of the republic, which are scientific and industrial centers of the region. TISCs in aggregate annually work out at least 2,000 appeals on all aspects of intellectual property.

In many respects, due to the advantages in providing the TISC network with a range of services on free access to patent and non-patent information resources, electronic interaction when applying for patenting inventions and conducting office work, as well as conducting events with the participation of leading experts in the field of intellectual property, allowed to develop a regional intellectual property management system, and in 2018, 2019 NEFU was recognized as one of the best practitioners of the TISC in Russia.

Undoubtedly, the strength of the TISC project is the involvement of regional universities in carrying out scientific research, conducting thematic events implemented by WIPO and Rospatent. Thus, as part of a pilot project on the use of information that is part of the public domain, for economic development, where the diamond company ALROSA was the main respondent, primary mechanisms were developed for the industry sector «Subsoil Use». In addition, NEFU tested a new toolkit for determining and refining scientific and technological priorities based on searching and analyzing patent data «MON / ROSPATENT - Global Technological Analytics System» (PATSCAPE) developed by Rospatent together with the Ministry of Education and Science of Russia. The system is actively used by the scientific community of the region.

With the support of the Government of the Republic of Sakha (Yakutia), NEFU for the first time implemented a project to expand the availability of advisory assistance on intellectual property issues, within which more than 100 small and medium-sized innovative business entities are supported.

The main focus is to expand access to professional information for different groups of applicants. For this, new business contacts with Russian and foreign partners are being created, effective approaches are being introduced in solving commercialization issues of developments, scientific research in the field of intellectual property management is being supported, new Internet technologies are being used to disseminate knowledge in the field of intellectual property. NEFU continues to expand its work in these areas.

3.2. New mechanisms in the implementation of the university system of intellectual property management

Based on the results achieved over the past periods in the formation of the NEFU intellectual property management system, new tasks have been set to improve the system capable of creating in-demand innovations for the goods and services market based on the support of the «intellectual economy» processes as the final stage of the innovation chain of science and technology development.

In this case, «intellectual economy» means a reasonable economy based on knowledge, and focused not only on the satisfaction of material needs, but also on the satisfaction of other needs, ensuring sustainable development and social partnership. The purpose of the intellectual economy (IE) is to establish control over new scientific and technical knowledge, i.e. the creation of rules for its production and distribution and the establishment of sanctions for their violation, securing knowledge of specific attributes (restrictions) [6].

Thus, new tasks should be aimed at developing motivations and stimulating the effectiveness of intellectual activity, the system of intra-university activities for the formation of qualitatively new mechanisms to support invention and create innovations at the university.

Based on the foregoing, the objectives are to achieve the advanced positions of intellectual activity for creating a sustainable system of economic development of the university based on intellectual resources - the Center for Intellectual Economy of the University («CINTEC»), while the system being improved includes measures to develop the dissemination of knowledge in the field of intellectual property , staffing, training of specialists in all areas of knowledge management, regulatory and information management in the area of research and innovation activities, the construction of the patent and economic strategic planning in the development of technological innovations.

Achieving economic results from the commercialization of rights to the results of intellectual activity is the final stage of the innovation chain of development of science and technology.

It is well known that not all results can be claimed on the market at a specific stage, while opinions are credible that each such result can be the basis for the development of subsequent, more attractive for implementation and practical application of developments. The task of the university is to provide favorable conditions for the use of the newly created results. In this case, the intellectual economy will be based on meeting the needs of both the university itself, the author's employer and copyright holder, the author and the society acting as a consumer of the innovation. Moreover, the interests of those departments of the university (departments or laboratories) on the basis of which this result was created should be taken into account. From this, it proceeds that the more successful results for commercialization will be those that will be in demand in the intellectual property market at this stage of development, which may be, for example, predetermined or predicted by building commercial strategies for disposing of intellectual rights. For what, it is necessary to learn to use modern tools of patent and information analytics, to have the basics of knowledge management, based on the consolidation of related services for legal, economic and organizational support.

To assess the effectiveness of the implementation of measures to create a platform of intellectual economy, you can develop a number of target indicators. But the main ones should give a clear idea of the state of affairs and the place of the university in the field of commercialization of intellectual rights, taking into account the quantitative and qualitative composition of transactions and their profitability, for example, depending on the annual accounting value of intellectual value.

The goal of the CINTEC project is to improve the university intellectual property management system. At the same time, work is planned in the following areas:

A1. Development of personnel potential and competences in the field of innovation activity and intellectual property;

A2. Improving the protection and enforcement of intellectual property rights;

A3. Monitoring and analysis of intellectual property performance;

B. Intellectual economy - as a factor in the sustainable development of the university.

The development of human resources and the wide dissemination of knowledge in the field of intellectual property among all students and employees of the university is the key to improving the university's system of intellectual property management, based primarily on the university's intellectual property policy.

The training of specialized personnel (direction A1) is explained by the versatility and interdisciplinary intellectual property. To ensure full-fledged management of innovation processes, not only patent specialists are demanded, but also analysts, marketing specialists, economists and appraisers, lawyers and attorneys, mediators, experts and specialists in patent strategy. Adjustment of the direction and type of activity of intellectual property management specialists takes place on an ongoing basis as science and technology develops, innovations are introduced into the norms of legislation and conditions imposed by the market. For the same reason, the work on training and development of competences among students and employees of the university, taking into account the specifics of the constant renewal of their composition, should be carried out on an ongoing basis.

Personnel training and competence development are the primary and fundamental activities of the base A block of the project. The main results of the implementation of the A1 direction are:

- introduction of a unified policy of NEFU in the field of intellectual property;
- the creation of a training center to provide training processes for advanced training and professional retraining of specialists in intellectual property of organizations in the region, to form a platform for interaction in the framework of cooperation with national and foreign partners.

The need to improve the work on ensuring legal protection (direction A2) is explained by the fact that all recorded results of intellectual activity that meet the requirements of current legislation for determining protectability are subject to such protection: novelty, inventive step, industrial applicability, originality, creative input and etc.

It is important to timely identify such results and ensure timely legal protection through official examination and registration. However, it is advisable to conduct a preliminary analysis and build a patent strategy on the identified (expected) results in order to determine the dominant positions in priority scientific areas. At the same time, different approaches can be taken for a specific result. First, the analytical group should present a coordinated protection regime (patenting or production secret) and determine the composition of the right holder, for example, either solely by the employer or joint ownership with the author, or by the individual himself. Secondly, in cases of a positive assessment of patent analytics, a patent strategy should be built to further commercialize the identified technical result, including defining exceptional approaches to working with a scientific group of authors and introducing the development to the market for subsequent high economic and social results from use.

The practice of introducing preliminary patent analytics is included in the base A block of the project and includes two main areas:

- introducing into the practice of carrying out scientific research on the order of analytical research at the stage of requesting topics, in order to be more confident in obtaining potentially attractive results for commercialization by the scientific group, preliminary work should be performed to determine the level of technology in the studied area and identify the most relevant for the near future areas of research and development. Thus, science from the very beginning must be aimed at the needs of the national economy and society and strives to obtain new demanded results. At the same time, analytical studies of the state of the art with a development forecast are carried out using patent information, which is the only reliable source of new technical achievements at any point in time;
- carrying out an analytical study of the results of scientific research regarding the availability of protectable and commercially attractive developments for the timely adoption of measures to ensure legal protection and the construction of an implementation strategy.

In addition, in order to resolve patent disputes, it is necessary to form an advocacy group on the protection of intellectual rights, actively using, among other things, methods of pre-trial problem solving, for example, mediation methods.

Monitoring and project-analytical project management are the activities of the base unit A of the project, are inter-unit in nature and are aimed at the timely identification of protectable and commercially promising research results to take measures according to the form of legal protection and building an implementation strategy (practical application) to the market (direction A3). For this purpose, advanced technology analysts, estimates and expertise by comparing the identified result with the capabilities and needs of a sector of the market for goods and services are used. Proper analytics can help a university achieve high economic results from using its own or acquired results of intellectual activity.

In addition, it is important to conduct observations of promising technologies on a global scale, which are taken into account when shaping the research and development topics. Such work can be performed on specific requests of research teams and presented in the form of an analytical report. At the same time, in those areas that are in demand in the region, but not mastered by the university at the moment, recommendations on the formation of new research directions on the basis of acquired technologies belonging to third parties can be formed.

Achieving economic results from the commercialization of the rights to innovations is the final stage of the innovation chain of development of science and technology (direction B).

The processes of introducing new results are accompanied by the execution of official procedures for registering the fact of a transaction, for which, contractual obligations must be competently executed, taking into account all the conditions of control by the right holder over the licensee's use of the rights to the transferred intellectual property.

IV. Conclusion

In order to enhance inventive activity in the Russian Federation, it is planned to include intellectual property in the indicators characterizing the effectiveness of scientific research, government programs, scientific and technical programs and projects. In addition, changes will be made to the legislation on service inventions in order to increase the creative activity of workers and develop systems of professional standards for all activities in the field of intellectual property. At the same time, the Strategy for the Scientific and Technological Development of the Russian Federation for 2017–2019 was defined as the main strategic planning document.

Improving the university's intellectual property management system in order to create a new university-based economy based on knowledge and focused on meeting the needs of the university, ensuring sustainable development and social partnership, is aimed at fulfilling the objectives of infrastructure support and attaining advanced positions in the field of intellectual activity.

At the same time, directions for the development of personnel potential and competences in the field of intellectual property, improvement of legal protection and protection of intellectual rights, monitoring and analysis of the effectiveness of intellectual activity and the formation of the university intellectual economy as a factor of its sustainable development were determined. The project will achieve the following key results:

- introduction of a uniform policy in the field of intellectual property;
- creation of educational programs for the development of competencies in intellectual property issues;
- formation of a platform for interaction in the framework of cooperation with national and foreign partners;
- achievement of the level of leading universities in the performance of intellectual activity;
- introduction of the practice of building a patent strategy, incl. based on the results of marketing research on a global scale;
- improvement of indicators of intellectual economy of the university, based on the achievement of profitability from the use of the results of intellectual activity, which is at least 200% of the annual accounting value of intellectual rights.

References

1. Послание Президента Федеральному Собранию от 01 марта 2018 года. URL: http://kremlin.ru/events/president/news/copy/56957 (дата обращения 20.03.2019). (Message of the President to the Federal Assembly of March 1, 2018. URL: http://kremlin.ru/events/president/

news/copy/56957 (appeal date 03/20/2019))

2. Отчет о деятельности Роспатента за 2018 год. Ежегодное официальное издание Федеральной службы по интеллектуальной собственности (Роспатент) // Под общей ред. Г.П. Ивлиева. – М.: Издательство ФИПС, 2019. - 200 с. (Report on the activities of Rospatent for 2018. Annual official publication of the Federal Service for Intellectual Property (Rospatent) // Ed. G.P. Ivlieva. - M .: Publishing house FIPS, 2019. - 200 p.)
3. Распоряжение Правительства Российской Федерации от 24 июня 2017 года № 1325-р «Об утверждении плана реализации Стратегии научно-технологического развития России». URL: http://static.government.ru/media/files/g5OvkCKBOKLEhAXjN94ogSBElV39ObPA.pdf (дата обращения 20.03.2019) (Order of the Government of the Russian Federation dated June 24, 2017 No. 1325-p «On approval of the implementation plan for the Strategy for the Scientific and Technological Development of Russia». URL: http://static.government.ru/media/files/g5OvkCKBOKLEhAXjN94ogSBElV39ObPA.pdf (appeal date 03/20/2019).
4. Распоряжение Правительства Российской Федерации от 28 июля 2017 года № 1632-р «Об утверждении программы «Цифровая экономика Российской Федерации». URL: http://static.government.ru/media/files/9gFM4FHj4PsB79I5v7yLVuPgu4bvR7M0.pdf (дата обращения 20.03.2019) (Order of the Government of the Russian Federation of July 28, 2017 No. 1632-p «On Approval of the Digital Economy of the Russian Federation Program». URL: http://static.government.ru/media/files/9gFM4FHj4PsB79I5v7yLVuPgu4bvR7M0.pdf (appeal date 03/20/2019)).
5. Распоряжение Правительства Российской Федерации от 25 августа 2017 года № 1817-р «Об утверждении плана мероприятий, направленных на стимулирование инновационного развития РФ, на 2017-2018 гг.». URL: http://static.government.ru/media/files/RnuuWjjVn1ACDQ9wYmkgXfINcjcE732A.pdf (дата обращения 20.03.2019) (Order of the Government of the Russian Federation of August 25, 2017. No. 1817-p «On approval of the plan of measures aimed at stimulating the innovative development of the Russian Federation for 2017-2018». URL: http://static.government.ru/media/files/RnuuWjjVn1A

CDQ9wYmkgXflNcjcE732A.pdf (appeal date 03/20/2019)).

6. Наумов Е.А., Понукалин А.А., Бенуа А.Е. Интеллектуальная экономика и устойчивое развитие в свете теории институционального конструктивизма. // «Международный электронный журнал. Устойчивое развитие: наука и практика». 1(10), 2013, С .66-74. (Naumov, EA, Ponukalin, A.A., Benoit, A.E. Intellectual economics and sustainable development in the light of the theory of institutional constructivism. //International electronic journal. Sustainable development: science and practice. 1 (10), 2013, pp .66-74).

ARCTIC SPACE AS A METHOD OF PRESERVING ETHNIC SELF-IDENTIFICATION

Larisa Yurievna Pisareva
Candidate of Sciences in Sociology, Associate Professor, Institute of Economics and Finance, NEFU
pisareva@inbox.ru

Abstract.

The article analyzes the problems of sustainable development of the territories of traditional nature usage of small indigenous peoples of the North. The study was conducted with the support of grant # 18-49-140005 "Transformations of socio-cultural image of indigenous population of Coastal Arctic of Yakutia in the conditions of modernization: experience of interdisciplinary study" financed by Russian Scientific Foundation. An analysis of the models of traditional life being shows significant transformations in the way of life of Northern people associated with the extraction of mineral resources in the Arctic. From the nomadic way of life - to the typically rural way of life: a short distance had been covered. Further narrowing of the living space raises for the indigenous people of the North the question of losing their ethnic identity. For the indigenous people of the North, the question of preserving the traditional way of life has been remaining the most important over a long period of time. However, this period is not comparable in duration with the history of the Arctic civilization which fragments are concealed in the descendants of the people who inhabited the northern latitudes of different continents on the Earth. The small ethnic population of the North carry a unique code linking them with the history and existence of the Arctic civilization.

Keywords: Arctic space, Arcticl social indicators (ASI), socio-economic development, level of living, indigenous peoples of the North, civilization, sustainable development, traditional model of livelihood, Coastal Arctic regions.

I. Introduction

The term "Arctic civilization" was introduced by Yu.V. Yakovets and U.V. Vinokurova who were inspired by the ideas of M.Ye. Nikolayev describing the Arctic philosophy of sakha people. In his numerous works there were discussed the achievements of people living in extremely cold natural and climatic conditions that formed a special circumpolar civilization. According to him the Arctic civilization is a civilization of survival, which is based on folk wisdom [1].

The end of the twentieth century, therefore, marked a turn to a new look at the Arctic. There happened a change of perception of the area. The Arctic had lost the context of a place associated with emptiness, immensity and whiteness and started to develop a system of ideas that include human presence, but ignore human experience in this area [2]. In Arctic space there occurred the collision of Western and Arctic civilizations.

The West with its technologies and industrial economy, consumer lifestyle, mass culture and alter faith rushed to the Arctic displacing and changing the way of life of indigenous people, depriving them of their traditional lifestyle, changing the outlook of the younger generation, spreading alcoholism, diseases and new moral values.

The economic and socio-cultural clash of civilizations has raised the question of its consequences. The acuteness of the influence of the intervention of the West and its industrial culture in the Arctic society manifested itself in the late twentieth century when the Declaration on Environment and Development signed at the Earth Summit in Rio de Janeiro in 1992 had changed the attitude of mankind to the surrounding space forever. The report "Our Common Future" prepared under the leadership of G.H. Bruntland [3] presented a picture of the edge where the mankind found itself in its egoistic desire to take the maximum profit from the environment, to transform the resources in order to increase their own comfort and after all to leave the places where necessary resources were located lifeless, polluted wastelands that have lost their original natural basis.

The environmental aspect of human activities has acquired a significant role in the development and adoption of any managerial decisions.

II. Social and economic indicators of living standards of the population of the Coastal Arctic regions of the Republic of Sakha (Yakutia)

2.1. Demographic characteristics

Between 2006-2009 foreign researchers under the leadership of the Arctic Institute named after V. Stefanson (Iceland) developed tools to ensure monitoring of the level of socio-economic development of the Arctic territories. The researchers focused on the regions located in the coastal areas of the Arctic Ocean. Accordingly the territory and population of the Republic of Sakha (Yakutia) was included in the monitoring of indicators which were called Arctic social indicators (ASI).

In the report "ASI-II: Implementation" [8] prepared as the results of testing the monitoring methodology of Arctic social indicators data for the Republic of Sakha (Yakutia) characterized the entire population of the region not taking into account and not distributing it by ethnicity which was one of the key shortcomings of the assessment.

For a more objective assessment of the current level of socio-economic development of the indigenous population of the Arctic zone in the interests of which Arctic social indicators were developed it is necessary to use more detailed statistics which unfortunately is not available in the statistical reporting forms.

The solution to this problem was drawn to the attention of the participants of the VII

Table 1. The population of the coastal regions of the Arctic zone of the Republic of Sakha (Yakutia) (people)

Name of the region	Urban population				Rural population			
	2011	2015	2016	2017	2011	2015	2016	2017
Allaikhovsky	2,344	2,118	2,068	2,095	678	615	614	623
Anabarsky	-	-	-	-	3,501	3,387	3,431	3,500
Bulunsky	5,178	4,557	4,556	4,604	3,961	9,847	3,810	3,800
Niznekolymsky	2,841	2,639	2,605	2,600	1,805	1,787	1,781	1,766
Ust-Yansky	4,370	3,878	3,926	3,920	3,681	3,366	3,316	3,282

Source: Statistical data of the Territorial Office of the Federal State Statistics Service for the Republic of Sakha (Yakutia), provided as part of comprehensive scientific research of RS (Y) 2017.

international forum "Arctic: Present and Future." The final resolution included a clause on the need to prepare a special statistical release "Economic and Social Indicators of Indigenous Areas of the North" gathering information throughout the Russian Arctic.

Describing the macroeconomic situation that has developed since 2010 in the coastal uluses of the Arctic zone of the Republic of Sakha (Yakutia) it should be noted that modernization and industrial development processes that affected mainly the Anabar region where placer diamonds are mined ("Almazy Anabara" company) have a significant impact on the growth and dynamics of socio-economic indicators of the region. The workers of the company's shift camps are specialists recruited from different parts of Yakutia.

Only in the Anabar district during the period of the company's operation it was possible to stabilize the indicators in terms of the number of residents (Table. 1). In other areas there has been a decrease in numbers. For the period from 2011 to 2017 the decrease in the number averaged: among the urban population - 10.5%, among the rural - 6.5%.

In the Anabar region there are high rates of natural (12.7 per 1000 people) and migration growth (72.1 per 10,000 people). Second place gets Allaikhovskiy area (10.7 and 25.9 respectively). In other regions the natural increase does not exceed 10.0 per 1000 people (Bulunsky-6, Nizhnekolymsky - 4.5, Ust-Yansky - 5.4) and there is a migration decrease.

The highest level of the indicator concerning the employment structure of the economically active population is in the Anabar region - 85.6% (2010) and 80.6% (2016) (Table. 2). At the same

Table 2. Employment structure of the economically active population of the coastal regions of the Arctic zone of the RS (Y) (person)

Name of the region	Economically active population		The average number of employees of organizations		Employment rate in economically active population	
	2010 г	2016 г	2010 г	2016 г	2010 г	2016 г
Allaikhovsky	1,580	1,493	1,263	1,044	79.9%	70.0%
Anabarsky	2,493	1,954	2,135	1,576	85.6%	80.6%
Bulunsky	4,639	4,086	3,502	2,970	75.4%	72.6%
Niznekolymsky	2,557	2,370	1,972	1,615	77.1%	68.1%
Ust-Yansky	4,750	3,921	3,432	2,506	55.7%	63.9%

Source: Statistical data of the Territorial Office of the Federal State Statistics Service for the Republic of Sakha (Yakutia), provided as part of comprehensive scientific research of RS (Y) 2017.

Table 3. The average monthly nominal wage of the coastal regions of the Arctic zone of the Republic of Sakha (Yakutia) (rubles)

Name of the region	The average monthly nominal wage of employees of organizations			Including mining		
	2010 г	2016 г	Темп роста	2010 г	2016 г	Темп роста
Allaikhovsky	25,567	53,680	209%	-	-	
Anabarsky	36,902	95,944	259%	51,902	160,393	309%
Bulunsky	24,769	52,468	252%	35,486	166,598	469%
Niznekolymsky	24,816	51,628	208%	27,093	-	
Ust-Yansky	25,117	54,760	218%	61,462	109,668	178%

Source: Statistical data of the Territorial Office of the Federal State Statistics Service for the Republic of Sakha (Yakutia), provided as part of comprehensive scientific research of RS (Y) 2017.

time there is a general tendency to reduce the average number of employees of organizations in all areas of this territory.

A significant quantitative increase in the average monthly nominal wage is also noted in the Anabar district (Table. 3).

2.2. Economic characteristics

The average subsistence cash income of the population in the coastal regions of the Arctic zone of Yakutia is 40,001 rubles, while the highest figure in the Anabar region is 58,141 rubles.

According to the indicators of traditional types of agricultural activity the Anabar district

Table 4. Number of reindeer per capita in Coastal regions of the Arctic zone of the Republic of Sakha (Yakutia) (heads)

Name of the region	Population (people)	Stock of reindeer (heads)		
		2010	2016	Per capita 2016
Allaikhovsky	2,718	1,766	-	
Anabarsky	3,500	17,333	15,407	4.4
Bulunsky	8,404	17,095	12,337	1.4
Niznekolymsky	4,306	18,425	19,920	4.6
Ust-Yansky	7,202	16,832	22,774	3.2

Source: Statistical data of the Territorial Office of the Federal State Statistics Service for the Republic of Sakha (Yakutia), provided as part of comprehensive scientific research of RS (Y) 2017.

Table 5. Retail trade, catering and the volume of paid services to the population of coastal regions of the Arctic zone of the Republic of Sakha (Yakutia)

Name of the region	Retail turnover per capita, rubles			The turnover of catering per capita, rubles			Volume of paid services per capita, rubles		
	2010 г	2016 г	Темп роста	2010	2016	Темп роста	2010 г	2016 г	Темп роста
Allaikhovsky	72,620	149,031	205%	315	1,659	526%	14,953	20,041	134%
Anabarsky	86,938	192,327	221%	397	1,445	363%	11,878	18,294	154%
Bulunsky	60,167	129,233	214%	748	978	130%	9,849	18,284	185%
Niznekolymsky	68,470	169,893	248%	316	506	160%	18,109	29,384	162%
Ust-Yansky	68,505	159,651	233%	362	1,209	333%	19,977	22,192	111%

Source: Statistical data of the Territorial Office of the Federal State Statistics Service for the Republic of Sakha (Yakutia), provided as part of comprehensive scientific research of RS (Y) 2017.

along with the Nizhnekolymsky district reached certain indicators for reindeer husbandry. The number of deer per capita in the Anabar district is 4.4, and in the Nizhnekolymsky region - 4.6 (Table. 4).

However the volume of domestic consumption in the Anabar region does not exceed the indicators of other coastal Arctic regions (Table. 5). Higher incomes of the population do not significantly affect the activation of trade and stimulate the economy of the region. The reason may be the lack of leisure infrastructure and the variety of services provided. Funds are either accumulated or spent outside the Arctic zone.

In Anabar district the housing stock is being actively updated. The share of housing built

Table 6. Produced products and services and profitable enterprises of coastal regions of the Arctic zone of the Republic of Sakha (Yakutia)

Name of the region	The volume of shipped goods of own production, work and services performed (million rubles)			The proportion of profitable enterprises and organizations		
	2010 r	2016 r	Growth rate	2010 r	2016 r	Growth rate
Allaikhovsky	72.1	150.6	208%	12.5%	-	-
Anabarsky	8329.8	13536.7	162%	57.1%	100%	143.9%
Bulunsky	947.4	4637.7	489%	55.6%	20%	-125.6%
Niznekolymsky	121.1	194.5	160%	28.6%	100%	172.4%
Ust-Yansky	232.0	721.8	311%	55.6%	25.0%	120.6%

Source: Statistical data of the Territorial Office of the Federal State Statistics Service for the Republic of Sakha (Yakutia), provided as part of comprehensive scientific research of RS (Y) 2017.

after 1995 is 40.4%. In other coastal territories of the Arctic zone of Yakutia the main housing development was carried out in 1971-1995 (an average of 78.9%). Anabar district is also a leader in terms of output and in the proportion of profitable enterprises (Table. 6).

During the analyzed period 2 objects of social infrastructure were put into operation in the Anabar district - a new kindergarten with 50 beds and a hospital with 25 beds. In other areas - one object. In particular, in the Nizhnekolymsky district - a school for 275 places, in Allaikhovsky and Bulunsky - gyms with an area of 1416 sq.m. and 288 sq. m., in Ust-Yansky - a kindergarten for 25 children.

The economic situation in the regions of industrial development of Arctic resources tends to increase indicators of employment and income. The content analysis of the regional newspapers also indicates the positive content of news publications. In the newspaper "Anabyr Light" (Anabyr Uottara) all events describe the active involvement of residents in projects and programs for the development of the district. In the information flow there are stories about events of a socio-economic orientation, in particular, about commissioned housing (photo 1).

In general, the emergence of industrial production in the Arctic region has a significant impact on the dynamics of the socio-economic indicators of the territory. This conclusion is well illustrated by the opinion of the journalist of the republican newspaper Our Time (Our time, No. 29, 07/31/2015, Evgeny Vasiliev): "Now they talk a lot about the industrial development of the

Photo 1. In Saskylakh young specialists were handed the keys to new apartments

(http://ulus.media/2018/05/03/v-saskyilahe-molodyim-spetsialistam-vruchili-klyuchi-ot-novyih-kvartir)

North of Russia. But few people manage to bring this to life. What we saw with our own eyes in the Anabar and Oleneksky uluses indicates that the North is really actively mastering the forces of a single enterprise. With a wide coverage of a vast territory. With the active involvement of the local population in industry. Replenishing the federal and local budgets with paid taxes. Step by step, year after year. Strengthening confidence in people of tomorrow."

However, as noted above, according to the indicators of the methodology of Arctic social indicators, the situation may appear from a different angle, through the prism of the standard of living of the indigenous peoples of the North, who are forced to share the once-limitless Arctic space with subsurface user companies.

The lack of statistical observation for this category of the population of the republic makes the analysis of ASI indicators extremely difficult. Alternatively, some indirect statistics were used.

According to indicators of the level of material well-being of the indigenous population,

Table 7. The level of material well-being of the population engaged in traditional environmental management in the coastal regions of the Arctic zone of the Republic of Sakha (Yakutia) (rubles)

Name of the region	Hunting and breeding wild animals			Reindeer breeding			Fishing		
	2010 г	2016 г	Growth rate	2010 г	2016 г	Growth rate	2010 г	2016 г	Growth rate
Allaikhovsky	-	-	-	-	-	-	12,098	21,767	179%
Anabarsky	5,217	21,000	402%	10,614	21,815	205%	-	-	-
Bulunsky	2,902	-	-	8,753	19,085	218%	8,133	13,601	167%
Niznekolymsky	7,846	-	-	10,805	22,378	207%	31,746	23,056	- 137%
Ust-Yansky	4,243	-	-	8,074	19,785	245%	6,251	28,972	463%

Source: Statistical data of the Territorial Office of the Federal State Statistics Service for the Republic of Sakha (Yakutia), provided as part of comprehensive scientific research of RS (Y) 2017.

data were used on the average monthly wage for certain types of activities, in the context of hunting, fishing, and reindeer breeding (Table 7). There is an increase in the wages of this category of workers, but the quantitative parameters remain low with a difficulty ensuring the minimum wage which in 2016 amounted to 16824 rubles in Yakutia.

Comparison with the level of average wages in districts shows that the labor of the population employed in the field of traditional environmental management is paid 3 times less. The average salary in the coastal regions of the Arctic zone in 2016 was 63,165 rubles a month, in the field of traditional nature management - 21,204 rubles.

According to the passport of the Bulunsky Evenki village (village of Kyusyur) [9] where 1418 people live, mostly indigenous minorities, the total number of employable people is 668 persons, including people of retirement age, of which 436 people are employed in the economy (65.2 %). Employment in traditional activities is - 40.3%. Employment in the public sector - 54.6% (Figure 1.). The number of individual entrepreneurs is 19 (construction, trade, mining).

Out of 280 families, 242 are considered to be poor, i.e. having a family income below the subsistence level. The total number of poor - 811 people, which is 57.1% of the whole

Figure 1. The structure of employment of the village of Kyusyur of the Bulunsky Evenki national nasleg (according to the data of the local statistics (passport of the nasleg) 2016 - http://old.sakha.gov.ru/node/10360)

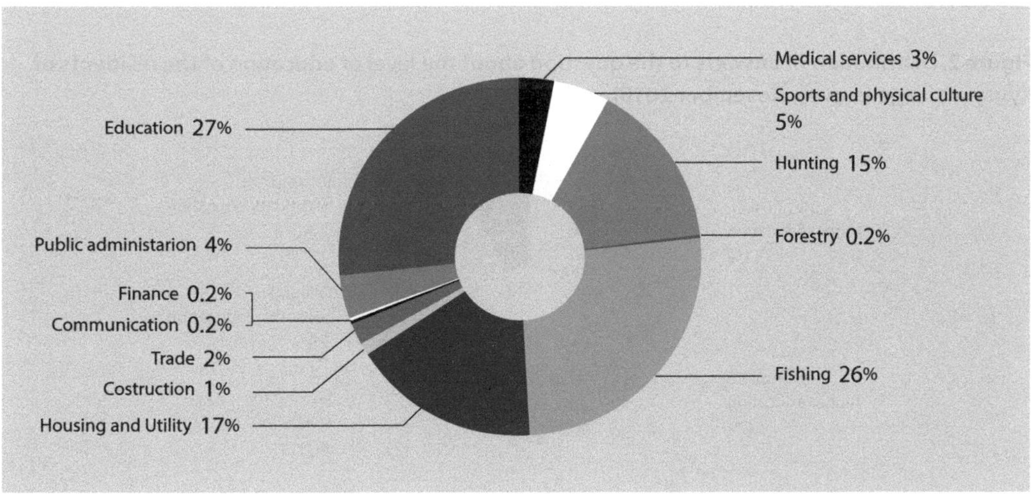

population - 1418 people (2016). The average family composition is 5 people. There are 66 disabled people living in the village. The average pension is 7014 rubles per month.

Thus, we can assume that for half the number of households in the village of Kyusyur, family incomes are in the range of 20,000-25,000 rubles per month. It should be assumed that this category includes older people who receive a low pension and low salary from employment in traditional crafts.

2.3. Social characteristics

When assessing the level of health care Arctic social indicators suggest the use of infant mortality rate. Unfortunately, there are no data on indigenous ethnic groups in this section. Assessment of the state of public health in this study was made using methods of sociological analysis. To the question "How would you rate your health?" 44.7% of the surveyed residents of the village of Kyusyur of the Bulunsky Evenksky national nasleg answered "satisfactorily (I'm not ill very often, I feel normal)." According to the survey these people seek medical help no more than 1-2 times a year. Often about 15% of the survey participants are sick and feel tired. 20.8% constantly take medication. Assessing the quality of medical care, 39.5% of the population surveyed consider it "satisfactory" and 26% - "bad." 36.4% believe that there are no necessary medicines on sale. 25% cannot afford to buy the necessary medicines. At the same time, the

Figure 2. Distribution of answers to the question about the level of education of the residents of Kyusyur village (survey, November 2018)

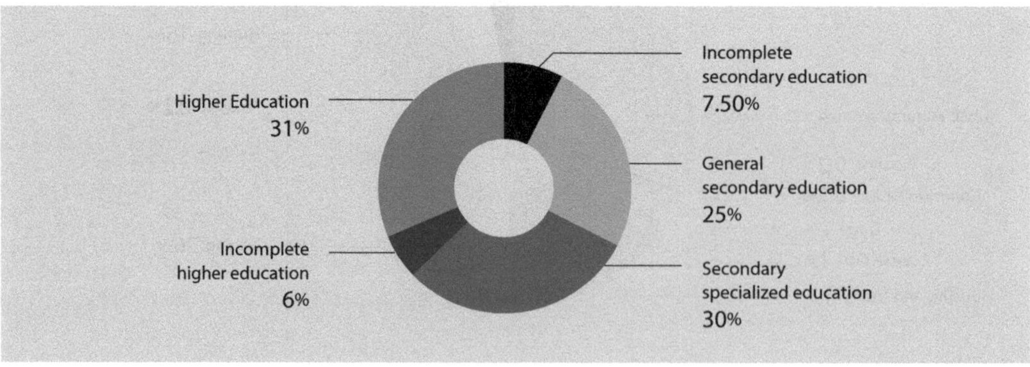

correlation of the survey data shows that the population will not experience significant health problems in the range from 16 to 45 years. After 45 years self-esteem of health worsens, and the estimation of quality of the health care system in rural areas also worsens.

Among the indirect indicators for applying the ASI methodology in terms of population health parameters in this study we can attribute the birth rate as well as the rate of natural growth of the indigenous population. According to the passport of the village of Kyusyur in 2016 the natural increase was 11.2 per 1000 people (31 born to 15 dead) which is almost two times higher than the figures for the Bulunsky district as a whole (6.0 per 1000). High natural growth shows a positive trend in the sustainable development of society.

Arctic social indicators as the main indicator of the level of education of the population consider the number of people enrolled in secondary, higher and continuing education programs. As a substitute indirect indicator this study analyzed the data of a population survey in the village of Kyusyur which showed in the educational structure of the indigenous population the dominance of people with higher, incomplete higher and secondary specialized education - 67.5% (Figure 2).

An analysis of the level of the presence of native language in everyday communication was also carried out according to a sociological survey of the population of Kyusyur village. Most of the respondents ethnically identified themselves as Evenks (55.2%) (Figure 3).

Figure 3. Distribution of answers to the question about the nationality of the residents of Kyusyur village (survey, November 2018)

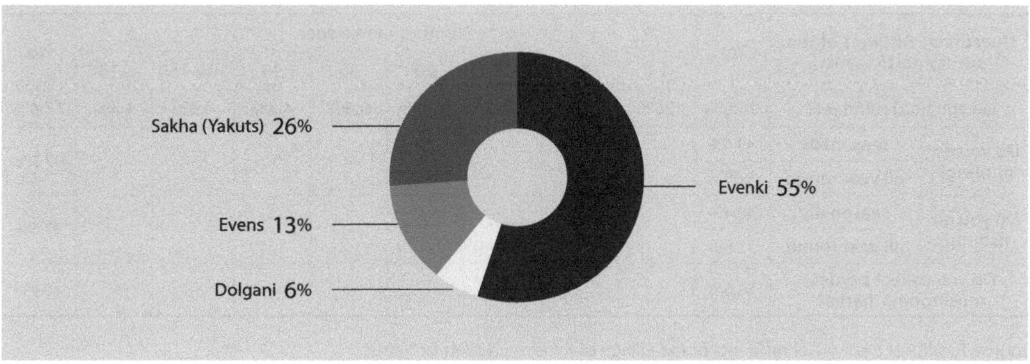

The answers to the question about the native language were distributed mainly in favor of Yakut language (81.2%). 18.3% called Russian as their native language. Only 0.5% of the surveyed villagers indicated the Evenk language as their mother tongue. To the question: "What language do you mainly speak at home?" 95% answered that they communicate in Yakut language. 46.4% use Russian in addition.

An indicator of the level of interaction with nature is characterized by data on the role of traditional crafts in the livelihoods of a family of indigenous ethnic groups in the Arctic zone (the level of production and consumption of environmental products).

According to the survey the majority of residents are involved and prefer to gather wild plants - 89.6% (Table. 8). Hunting and fishing play a significant role for only half of the surveyed population. 52.4% go hunting, 62.8% go fishing. Most residents do not breed reindeer in their personal households (73.4%). For those who contain reindeer the stock is mostly insignificant - from 1 to 6 heads (26%). Only few families have large herds: from 100 to 213 heads.

At the same time the diet for 31.9% of respondents living in Kusyur is entirely composed of ethnic food. For 30.9% of the survey participants ethnic diet coposes half of the ration and for 23.7% - more than half of the ration is represented by products of traditional crafts. 12.3% - a quarter of the diet. In general the population to a large extent prefers and depends on traditional

Table 8. Distribution of answers to a question about occupations by traditional crafts of residents p. Kyusyur

Questions / Answers of the survey participants		Yes	Number of reindeer								No
			1-6	10	15	20	30	96	100-150	213	
Do you hold reindeer?		26.6%	26%	8.6%	8.6%	4.3%	8.6%	4.3%	4.3%	4.3%	73.4%
Do you go hunting?	seasonally	49.4%	-	-	-	-	-	-	-	-	47.5%
	all year round	3.09%									
Do you go fishing?	seasonally	49.4%	-	-	-	-	-	-	-	-	37.6%
	all year round	13.4%									
Do you collect berries, mushrooms, herbs?		89.6%	-	-	-	-	-	-	-	-	10.4%

Source: Results of a survey of residents of the village of Kyusyur, November 2018

products. Every day they consume venison - 86.5%, fish - 59.7%, wild plants - 24.7%, game - 8.24%. 32.9% do not manufacture national clothes. 41.2% make only some elements. Of the traditional clothes only fur hat (72.1%) and high boots (92.7%) are actively used in everyday life. The fur coat (14.4%) and the fur jacket (23.7%) are less important today for the indigenous population. Only 32.3% of respondents prefer to wear jewelry with a national ornament.

According to the indicator of control over land resources the data of a population survey show that the majority do not own pastures (80.4%), areas for hunting (77.3%) and fishing (70.1%). Only 1% own rangelands (4 ha). 16.4% of respondents have a specific hunting area, 25.7% have a fishing area.

Nevertheless, the population is very concerned about the possibility of further modernization and reduced access to the Arctic. 50.5% of respondents believe that the condition of traditional land over the past 10 years has already worsened. 62.8% have a negative attitude to the industrial development of the district. 53.7% believe that development will violate the ecology of the area. 36% are sure that the commissioning of industrial facilities will worsen the indicators of public health and reduce the quality of life. 23.7% of respondents are ready to speak out and support the action of the movement against the construction of large industrial

Table 9. Key indicators of agriculture Kyusyur 2016 (according to local statistics of the settlement)

Main indicator	Amount	Peasant farms and tribal communities	State enterprises	Personal households
Number of households, including	9	-	-	-
- state unitary enterprise	1	-	-	-
agricultural cooperatives	5	-	-	
peasant farms	1	-	-	-
- tribal communities	2	-	-	-
The number of agricultural animals, including	2905	-	-	-
- horses	5	-	-	5
- reindeers	2905	-	2007	893
The volume of agricultural production, including (tons)	273,59	-	-	-
- fishing	273,59	-	--	-

Source: Passport of the Bulunsky national (Evenki) nasleg, 2016

facilities.

According to the passport of the nasleg the main role in the village was assigned to state agricultural enterprises where the main number of reindeer is kept. In the village there are 2 tribal communities, 1 peasant farm, 5 agricultural cooperatives and 7 pasture land owners (Table 9).

Thus, it is obvious that on average a family contains only 3 reindeer (893 heads / 280 families). A family does not have its own pastures and is extremely concerned about the prospects for further industrial development of the Arctic space.

The geoculture of development has led the ethnic minorities of the Arctic to a deadlock, a way out of which is seen only in the ability of the local elite to establish the right dialogue with the state and mining companies.

III. Arctic space and geoculture of development

3.1. Arctic geoculture specifics

In this context Arctic issues have taken a leading position in the world agenda by the number of emerging structures and initiatives aimed at ensuring its sustainable development. Abroad these are the Arctic Council, the University of the Arctic. In Russia - the Association of Indigenous People of the North, Siberia and the Far East, the Northern (Arctic) Federal University, the Interregional Public Organization “Association of Polar Explorers” and many others.

It has been prepared a number of reports on human development in the Arctic. The methodology of Arctic social indicators has been developed and applied.

Every year a series of conferences, forums, symposiums on the problems of the Arctic is held in different parts of the world. At the same time large-scale projects of a new invasion into the Arctic are developing in parallel. The Final Public Resolution of the VII International Forum “The Arctic: Present and Future” held in December 2017 clearly shows Russia’s active interest in the permanent extended presence in the Arctic zone [4]. It is not possible to stop further narrowing of the Arctic space by industrial development.

There is a desire to make this onslaught more balanced among various structures involved in the modernization of the Arctic space, but the practical realization of these intentions goes beyond the scope of the declared obligations. According to the Deputy Prime Minister of the Russian Federation, the Chairman of the State Commission for the Development of the Arctic D.O. Rogozin, "the purpose of these changes is not the development of natural resources, not the militarization of the Arctic. Our goal is to preserve human presence in the Arctic, to build visible long-term life prospects for it. The exceptional attitude of people towards the region, their desire to go to the Arctic and permanently associate their fate with it should be the main indicator of our effectiveness."

Thus, a personnel strategy was formulated to fill the Arctic space with new human resources. Any personnel strategy is always the answer to the primary and basic goal. In this case, it is undoubtedly a new round of industrial development of Arctic resources.

In this perspective, the participation and assistance of the scientific community in providing expert opinion on sustainable development issues is of key importance.

The historical path traversed by the indigenous people is incomparably longer than the path of other ethnic groups. It is this incomparably different experience of life being that represents a unique phenomenon that requires ever deeper study and reflection.

Yet 100-150 years ago the indigenous people of the North remained free nomads who used the resource potential of northern landscapes by means of traditional nature management while maintaining a high dependence on the natural conditions of being and, accordingly, on the geographical environment that their unique society possessed. To maintain the tradition it is required to save space. The twentieth century became a turning point in the fate of the northern ethnic groups, when Western civilization made inroads into life being of people that had been very superficially known to them and this knowledge was descriptively-ethnographic in nature. From the heroes of ethnographic articles and publications, at the turn of the century, the indigenous people of the North turned into neighbors in the territory of residence.

Onslaught similar to the beginning of the industrial development of the Arctic territories the indigenous population have never experienced before.

What happened as a result of mixing different types of civilizations? Could Arctic civilization not resist the onslaught? Or had it took a hybrid form incorporating the components of Western civilization and taking the form of geoculture of development?

In one of the recent works by N. A. Smirnov the original compositional structure of Arctic geocultures is presented. Understanding geoculture as a spatial form of colonization [5] and the formation of new social forms in space, he identifies three types of geocultures that are present today in parallel in the Arctic society. This is, firstly, the geoculture of the indigenous people of the Arctic, secondly, the geoculture of Soviet colonization settlements and, thirdly, the post-Soviet neoliberal geoculture with rhetoric of traditions.

The author presents such combination of geocultures as a peculiar lattice of accretions which arose with each successive wave of colonization. Thus, the Arctic is a space that has absorbed a unique multi-layered composition of geocultures of gradual layering, mixing, sharing of various ethnic groups into the root geoculture established over the millennial history. At the same time, according to N.A. Smirnov, the issues of national identity were not inherent [5] to these groups of people.

3.2. Values of traditional model of livelihood

They defined themselves as "real people." It was only at the turn of the nineteenth and twentieth centuries that the cataloging of the tribes inhabiting the northern territories had began with the identification of ethnic features and the appropriation of ethnic identification.

All the previous industrialization stages of the so-called "colonization" took place without damage to the traditional model of livelihood. The principal features of that model can be considered as [6]:

First, the use of natural biological resources as the basis of economic activity and foodstuffs security;

Secondly, the need to preserve the biological diversity of the flora and fauna resources to support economic activity and foodstuffs security.

Based on these features there can be distinguished several main parameters of the traditional model of livelihood:

- traditional method of housing;
- traditional method of getting food;
- traditional way to provide households with clothing, household items, tools;
- traditional way of upbringing and education of the younger generation;
- traditional way to manage, organize and interact within the community.

Taking into account the distinguished parameters it can be formulated the so-called ideal type of the traditional household:

1. A family where husband and wife are indigenous people;
2. A family where husband and wife are engaged in hunting, reindeer herding, horse breeding, gathering, fur trade;
3. A family that does not have a permanent place for living;
4. A family exchanging natural products for household goods and tools;
5. A family making outerwear for family members;
6. A family that provides education and upbringing of children for their further inclusion in traditional livelihoods;
7. A family that is a part of the tribal community that provides the unification of households for their interaction.

This model ensured the preservation of the ethnic gene of the indigenous people of the North during unusually long period in the history of mankind but it could not withstand industrial intervention. Gradually filling the once limitless expanses of the Arctic the new population had constricted and narrowed the usual habitats of steady existence.

At the first stage it took place the language assimilation. Indigenous people began to use the advantages of Sakha and Russian languages for more complete self-expression and more complete interaction and providing the necessary contacts. A sharp clash with a different civilization in the Soviet period did not leave the indigenous minorities of the North to choose the path for self-preservation. The only possibility was the adoption of a new model. In my opinion, Soviet government collectivization and further development of state farms played a significant role in this process.

The way of life of the indigenous people of the North has undergone a historically abrupt transition from the traditional to the Soviet agricultural model of livelihood. Under the influence of forced collectivization and state farm building there was an undermining of value's system of the indigenous minorities of the North. Nature and the Arctic space as the basis of family well-being were replaced by state farm workdays and salary.

The values of a measured, rational interaction with the environment were replaced by the Communist party's ideology aimed at the formation of a new man who gives up his work for the benefit of the Soviet common construction. The results of subordination to the requirements of the party leadership were the desire to obtain vocational secondary and higher education, the increased number of inter-ethnic marriages, the choice of Yakut identification, raising children in boarding schools as well as the abandonment of traditional customs and traditional methods of treatment, an increase in morbidity and alcoholism.

One of the main mechanisms of self-preservation in these conditions was the principle of ensuring communication with the Arctic space and keeping the place of residence as a source giving strength to preserve the basic components of the value structure of its elusive culture.

IV. Conclusion

Keeping adherence to the original territory of residence the indigenous ethnic groups of the Arctic ensured the inclusion of the geoculture of their people in the compositional mix that is currently being experienced.

As a part of the post-Soviet neoliberal geoculture it is being formed the basis for a return to the traditional components of the culture of the Northern ethnic groups, to the revival of languages, rituals, ceremonies, full ethnic self-identification and, in general, the traditional way of life and livelihood.

The high level of education among the representatives of the indigenous people of the North accumulated as a result of the influence of the Soviet party ideology has formed the elite that can adequately respond to the challenges of any new wave of so-called "colonization."

The increase in social guarantees for representatives of the indigenous small ethnic groups of the North contributed to the growth of ethnic identity which was recorded in the 2010 census.

Using the effects of the Soviet agricultural model of livelihoods, the indigenous people of the North formed a mixed type of livelihood based on a combination of two sources of income:

- Monetary source - in the form of getting wages and employment at enterprises of the public sector;
- Non monetary source - in the form of natural bio recourses usage (hunting, fishing, wild plants gathering).

In modern conditions of livelihood the Arctic family seeks to use all the advantages of modernization, combining them with the possibilities of free nature usage that are provided by the Arctic space.

However, at the same time modernization narrows the space of the Arctic. It is the Arctic space that allows society to preserve the memory of previous generations and maintain the main traditions. Arctic space provides an opportunity to engage in traditional activities that for indigenous people is an integral part of their lifestyle.

References

1. Попков Ю.В., Е.А. Тюгашев Арктическая философия народа саха (якутов) // Вестник Северного (Арктического) федерального университета, №4, 2015, С.58-66 (Yu.V.Popkov, E.A. Tyugyashev. Arctic philosophy of Sakha (Yakuts) in the interpretation of M.E. Nikolaev // Bulletin of the Northern (Arctic) Federal University, № 4, 2015)
2. Даниель Шартье. Что такое воображение Севера? // Геокультуры Арктики: методология анализа и прикладные исследования. Москва. 2018, С.17 (Daniel Shartier. What is the imagination of the North? // Arctic Geocultures: methodology of analysis

and applied research. Moscow. 2018. p.17)

3. Наше общее будущее // Доклад Всемирной комиссии по окружающей среде и развитию под председательством Г. Брунтленда. Генеральная Ассамблея ООН. 42-я сессия, 4 августа 1987 г. (Our common future // Report of the World Commission on Environment and Development under the chairmanship of G. Bruntland. UN General Assembly.- 42nd session, 4 August 1987 - Electronic resource - http://www.un.org/ru/ga/pdf/brundtland.pdf - the date of access 12.12.2018)
4. Итоговая резолюция о социально-экономическом развитии Арктической зоны Российской Федерации // 7 Международный форум «Арктика: настоящее и будущее» - С-Петербург, 2017 (The final public resolution on the socio-economic development of the Arctic zone of the Russian Federation // VII International Forum "Arctic: Present and Future." IES "Association of polar explorers." - St. Petersburg. 2017)
5. Н.А. Смирнов. Композиция геокультур Арктики: новые основания геокультурного анализа // Геокультуры Арктики: методология анализа и прикладные исследованияю Москва. 2018, С.47-49 (N.A. Smirnov. Composition of Arctic geocultures: new foundations of geocultural analysis // Arctic geocultures: methodology of analysis and applied research. Moscow. 2018. P.47-49)
6. Л.Ю. Писарева. Образ жизни коренных жителей Арктической зоны Якутии: социально-экономический аспект// Социология, №4, С.201 (L.Yu. Pisareva. Lifestyle of the indigenous ethnic groups of the Arctic zone of Yakutia: socio-economic aspect // Sociology, №4, 201)

CONCEPTUAL MODEL OF THE DEVELOPMENT OF AUTONOMOUS LEARNING SKILLS AMONG YAKUT NATIVE STUDENTS

Uliana Semenovna Borisova
Doctor of Sociology, Professor, HR and Sociology Department, Institute of Finance and Economy, North-Eastern Federal University
ulsem2012@mail.ru

Galina. Mikhailovna Parnikova
Doctor of Education, Professor, Institute of Foreign Languages and Regional Studies, Foreign Languages Department for Non-linguistic Institutes, North-Eastern Federal University

Abstract.

The issues addressed in the article are of particular relevance, being in line with the main current trends in methodology of teaching foreign languages in Russia and abroad. The aim of the article is to present results of building a conceptual model of the development of autonomous learning skills among Yakut native students. The research has revealed that there is a strong correlation between the content of the foreign language teaching in Russia and the development trends of the Russian society; the level of development of students' personal qualities and sets of competencies and the utilization of the potential of this academic discipline; and the demand for a young professional in a competitive labour market and her/ his ability to work independently. This study presents the results of the predictive theoretical modelling of the level of development of autonomous learning skills among Yakut native students achieved through studying foreign languages.

The unified all-Russian system of foreign language teaching at non-philological higher educational institutions does not take into account the specifics of such sub-national region as Yakutia. Therefore, the experimental research was conducted on the basis of a federal university located in the North-East of Russia. The contradictions existing in the practice of higher education in Yakutia make it highly relevant to build a conceptual model based on data related to a particular region. Each component of the model reflects its specific character and is designed to change the content and methods of foreign language teaching, taking into account the real regional situation.

The developed conceptual model increases efficiency of developing autonomous learning skills among students of non-philological higher education institutions through studying foreign languages. It is an integral system consisting of the following components and clusters of elements: regional social policies (requirements of federate state standards of higher education regarding foreign language teaching at non-philological higher education institutions, strategic plans for regional development, competition in the regional labour market); strategic goals (learning objectives and principles¬); tactical elements (methodological approaches, learning environment and stages of its implementation); content components (methodology, content, techniques, forms, methods, means and approaches to teaching foreign languages at non-philological higher education institutions); assessment of results (autonomous learning components; levels, criteria and indicators of its formation); and systemic framework components (goal setting, reflection). The research results have practical significance for linguists, methodologists and educators dealing with the issues of training non-linguistic specialists of native background with foreign language skills.

Keywords: Yakut native students, conceptual model, development of autonomous learning skills

I. Introduction

Our study of the regulatory documents (Nacional'naja doktrina obrazovanija Rossijskoj Federacii, 2000; Federal'nye gosudarstvennye obrazovatel'nye standarty vysshego obrazovanija, 2016) and analysis of studies on modernization of the Russian higher education system (Baydenko, 2007; Grebnev, 2011) and on improvement of the language teaching quality (Safonova, 2014; Sergeeva, 2014; Solovova, 2013; Ter-Minasova, 2015) have allowed us to identify a number of possible directions for developing the methods of teaching foreign languages in Russian higher education institutions, and in non-philological higher schools in particular: orientation to international requirements and standards of higher education; lifelong learning; professionally-oriented content of language teaching curricula; changes in the correlation between classroom hours and students' independent work; differentiation and individualization in teaching foreign languages.

The issues of training Yakut native students have been considered in the works of the leading educators of the analysed region (Barakhsanova et al., 2016; Neustroev et al., 2016). Our review and analysis of foreign works on methods of foreign language teaching and on autonomy in teaching and learning, autonomous learning skills and independent learning issues confirm that our research into development of autonomous learning skills among students studying foreign languages is of particular relevance (Benson, 2007; Byram, 2011; Gremmo & Riley, 1995; Holec, 1985; Voller, 1997).

The aim of the article is to present results of our research into building a conceptual model of the development of autonomous learning skills among Yakut native student through studying foreign languages.

II. Materials and Methods

2.1. Model

The conceptual model of the development of students' autonomous learning skills was created on the basis of the specific principles, methodological approaches and the learning environment practically implemented as a theoretical and methodological strategy of experiential program of teaching foreign languages at a non-philological higher education institution.

The initial phase of the modelling process involved identification of initial preconditions for creating the above-defined model (Parnikova, 2016a) and understanding of opportunities provided by the academic discipline "Foreign Language" for the personality development of students at non-philological higher education institutions (Parnikova, 2013). Our research has revealed that there is a strong correlation between;

- The content of the foreign language teaching in Russia and the development trends of the Russian society;
- The level of development of students' personal qualities and sets of competencies and the utilization of the potential of this academic discipline;
- The demand for a young professional in a competitive labour market and her/his ability to work independently.

The conceptual model is an integral system consisting of a number of elements. Some systemic framework components, ensuring interaction between all systemic elements, are also essential part of its structure.

It has been found out that the unified all-Russian system of foreign language teaching at non-philological higher educational institutions does not take into account the specifics of such sub-national region as the Republic of Sakha (Yakutia) (Parnikova, 2016, p.2):

- regional socio-economic, cultural, historical and ethno-linguistic features;
- psycho-physiological, social, educational and linguodidactic characteristics of Yakut native students;
- challenges faced by this category of students in the process of foreign language learning at non-philological higher education institutions;
- objective and subjective factors affecting demand for young professionals in the regional labour market.

In view of the above, we consider that the content of the regional social policies is the starting point for building the model of developing autonomous learning skills among students of non-philological higher education institutions through studying foreign languages, because the main consumer of educational services is a specific subject of the Russian Federation. This element of the model includes not only the requirements stipulated in the Russian regulatory documents but also strategic plans for the development of the region, its demand for highly qualified professionals of native background with knowledge of foreign languages in the environment characterized by strong competition from specialists arriving (invited) from other regions. The regional social policies dictate certain requirements for the quality of foreign language training of students at non-philological higher education institutions, permeating the entire model and affecting its structure and content of its components.

As the contradictions existing in the practice of higher education in the Republic of Sakha (Yakutia) make it highly relevant to build a conceptual model of the development of autonomous learning skills among students of non-philological higher education institutions through studying foreign languages, based on data related to a particular region, each component of the developed conceptual model should reflect its specific character designed to change the content and methods of foreign language teaching, taking into account the real regional situation.

The strategic element of our model includes the purpose and principles of foreign language teaching in higher education institutions. We consider it logical to specify the general purpose and principles of education, based on the current regional methodological status and the social policies of the particular subject of the Russian Federation determining demand for trained specialists with the knowledge of a foreign language. It should be noted that the formulated purpose and principles do not contradict provisions of the regulatory document but further specify and complement them. Thus, we define the specific purpose of the methodology of teaching foreign languages to Yakut native students as a methodological background for meeting the regional demand for training such independent-thinking indigenous specialists with the knowledge of foreign languages that would be most likely to be employed in the competitive local labour market; such training should be based on the rational use of technologies, forms, methods and means and take into account the national specific characteristics of the students.

The specific principles of teaching foreign languages to students of Northern indigenous ancestry can be grouped as follows:

- principles of group I reflect compliance of the system of teaching foreign languages at non-philological higher education institutions with the requirements of regional social policies;
- principles of group II take into account the local cultural and historical heritage and traits of national character;
- principles of group III disclose possibilities of multilingualism in the multicultural region.

The general strategy of teaching foreign language requires a systematic and consistent implementation of appropriate approaches, learning environment and stages presented in the tactical part of our model. An essential precondition for formation of autonomous learning skills among students of non-philological higher education institutions is the implementation of a number of theoretical propositions related to the humanistic paradigm of education, close relationship between activities and personality development and a complex of general pedagogical, methodological specific principles and ideas of systemic, competence-based, hermeneutic, synergistic and ethno-cultural approaches and the learning environment. The learning environment includes the following:

- Organisation of the process of foreign language learning, taking into account the experience accumulated by the regional system of education in upbringing younger generations, in order to meet the regional demand for training competitive local specialists;
- Establishment of a specially organized foreign language environment, based on coping strategies that take into account the relationship between independent educational activities of students and determination of personal activity, initiative and awakening of creative possibilities of students through learning foreign languages;
- Optimisation of students' autonomous learning, including practice-oriented focus, use of applied learning materials and active and interactive methods of foreign language learning;

- Implementation of methodological framework components for the development of students' autonomous learning skills in the process of foreign language learning, taking into account the existing natural Yakut-Russian bilingualism in the multicultural region.

2.2. Implementation

The practical implementation of the learning environment includes the following stages: 1) organisation and preparation, 2) realisation, 3) results. All the stages reflect the integration of foreign-language education activities and formation of autonomous learning skills among students of non-philological higher education institutions.

The preparatory stage includes the following:

- determination of the specific character of the Northern area of Russia, demand for professions in the local market and specific features of Yakut native students;
- identification of challenges faced by the studied category of students in the process of learning foreign languages;
- identification of potential of the academic discipline for the development of autonomous learning skills;
- identification of components, content, levels, criteria and indicators of formation of autonomous learning skills as a personal characteristic and formulation of the techniques of developing such skills;
- overall alignment of goals, objectives and methods of implementation of the studied process;
- planning of stages for the foreign language learning;
- forecasting results of the experimental activities.

As part of this stage, the following activities are necessary to prepare students for the development of their autonomous learning skills through foreign language learning:

- motivating students to study the academic discipline, engage into autonomous learning activities and accumulate positive experience and emotions;
- students' understanding and actualisation of their own experience of foreign language

learning;

- students' awareness of the relationship between foreign-language learning activities and formation of autonomous learning skills for further realisation of their personal career goals;
- mastering autonomous learning strategies in the process of foreign language learning;
- introduction to using general methods of self-assessment of abilities and knowledge;
- assessment of students' readiness to autonomous learning of foreign languages at a non-philological higher education institution.

The second stage is oriented to the practical realisation of earlier formulated theoretical provisions, ideas, patterns, principles, approaches and requirements to the environment for foreign language learning in order to achieve the set goals. At this stage, the organization of activities of the educational process subjects takes place. The students start learning foreign languages on the basis of the newly developed model. The studied process is aimed to enhancement of students' learning abilities and provides for the correction and minimisation of challenges faced by Yakut native students in foreign language learning, which determines the choice of methodological requirements, content of training materials and techniques, forms, methods and means for fulfilling the set objectives – all these components constitute the content of our model.

At the process of realisation, foreign language learning is combined with the enhancement of emotional, volitional, informative, cognitive, motivational, assessing and reflective components of autonomous learning skills, which are developed through studying the foreign language. The following methodological requirements to organisation of the process of foreign language learning are very important for overcoming challenges faced by Yakut native students:

- differentiation and individualization of the used methods and techniques for the students of both cycles of higher education, based on the individual character of challenges faced by each of them during studying the academic discipline and mastering their knowledge and the level of autonomous learning skills;
- application of productive coping strategies during adaptation to the new environment,

conditions and situations;

- use of the native language (Yakut or Russian) to explain the most difficult issues of the foreign language, looking for analogues, parallels or differences for better understanding of the foreign (e.g. English) language;
- group-based organisation of the training process for overcoming inertia of mental activities occurring in Northern natives along the following lines: teamwork – work in small groups – student's individual work;
- co-learning of languages and cultures of foreign countries to promote a cross-cultural dialogue and tolerant attitude to other values and cultural and historical heritage, while carefully preserving identity of own people and the native country;
- practical, job-oriented teaching in foreign languages at a non-philological higher education institution;
- creation of the situation of success and positive motivation to learn the academic discipline and to improve autonomous learning skills in order to form readiness for such activities among students through learning foreign languages;
- creation of favourable atmosphere and comfortable environment in the foreign language classroom, contributing to the reduction of the level of anxiety, nervousness and lack of self-confidence among students;
- stimulation of personal activity, initiative and self-reliance through alternation of active and interactive methods, tools and techniques of foreign language teaching to overcome passive attitudes to communication and speech activities ;
- gradual inclusion of students in autonomous learning activities through studying foreign languages with a consistent increase in complexity, creation of a positive attitude and confidence in their abilities;
- simultaneous loading of students' auditory and visual channels of information perception, use of schemes and tables for explanation of grammatical materials, based on the intrinsic abilities of students to perceive the surrounding reality and handle images;
- use of reflection, assessment techniques, self-evaluation and analysis of the performed

autonomous learning activities during foreign language learning;

- involvement of students in extracurricular individual activities in foreign languages organized by the NEFU non-linguistic departments: participation in regional, all-Russian and international language competitions, contests, conferences and other educational events;
- organization of joint events with senior students, listeners of master programs and higher school graduates trained in a foreign university in order to overcome the low need in manifestation of individuality;
- provision of students with free access to basic and additional reference literature and textbooks, informative and analytical professional directories and dictionaries at the Methodology Office of foreign language divisions of the NEFU non-linguistic departments;
- access to regularly updated resources, educational sites and other sources of necessary information in English (for example, sites of British newspapers) that are publicly available on the Internet;
- methodological assistance in creating students' personal accounts (profiles) of the university system Moodle to perform assignments within the frameworks of independent work and to communicate with the teacher.

III. Results and Discussion

3.1. Content of foreign language learning

The methodological background provides necessary mechanism for the development of autonomous learning skills through studying foreign languages. The listed methodological requirements to organisation of the process of foreign language learning by Northern native students can greatly facilitates the achievement of the level of foreign language competence specified in the regulatory documents of higher professional education.

The content of foreign language learningis aimed at the formation of students' readiness, ability and stable need of demonstrating independence in their learning activities and at promoting a positive attitude to the entire process and the results of its implementation. Therefore, the following components of the foreign language learning content were selected to contribute to the development of students' autonomous learning skills through studying foreign languages: the sphere of communication, situations and subjects; means of communication; oral and written skills of communication in a foreign language; learning skills.

The contemporary social development is characterized by the growth of international contacts in all spheres of human activity, and today's young graduates of non-philological higher education institutions are interested, first of all, in the pragmatic language competence. Joint productive professional activities with foreign partners or colleagues presuppose communication in oral and written forms. This is dictated by the current state of the regional economy, education, science and cultural space, as well as by the long-term plans of future development of the Republic of Sakha (Yakutia).

The nature of the speech activity of students, influencing the choice of linguistic means and norms of communication, depends on the target sphere of activity (business, science or culture). Communication in a foreign language is carried out within the frames of learning situations: predictable and non-predictable. Such speech situations are used to train students in analysing professional speech in a foreign language from the point of view of some set parameters (purpose, content, structure and conditions of communication), which actualizes development of conscious attitudes.

The proper use of grammatical constructions in a foreign language is very important, and it is mastered in the process of their practical use in learning situations, imitating actual speech communication. Involvement of students in situations of actual use of a foreign language gives them an opportunity to shift the focus from the linguistic component to the informative one and concentrate attention on actual problems rather than on the academic discipline itself, which reduces/minimizes challenges (fear/doubts/lack of self-confidence) faced by students during foreign language learning.

Therefore, it is necessary to choose a number of typical situations with a definite practical value for the development of professional communication skills on the basis of an analysis of real communicative situations in the respective sphere of activity. The communication themes should, in turn, reflect issues of the actual sphere of activity. The preliminary selection of themes is caused by the necessity to choose specific lexical materials, texts of various genres and styles, and diverse information sources.

The next element of the foreign language content is means of communication: lexical units, grammatical forms and constructions, formulas of speech communication, socio-cultural and cross-cultural knowledge. Specialisation of training materials is one of the important conditions for mastering professional vocabulary. Learning foreign language vocabulary by students of non-philological higher education institutions implies the selection and consolidation of "primary" information and processing of the extracted data, preparation of own records for further reference and their interpretation and reorganization for future use, i.e. studying foreign languages not only stimulates development of students' autonomous learning skills but also helps to improve their self-control.

Learning grammar includes the following stages: acquaintance, initial consolidation of knowledge, formation of skills and abilities of grammar use in both verbal and non-verbal communication. Students' learning autonomy is expressed in independent acquaintance with the form and meaning of grammatical forms and structures, ability to keep records, make comments, adequately use grammatical conceptual apparatus and to register grammar material in the form of diagrams or tables.Verbal communication formulas convey various communicative intentions of students. A cultural, well-educated person is characterised by the ability to adequately assess the situation, skilfully enter into and carry out communication and to convey thoughts clearly.

Other components of the content of foreign language learning at non-philological higher education institutions include the linguistic skills that form the basis of speech abilities, promote the development of language abilities and suggest the presence of the formed automatism of using linguistic materials of different levels of complexity in the process of verbal and non-verbal communication. The unique and non-repeatable nature of individual skills of using a foreign language as a means of communication in different spheres and communication situations contributes to creativity of autonomous learning activities.

Another contentive component includes the learning skills, after mastering of which students are able to use independently all the necessary cognitive techniques of searching, retrieving, recording, analysing and processing the relevant information; to systematize linguistic means; to use basic and supplementary study materials, as well as reference and specialized literature and literary sources; to carry out self- assessment and self-control and continue their self-education.

During our study, we have also confirmed that the content of foreign language learning activities also provides for acquiring linguistic and professional experience when using coping strategies to mitigate challenges during adaptation to new/unknown conditions and situations (Amirkhan, 1990; Carver C.S. et al, 1989; Lazarus, 1966; Lazarus & Folkman, 1984; Murphy, 1962). Our choice of the productive coping strategies is based on:

- the genetic predisposition to group-based organization of labour in the studied categories of students, challenges of the adaptation period, psychological and physiological characteristics (coping through communal support);
- the basic idea of our methodological concept on relationship between active foreign language learning and efficient formation of students' autonomous learning skills (coping through problem solving).

Our study, in general, presupposes group-based organisation of foreign language learning at non-philological higher educational institutions: language teachers bring together representatives of different uluses (districts) or ulus groups into student groups or microgroups (Baccalaureate cycle) and graduates of different Baccalaureate specialities (Magistrate cycle) with different native languages (Yakut or Russian) and varying levels of both foreign language knowledge and autonomous learning skills. First, at the initial stage of training at a higher education institution students have not established stable interpersonal relationships, so teacher's decisions play a leading role. Second, such organization of the educational process is dictated by the desire to teach the students to leave the comfortable environment and to operate effectively in the new conditions.

Thus, the content of foreign language learning reflects the process of the development of autonomous learning skills and its result. The described model provides for teaching foreign languages on the basis of a specially developed practice-oriented methodology of foreign language teaching with the use of teaching technologies, forms, methods and means, which will be described in detail in our future papers.

3.2. Assessment and evaluation

The final stage (assessment of results) includes assessment and evaluation of the level of development of autonomous learning skills among students of non-philological higher education institutions through studying foreign languages:

- monitoring of the entire educational process by the teacher;
- correction and consolidation of the achievements and the positive dynamics of students' autonomous learning activities by the teacher;
- teacher's assessment and analysis of the levels and indicators of formation of autonomous learning skills among future specialists;
- ongoing assessment and analysis of the personal readiness and ability to perform autonomous learning activities during foreign language learning by students themselves;
- students' forecasts regarding future application of the results achieved during autonomous learning in their future professional activities.

Such assessment should not be reduced only to identification of deficiencies, mistakes or shortcomings. It should be considered as a critical analysis of foreign language learning activities for a more accurate determination of the directions of improvement, i.e. at this stage the main goal is to improve the quality of work of a particular individual and to stimulate further independent learning activities in line with the life objectives.

So, the research results are expressed in positive qualitative changes in the structure of the studied skills and related personal traits of the student. The indicators of students' motivation to study an academic discipline and carry out autonomous learning activities are the presence of internal and external positive motivation, personal need of autonomous learning activities and students' industriousness.

The level of personal activity can be measured by the formation of special skills and meta-skills, manifestation of initiative and readiness to take efforts to overcome challenges. The extent of students' independence is demonstrated through ability to perform autonomous learning activities in studying foreign languages and low dependence on external evaluation by classmates or the teacher. Students' awareness of the importance of autonomous learning activities is manifested through their personal assessments of its significance and self-assessment of their own activities. The reflection dynamics is characterized by the ability to perform self-analysis of autonomous learning activities, as well as the ability to assess the learning situation and the results of autonomous learning activity.

The following main criteria of the development of autonomous learning skills have been selected: motivation, activity, student's independence and awareness of importance of autonomous learning activities, and reflection indicators. We have identified three levels of the development of autonomous learning skills: 1) reproductive (low); 2) productive (medium); 3) productivity creative (high). They allow monitoring the progress of the development of the required qualitative characteristic of the student's personality.

So, the realisation of the above-described stages provides us with the opportunity to implement in practice the process of the development of autonomous learning skills among students of non-philological higher education institutions through studying foreign languages, from the analysis of the requirements of regional social policies to assessment of the achieved results. Systemic framework components (goal setting, reflection) are the last but not least important element of our conceptual model – they integrate individual elements into a unified whole to stabilize the model.

IV. Conclusion

Summarizing the research findings, we can state that the developed conceptual model increases efficiency of developing autonomous learning skills among students of non-philological higher education institutions through studying foreign languages and should be considered as an integral system consisting of the following components and clusters of elements:

- regional social policies (requirements of federate state standards of higher education, strategic plans for regional development, competition in the regional labour market);
- strategic goals (objectives and principles¬ of teaching foreign languages at non-philological higher education institutions);
- tactical elements (methodological approaches, learning environment and stages of its implementation);
- content components (methodology, content, techniques, forms, methods, means and approaches to teaching foreign languages);
- assessment of results (autonomous learning components; levels, criteria and indicators of its formation); and systemic framework components (goal setting, reflection).

References

1. Байденко В.И. Новые стандарты высшего образования: методологические аспекты / В.И. Байденко // Высшее образование сегодня. – 2007. – № 5. – С. 4-9. (Baidenko V.I. New Standards of Higher Education: Methodological Aspects). Vysshee obrazovanie segodnja (Higher Education Today), 2007, no. 5, pp. 4-9).
2. Гребнев Л.С. Болонский процесс и «четвертое поколение» образовательных стандартов / Л.С. Гребнев // Высшее образование в России. – 2011. – № 11. – С. 29-41. (Grebnev L.S. The Bologna Process and the "Fourth Generation" of theEducational Standards). Vysshee Obrazovanie v Rossii (Higher Education in Russia), 2011, no. 11, pp. 29-41).

3. Национальная доктрина образования Российской Федерации // Бюллетень Минобразования РФ. – 2000. – № 11. – С. 4-13. (The National Doctrine of Education in the Russian Federation). Bulletin of the Ministry of Education of the Russian Federation, 2000, no. 11, pp. 4-13).
4. Парникова Г.М. Педагогический потенциал иностранного языка в формировании учебной самостоятельности студентов неязыковых вузов / Г.М. Парникова // Высшее образование сегодня. – 2013. – № 7. – С. 67-69. (Parnikova G.M. Educational Potential of Foreign Languages for Formation of Autonomous Learning Skills among Students of Non-philological Higher Education Institutions). Vysshee obrazovanie segodnja (Higher Education Today), 2013, no. 7, pp. 67-69).
5. Парникова Г.М. (1). Принципы обучения иностранному языку студентов из числа представителей коренных народов Севера в неязыковом вузе / Г.М. Парникова // Педагогическое образование в России. – 2016. – № 1. – С. 197-203 (Parnikova G.M. Principle for Teaching Foreign Languages among Students of Northern Indigenous Ancestry at Non-philological Higher Education Institutions). Pedagogicheskoe Obrazovanie v Rossii (Pedagogical Education in Russia), 2016a, no. 1, pp. 197-203)
6. Парникова Г.М. (2). Учет региональных особенностей при обучении иностранному языку в неязыковом вузе / Г.М. Парникова // Высшее образование сегодня. – 2016. – № 1. – С. 81-85. (Parnikova G.M. Consideration of Regional Specifics of Teaching Foreign Languages at Non-philological Higher Education Institutions). Vysshee obrazovanie segodnja (Higher Education Today), 2016b, no. 1, pp. 81-85).
7. Сафонова В.В. Соизучение языков и культур в зеркале мировых тенденций развития современного языкового образования / В.В. Сафонова // Язык и культура. – 2014. – № 1 (25). – Томск: Изд-во НИТГУ. – С.123-141. (Safonova V.V. Co-Learning of Languages and Cultures in the Context of Global Development Trends of Contemporary Linguistic Education). Jazyk i kul'tura (Language and Culture), 2014, no. 1 (25), Tomsk: NRTSU Press, pp. 123-141).
8. Сергеева Н.Н. Иноязычная коммуникативная компетенция в сфере

профессиональной деятельности: модель и методика развития / Н.Н. Сергеева // Педагогическое образование в России. – 2014. – № 6. – С.147-150. (Sergeeva N.N. Foreign Language Communicative Competence in the Sphere of Professional Activities: A Model and Development Methodology). Pedagogicheskoe Obrazovanie v Rossii (Pedagogical Education in Russia), 2014, no. 6, pp. 147-150).

9. Соловова Е.Н. Перспективные направления развития вузовской методики преподавания иностранных языков / Е.Н. Соловова // Вестник МГИМО. – 2013. – Выпуск № 6 (33). – С. 67-70. (Solovova E.N. Development Prospects for Methods of Teaching Foreign Languages at Higher Education Institutions). MGIMO-University Bulletin, 2013, no. 6 (33), pp. 67-70).
10. Тер-Минасова С.Г. Преподавание иностранных языков в современной России: прошлое, настоящее и будущее / С.Г. Тер-Минасова // Молодой ученый. – 2015. – №15.2. – С. 1-7. (Ter-Minasova S.G. Teaching Foreign Languages in Contemporary Russia: Past, Present and Future). Molodoy Ucheny, 2015, no. 15/2, pp. 1-7).
11. Федеральные государственные образовательные стандарты высшего образования [Электронный ресурс]. 2016. – Режим доступа: http://fgosvo.ru/fgosvo/92/91/4. – Дата доступа: 22.11.2016 (Federate State Standards of Higher Education). [Online]. 2016. Available at: http://fgosvo.ru/fgosvo/92/91/4. Accessed on 22.11.2016)
12. Amirkhan James H. A Factor Analytically Derived Measure of Coping: The Coping Strategy Indicator. Journal of Personality and Social Psychology, 1990, vol. 59(5),pp. 1066-1074.
13. Barakhsanova E.A., Savvinov V.M., Prokopyev M.S., Vlasova E.Z. & Gosudarev I.B. Adaptive Education Technologies to Train Russian Teachers to Use E-learning. IEJME-Mathematics Education – IEJME. Published Online: November 25, 2016. pp. 3447-3456. Article Number: iejme.2016.283.
14. Benson P. Autonomy in language teaching and learning: State of the art article. Language Teaching, 2007,vol. 40, pp. 21-40.
15. Byram M. The Common (European) CEFR of Reference – teaching foreign languages,

mediation and intercultural competence. Annual Review of English Learning and Teaching, 2011, vol. 16, pp. 63-70.

16. Gremmo M.-J., Riley P. Autonomy, self-direction and self-access in language teaching and learning: the history of an idea. System, 1995,23(2), pp. 151-164.
17. Holec H. On autonomy: some elementary concepts. InRiley (ed.) Discourse and Learning. London: Longman, 1985, pp. 173-190.
18. Lazarus R. S. & Folkman S. Stress, appraisal, and coping. New York: Springer, 1984, 445 p.
19. Murphy L. The child's way of coping: A longitudinal study of normal children. Bulletin of the Menninger Clinic, 1962, vol. 24, pp. 136-143.
20. Neustroev N.D, Nikolaeva A.D., Neustroeva A.N., Ivanova A.V. Problems and Modernization Trends of Ungraded Schools of the Russian North. IEJME-Mathematics Education – IEJME. Published Online: November 25, 2016, vol. 11, issue 10, pp. 3415-3424. Article Number: iejme.2016.280.
21. Voller P. Does the teacher have a role in autonomous learning? In P. Benson & P. Voller (Eds.). Autonomy and Independence in Language Learning. London: Longman, 1997, pp. 98-113.

THE USE OF LANGUAGES OF INDIGENOUS PEOPLES OF NORTH, SIBERIA AND FAR EAST IN SUBJECTS OF THE RUSSIAN FEDERATION IN ACTIVITIES OF PUBLIC AUTHORITIES AND LOCAL GOVERNMENTS

Ivan Vasilievich Yadreev
Senior Counselor of Justice, Prosecutor of the Churapchinsky District of the Republic of Sakha (Yakutia), Postgraduate student, Faculty of Scientific Personnel Training, University of the General Prosecutor's Office of the Russian Federation
kutlug@mail.ru

Abstract.

The article analyzes the current legal regulation of using of native languages of indigenous peoples of North, Siberia and Far East in the official spheres. None of the languages of indigenous peoples of North, Siberia and Far East is established as a state language of a subject of the Russian Federation. The fields of possible use of the indigenous peoples' languages that can be deduced from the provisions of laws are the following: the work of state authorities and local governments, the publication of normative legal acts, the organization and running of elections, the official paperwork, the writing of names of geographical objects, the road signs, the signboards. And the conditions for such use are the compact residence of native speakers and the necessity. The non-state languages' use can only be additional to that of state languages of the Federation and/or of the Republics. The article makes an evaluation of the completeness of the use of opportunities by regional legislation in the field of language-construction. Several conclusions can be drawn from the analysis of those laws: not every subject of the Federation in whose territory indigenous peoples live, has adopted regional laws regulating the legal status and the use of the languages; the languages of the indigenous peoples of the North, Siberia and the Far East, in most subjects of the Federation, do not have official status, with the exception of Dolgan, Chukchi, Evenki, Even, Yukagir in the Republic of Sakha (Yakutia) and the Nenets, Mansi, Khanty in Khanty-Mansi Autonomous Area - Ugra, where they are called “national.” In the rest of the subjects the languages have a not very clear status of “native”; there is no single approach to the indigenous peoples’ languages’ areas of use determining. All the subjects of the federation do narrow the scope of the use of indigenous peoples’ languages in comparison with the possibilities provided by federal legislation; in the legal regulation of the use of languages in all subjects of the Federation, except partially the Republic of Sakha (Yakutia), a discretionary rules are used: the use of the language in official spheres every time is dependent on necessity, on regional authorities’ and local governments’ decisions, on some conciliatory procedures implementation. Based on all analysis that we made in this article it is concluded that there is a need to reform the legislation of languages of subjects of Russian Federation.

Keywords: official language, native languages, indigenous peoples of North, Siberia and Far East, local government, language use, federalism, language policy, language construction.

I. Introduction

The Russian Federation is currently the largest multinational state in the world.This factor was and is the crucial one in the Russian state structure development on each of its historical stages [5].The legislation of the Russian Federation on the legal status of languages was adopted in the era of the contemporary Russian statehood formation [4].

The possibility of the use of a language in public authorities’ and local governments’ activities depends on its legal status.

Part 1 of the Article 68 of the Constitution of the Russian Federation provides that the

Russian language shall be the state language throughout the territory of the RF. Part 2 of that Article provides that the Republics shall have the right to establish their own state languages. Part 3 of the Article provides that Russian Federation shall guarantee to all of its peoples the right to preserve their native languages and to create conditions for study and development of those languages [8].

None of the languages of indigenous peoples of North, Siberia and Far East is established as a state language of a subject of the Russian Federation.It seems that this was caused by the peoples' status gradation originating in the Soviet historical period rather than the small number of native speakers.The remnants of this gradation are preserved in the internal structure of the Russian Federation.

For instance the number of Nenets language speakers is only slightly smaller than that of Altaian, Khakassian or Circassian, the last three being the state languages of the respective republics [7].

The Nenets and Chukchihave a hypothetical possibility of being recognized as state language of a subject of the Federation, as they have a significant number of speakers settled in relatively large proportions within the territories of the subjects of the Federation that can potentially obtain the status of a republic within the Russian Federation.

II. Indigenous languages usage in official legislation

2.1. Federal legislation on languages

Let's analyze the federal legislation in terms of the indigenous peoples' languages' possibility to be used in the official spheres.The Law of Russian Federation No. 1807-1 of October 25, 1991 "On the Russian Federation peoples' languages" (part 2 of the Article 3) provides that Republics have the right to establish their own state languages pursuant to the Constitution. According to the part 4 of the Article 3 the language of a people not having its own national-state or national-territorial entity or living outside such, in a territory of compact residence of such a people can be used in the sphere of official communication in addition to Russian and the state language of a republic. The rules for the use of languages in such territory are to be determined by the federal legislation and the legislation of the subject of the Federation.

The part 1 of the Article 11 of the above mentioned Law provides that the federal and, regional and local authorities' activities are to be carried out in the state language of the Federation. The part 2 of the Article 11provides that the republics shall have the right to use their state languages in the activities of regional and local authorities.

The rules of part 1 of article 15 of that Law stipulate that the state language of the Federation, the state languages of the republics and other languages of the peoples of Russia are to be used in the activities of government bodies and organizations and enterprises and institutions of the Russian Federation. However, the content of parts 2 to 6 of this article shows that it is only about citizens' rights to speak their language, to have an interpreter, to appeal and receive a reply in the language of the appeal, i.e. about the use of the language in some specified cases.

The article 13 of the Law in question provides that Russian shall be the language of regional normative legal acts and regional legislation, while republics shall have the right to publish the federal normative legal acts and to officially publish the regional normative legal acts in their state languages. It is also stated that subjects of the Federation may enact legislation governing the normative legal acts' publication in the other languages of the peoples of Russian Federation.

The article 14 provides that in holding the elections or referenda republics are entitled to use their state languages and the languages of the peoples of Russia (in the territories of those peoples' compact residence) in addition to Russian language.

According to the Article 16 of the Law in question the official paperwork of government bodies and organizations and enterprises and institutions is to be carried out in Russian as the state language of the Federation. The official paperwork in republics is also carried out in the state languages of the respective republics.

The rules for the use of languages in the official paperwork are to be determined by the federal legislation and the legislation of the republics.

Part 2 of that article stipulates that texts of documents (letterheads, seals, stamps) and sign-plates with the names of state bodies, organizations, enterprises and institutions are to be made in the state language of the Federation, state languages of the republics and other languages of the peoples of Russia, determined by the legislation of the republics.

Part 3 of that Article allows the official paperwork in the subjects of the Federation to be carried out in the languages of the peoples of Russia (in the territories of their compact residence) in addition to the state languages of the Federation and its republics. The rules for that are to be adopted by the subjects of the Federation.

The Article 23 of the Law in question provides that the republics may write the names of geographical objects and make road signs and other signs in the state languages of the republics in addition to the state language of the Federation.

Part 2 of that Article provides that in the territories of peoples' of Russia compact residence the names of geographical objects may be written and road signs and other signs may be made in such peoples' languages in addition to the state language of the Federation [13].

2.2. New definitions of languages in federal legislation

The adoption of the Federal Law No. 53-FZ of June 01, 2005 "On the state language of the Russian Federation" defined the spheres of languages' use more clearly.

Part 2 of the Article 1 of the above mentioned Federal law provides that the status of the Russian language as the state language of the Federation implies its mandatory use in fields defined by law.

Part 7 of that Article indicates that the obligation to use the state language of the Federation should not be construed as a denial or derogation of the right to use the state languages of the republics, and the languages of the peoples of Russia.

The article 3 provides that the use of state language of the Federation is mandatory in all official spheres: in the activities of public authorities and local governments including their paperwork; in the names of those authorities and governments; in holding the elections and referenda; in official publication of legal normative acts; in the interaction of the authorities and governments with citizens and associations; in the names of geographical objects, in road signs; in other fields specified by federal laws [11].

The Federal Law No. 82-FZ of April 30, 1999 "On Guarantees of the rights of indigenous peoples of the Russian Federation" does not provide for the use of languages of indigenous minorities in any official spheres [10].

The Federal Law No. 273-FZ of December 29, 2012 "On education" [9] and the Law of Russian Federation No. 2300-1 of February 07, 1992 "On protection of Consumer's rights" [12] and other federal laws have some provisions on languages' use but those provisions fall beyond the scope of our topic.

Thus the above analysis of laws allows to conclude that federal legislation does regulate the use of non-state languages of Russia in official spheres.

The fields of possible use of the indigenous peoples' languages that can be deduced from the provisions of laws are the following: the work of state authorities and local governments, the publication of normative legal acts, the organization and running of elections, the official paperwork, the writing of names of geographical objects, the road signs, the signboards.

And the conditions for such use are the compact residence of native speakers and the necessity.

The subjects of the Federation are commonly entitled by federal legislation to identify the existence of such necessity.

The non-state languages' use can only be additional to that of state languages of the Federation and/or of the Republics.

The legislation does not give a definition of compactness of residence of a people not having its own national-state or national-territorial entity or living outside such. However the "Russian classification of economic regions. OK 024-95" (approved by the Decision of the GosStandart of Russia No. 640 of December 27, 1995), can be helpful as its paragraph 13 indicates the regions of traditional residence of the indigenous peoples of Russia [14].

In some cases, such lists are adopted in the form of acts of the subjects of the Federation.For example the Law of the Republic of Sakha (Yakutia) of July 10, 2003, 59-Z N 121-III "On the List of Indigenous peoples of the North and traditional places of their residence and traditional economic activities in the Republic of Sakha (Yakutia)" [27].

III. Analysis of indigenous languages legislation in the subjects of Russian Federation

3.1. Legislation of the Republic of Sakha (Yakutia)

A subject of the Federation in whose territory the indigenous peoples of the North, the Siberia and the Far East reside, governs the status and the use of relevant languages.

The Republic of Sakha (Yakutia) has the most detailed legal regulation in this field, as compared to the Republics of Buryatia, Komi, Tuva and Khakassia.

In accordance with Article 46 of the Constitution of the Republic of Sakha (Yakutia), Sakha and Russian are the state languages of the Republic. The languages of the indigenous peoples of the North are official in the places of compact residence of these peoples [15].

The Law of the Republic of Sakha (Yakutia) No. 1170-XII of October 16, 1992 "On Languages in the Republic of Sakha (Yakutia)" (Article 6) recognizes Evenki, Even, Yukagir, Dolgan, Chukchi languages as local official languages in the places of residence of the peoples concerned and provides for their use alongside state languages.

However, the Article 12 of that Law provides that the languages of the local ethnic groups of the North are used only in the work of local governments in places of compact residence of those groups alongside the state language of the Republic and the state language of the Federation. The use of those languages in the work of other public authorities and public, organizations, enterprises, institutions is not provided for [31].

The Law of the Republic of Sakha (Yakutia) Z No. 461-III of March 31, 2005 "On the legal status of indigenous peoples of the North" (Article 30) has similar provisions [28]. And according to the part 2 of the Article 30, local governments shall determine the list of localities, economic, social, cultural objects, names of which are to be indicated in the languages of the indigenous peoples of the North.

At the same time, it is provided that, if necessary in the areas of indigenous peoples' traditional residence and economic activities the official paperwork can be conducted in the languages of these peoples, entities who are to use these languages not being specified (Article 9 of the Law of the Republic of Sakha (Yakutia) 111-Z N 243-III of February 20, 2004 "On the status of languages of the indigenous peoples of the North") [30].

It is stipulated that acts of bodies of local self-government should be adopted and published in Sakha, Russian and local official languages (Article 13 of the Law of the Republic of Sakha (Yakutia) N 1170-XII of October 16, 1992 "On languages in the Republic of Sakha (Yakutia)").

The Article 17 of that law provides for the use of the local official languages in official correspondence and postal and telegraphic communications. The Article 18 provides for the use of the local official languages in statistical and financial documentation of enterprises, institutions and organizations.

The Article 23 stipulates that in holding the elections or referenda,Sakha language, and the languages of the peoples of Russia (in the territories of their compact residence) may be used along with the state language of the Federation.

The Article 32 provides that the names of geographical objects on road signs and on other signs in the territory of the Republic are to be indicated in the state languages of the Republic of Sakha (Yakutia).

If necessary, these names may be additionally indicated in other languages of the peoples of Russia, taking into account the interests of the respective territory's population.

The Article 34 stipulates that texts of documents (letter heads, seals, stamps) and sign-plates with names of state bodies, organizations, enterprises and institutions are to be made in the state languages, and (if necessary) in local official languages.

The Article 35 provides that sign-plates with names of state and local authorities, names of enterprises and institutions and organizations are to be made in the state languages of the

Republic and (in the areas of compact residence of the indigenous peoples of the North) additionally in local official languages. The same requirements apply to the texts of signs and announcements and advertisements and other information media containing information in a visual form.

The Law of the Republic of Sakha (Yakutia) "On the status of the national administrative-territorial units in places of traditional residence and economic activities of indigenous peoples of the North of the Republic of Sakha (Yakutia)" 207-Z No. 419-III of January 27, 2005 (part 6 of the Article 6) [29] provides that the names of public enterprises and institutions in the territory of the national administrative-territorial unit shall be indicated in the state languages of the Republic and in the language determined by referendum or assembly (meeting).

So, the legislation of the Republic of Sakha (Yakutia), firstly, grants official status to the languages of indigenous minorities in the areas of native speakers' compact residence; secondly, it provides for mandatory use of these languages in the work of local governments, in publication of normative legal acts, in making of sign-plates with the names of authorities, enterprises and organizations, in texts of signs and announcements and advertisements and other information media containing information in a visual form. The rules regulating the use of languages in paperwork, in holding of elections, in official correspondence, in the names of geographical objects, in road signs and other signs, in the texts of documents (letterheads, seals, stamps), are discretionary: "if necessary."

Local governments have the right to decide on issues of indication of names of public enterprises and institutions and to determine the list of localities, economic, social, cultural objects, names of which are to be indicated in the languages of the indigenous peoples of the North.

3.2. Legislation of other republics of the Russian Federation

The other republics' legislation regulate the sphere in question to a considerably lesser extent.

The Law of the Republic of Buryatia No. 221-XIIofJune 10, 1992 "On languages of the peoples of the Republic of Buryatia" (Article 11) provides for the possibility of using the languages of the peoples of Russia in holding the elections [25]. Similar norms are found in the Law of the Altai Republic No. 9-6 of March 03, 1993 "On the languages of peoples living in the territory of the Altai Republic" [24]. In addition the article 4 of this law, recognizes the Kazakh as the official language in the areas of compact residence of its speakers.

The Law of the Republic of Khakassia no. 11 of October 20, 1992 "On the Languages of the peoples of the Russian Federation living in the Republic of Khakassia" [33] in addition to the rule on the possibility of using the non-state languages in holding the elections (Article 12) provides for the possibility of paperwork in languages of peoples (other than Russians and Khakass) compactly living in the Republic (Article 14) and for the possibility of geographical objects' names indication and making of road signs and other signs in cases of necessity (Article 21).

The laws of the Komi Republic [26] and the Republic of Tyva [32] do not regulate the use of the languages of indigenous peoples.

We shall consider the governing of the relations concerned in four autonomous areas, three of which being the parts of the Arkhangelsk and Tyumen Regions.

The laws of the Nenets [22], Yamal-Nenets [38], the Khanty-Mansi-Ugra Autonomous Areas [36], firstly, do list the languages of indigenous peoples living in these Areas, and secondly, refer to those as "native," and (in Khanty-Mansi Autonomous Area-Ugra) as "national (native)."

The laws of these Areas have close resemblance.

The Law of the Khanty-Mansi Autonomous Area No. 89-OZ of December 4, 2001 "On the languages of the indigenous peoples of the North living in the Khanty-Mansi Autonomous Area" (Article 6) provides that the right to use those languages is to be guaranteed by state authorities' and local governments' rules on official paperwork.

The Law of the Nenets Autonomous Area No. 4-OZ of March 18, 2013 "On the Nenets language in the Nenets Autonomous Area" (Article 9) provides for paperwork in Nenets language along with the state language, but only in local authorities, and stipulates this for cases established by the Area's Administration. Seals and stamps and letterheads with bilingual

(Russian and Nenets) texts can be used for that purpose.

The part 2 of the Article 9 allows making of sign-plates with the names of state authorities and local governments of the Area in the state language of the Federation and in the Nenets language, provided that the name of the relevant entity in Nenets is indicated in its constituent documents.

The Law of the Yamal-Nenets Autonomous Area No. 48-ZAO of April 05, 2010 “On the native languages of Indigenous peoples of the North in the Yamal-Nenets Autonomous Area” (part 3 of the article 1) provides that native languages are to be used in everyday communication, in fields of social relations that are important to those peoples, alongside the state language of the Federation. However the Article 7 of the Law in questioner stricts the use of native languages in official paperwork to only sending responses to citizens' appeals. Earlier, before amendments were made to the Law on June 09, 2019, official paperwork of local governments in Nenets, Khanty and Selkup languages was possible.

The rules on the adoption and translation of normative legal acts into the indigenous peoples' languages are as follows.

The above mentioned Law of The Nenets Autonomous Area of The Arkhangelsk Region (Article 8) provides for the translation and publication of a law or another normative legal act into Nenets if there is a special decision of the authority that adopted the act and only in the field of the Nenets people's rights' guarantees.

The law of the Khanty-Mansi Autonomous Area - Ugra (Article 7) establishes that normative legal acts of state authorities and local governments of the Area that affect the rights and freedoms of citizens, may be published in the languages of indigenous peoples along with the official publication of those acts.

The law of the Yamal-Nenets Autonomous Area (Article 6) regulates that the translation and publication of normative legal act into the languages of indigenous peoples of the North are possible provided that there is a decision of the issuing authority, and that the act relates to the field of the guarantees of rights of those peoples.

The use of languages in geographical objects' names indication is provided for in the laws of the Nenets and Yamal-Nenets Autonomous Areas and is not affected by the legislation of the Khanty-Mansi Autonomous Area-Ugra.

Article 10 of the law of the Nenets Autonomous Area stipulates that in places of compact residence of the Nenets people using the Nenets language, the names of geographical objects of the Area may be indicated and road signs (other signs) may be made in Nenets in addition to the state language of the Federation. This requires a decision of the Government of the Area issued in accordance with the interests of the population and on the basis of municipalities' heads' and Nenets people associations' proposals.

Under the Article 11 of that Law visual information such as street names, banners, advertisements, information plates and signs on cultural heritage sites of local (municipal) significance may be additionally (beside Russian) indicated in Nenets if the charters of the respective municipalities provide for that.

The law of the Yamal-Nenets Autonomous Area provides that names of geographical objects may be indicated in native languages of the indigenous peoples of the North (in addition to the state language of the Federation) under the decisions of the Government of the Area issuedat the proposal of the entities concerned and according to the procedure established by the Government. Such procedure has been adopted.

Under the Article 9 of the Law of the Autonomous Area indication of street names making of public authorities' and local governments' sign-plates, banners, advertisements, cultural heritage sites' information plates and signs in those native languages is also possible under a decision of local government if the charter of a municipality provides for that.

Thus, languages are declared native or national and not official.

The use of languages in the activities of state authorities and local governments is possible if this is provided for by relevant bodies' statutes, or in cases specially determined by the Area's administration (except for the Yamal-Nenets Autonomous Area).

Normative legal acts publication in the languages of indigenous peoples is due only for those acts directly affecting the rights of the peoples concerned, and requires a decision of the issuing authority on such a publication.

Languages are also used to a limited extent on road signs and other signs, in the naming of authorities, in visual information (including sign-plates) under the Area's government decision issued at the proposal of the entities concerned.

In contrast to rather detailed regulation of this sphere by legislation of the above considered Areas, the Law of the Chukotka Autonomous Area No. 65-OZ of October 23, 2017 "On the native languages of the indigenous peoples of the North, Siberia and the Far East of the Russian Federation living in the territory of the Chukotka Autonomous Area" [37] (part 2 of the Article 3) provides only that in the Area's state programs measures can be taken on the native languages' use in public life of the territories of the peoples' compact residence along with the state language of the Federation, including the indication of the names of geographical objects and the design of road signs and other signs.

Therefore, the solutions in this area are entirely the responsibility of the executive authorities of the Area.

We shall consider the legislation on languages of indigenous peoples of other subjects of the Federation in whose territory these peoples live.

The law of the Kamchatka Territory [18] establishes rules similar to those of the corresponding law of the Chukotka Autonomous Area.

The law of the Kemerovo region stipulates that by a decision of the Regional Administration's Collegium, the writing of names of geographical objects and the designation of road signs and other signs can be made in the languages of indigenous peoples (in the territory of their compact residence and taking into account the interests of the population) along with the state language of the Federation [19].

Similar rules are provided for by the laws of the Krasnoyarsk Territory [20], Sakhalin Region [34], Magadan Region [21].

Special laws on the languages of indigenous peoples of Russia have not been adopted In Trans-Baikal Territory, Primorye Territory [23], Khabarovsk Territory [35], Amur Region [16], Irkutsk Region [17], Tomsk Region, the Jewish Autonomous Region.

There is only legislation on general guarantees of the indigenous peoples' rights but not in each of the mentioned subjects of the Federation.

Some of the laws (e.g. in Sakhalin Region, in Kamchatka Territory) do list the indigenous peoples' native languages, and some do not.

IV. Conclusion

Several conclusions can be drawn from the analysis of those laws:

1) Not every subject of the Federation in whose territory indigenous peoples live, has adopted regional laws regulating the legal status and the use of the languages. This, apparently, is due to both the lack of practice of official use of these languages in the past, and the difficult situation of the languages as such.

2) The languages of the indigenous peoples of the North, Siberia and the Far East, in most subjects of the Federation, do not have official status, with the exception of Dolgan, Chukchi, Evenki, Even, Yukagir in the Republic of Sakha (Yakutia) and the Nenets, Mansi, Khanty in Khanty-Mansi Autonomous Area - Ugra, where they are called "national." In the rest of the subjects the languages have a not very clear status of "native."

3) There is no single approach to the indigenous peoples' languages' areas of use determining. All the subjects of the federation do narrow the scope of the use of indigenous peoples' languages in comparison with the possibilities provided by federal legislation. Thus the scope is often limited to the level of local governments.

4) In the legal regulation of the use of languages in all subjects of the Federation, except partially the Republic of Sakha (Yakutia), a discretionary rules are used: the use of the language in official spheres every time is dependent on necessity, on regional authorities' and local governments' decisions, on some conciliatory procedures implementation.

The legal regulation in the Republic of Sakha (Yakutia) certainly is not perfect too. For example, there is no indication that a particular language is official for a particular territory, it is only implied and this cannot be considered sufficient.

However, the most important and acute issue is the Republic's language legislation rules implementation which is not properly ensured.

V.Shadrin notes that most of the 70 localties (places of compact residence) of the indigenous peoples of the North in the Republic of Sakha (Yakutia) show no visible signs of the language official status, i.e. use of language in official sign-plates, street names, attributes and information. In none of the localities the languages of the peoples of the North are used in the authorities' work process and document flow, including the translation of the main normative legal acts into them [6].

It should be taken into account that language legislation implementation problems exist in all the subjects of the Federation (republics are included) particularly in the law-making process.

L. Vasil'eva notes that the legislative process in the republics is carried out mostly in one language. For example in the National Assembly of the Republic of Mordovia texts of laws are being prepared, discussed and adopted only in Russian. Some researchers consider translations of laws into Moksha and Erzya (state languages of the Republic) and their subsequent publication as having informational rather than legal value [1].

However, the languages of indigenous peoples are in a more difficult position as compared with that of the republics' state languages.

For example, the use of the Russian language as the language of interethnic and business communication in the Ugra is due to the dominance of Russian residents (more than 60% of the total), the multi-ethnicity (125 nationalities) of the region's population, and other factors. 83% of respondents choose Russian as a means of communication [3].

Indigenous peoples, living in a predominantly Russian-speaking society, gradually lose their native (national) languages and are in need special state support. Particular attention should be paid to the preservation of indigenous languages, to fully ensure the right to use them. Language being a sign of belonging to an ethnic group serves as an effective means of national identity preservation.

However, the adoption of special measures for the development of these languages should in no case be regarded as discrimination against native speakers of the Russian language, but should contribute to the development of non-state languages and the achievement of equal rights for native speakers of these languages and the rest of the population [2].

Ensuring of the language functioning in all spheres of life, including the official sphere, is essential for its vitality.

Thus, the subjects' of the Federation legislation on the use of the indigenous peoples' languages needs to be changed, aiming primarily at using all the opportunities provided by federal legislation. Also of great importance are the measures aimed at the existing legislation implementation.

In addition, it is necessary to consider the foreign countries' experience in the legal regulation of the use of indigenous peoples' languages.

Only full use of languages of Russia is the key to safe and stable coexistence of the peoples of our country.

References

1. Васильева Л.Н. Двуязычие нормативных правовых актов в Российский Федерации: совершенствование правовой основы // Журнал российского права. – 2008. – N8. (Vasil'eva L.N. Dvuyazychie normativnykh pravovykh aktov v Rossiyskoy Federatsii: sovershenstvovanie pravovoy osnovy [Bilingualism of normative legal acts in the Russian Federation: improving the legal framework]. Journal of Russian Law.2008, no. 8.)
2. Гарипов Р.Ш. Право на использование и охрану родного языка у коренных малочисленных народов России [Электронный ресурс] — Режим доступа: https://wiselawyer.ru/poleznoe/59843-pravo-ispolzovanie-okhranu-rodnogo-yazyka-korennykh-malochislennykh (дата обращения 22.09.2019). (GaripovR.Sh. The right of the indigenous peoples of Russia to use and protect their native languages. Available at: https://wiselawyer.ru/poleznoe/59843-pravo-ispolzovanie-okhranu-rodnogo-yazyka-korennykh-malochislennykh (Accessed on September 22, 2019).
3. Исламова Ю.В. Сферы распространения языков обских угров в Кондинском

районе Ханты-Мансийского автономного округа – Югры // Филологические науки. Вопросы теории и практики [Электронный ресурс] — Режим доступа: https://cyberleninka.ru/article/n/sfery-rasprostraneniya-yazykov-obskih-ugrov-v-kondinskom-rayone-hmao-yugry. (IslamovaYu.V. Sfery rasprostraneniya yazykov obskikh ugrov v Kondinskom rayone Khanty-Mansiyskogo avtonomnogo okruga – Yugry [Spheres of distribution of languages of the Ob Ugrians in the Kondinsky district of the Khanty-Mansiysk Autonomous Area – Ugra].Filologicheskie nauki.Voprosy teorii i praktiki. Available at: https://cyberleninka.ru/article/n/sfery-rasprostraneniya-yazykov-obskih-ugrov-v-kondinskom-rayone-hmao-yugry.

4. Каримов А.С. Коллизионные проблемы развития законодательства о языках субъектов РФ // Российская юстиция. – 2015. – N12. (Karimov A.S. Kollizionn yeproblemyrazvitiyazakonodatel'stva o yazykakhsub"ektov RF [Conflict problems of the development of legislation on languages of constituent entities of the Russian Federation]. Rossiyskayayustitsiya.2015, no. 12.)
5. Таева Н.Е. Реализация принципа равноправия и самоопределения народов в республике Крым и Севастополе // Lex russica. 2017. – N2. (Taeva N.E. Realizatsiya printsip ravnopraviya i samoopredeleniya narodov v respublike Krym i Sevastopole [Implementation of the principle of peoples equality and self-determination in the Republic of Crimea and the city of Sevastopol]. Lexrussica.2017, no. 2.)
6. Шадрин, В.И. Основные вопросы функционирования языков коренных малочисленных народов Севера Республики Саха (Якутия) (доклад на заседании Совета по языковой политике при Главе РС (Я), с. Иенгра, 9 апреля 2015 г.): [Электронный ресурс] — Режим доступа: http://yakutiakmns.org/archives/3423 (дата обращения 22.09.2019) (Shadrin, V.I. The main issues of the Sakha (Yakutia) Republic indigenous peoples languages functioning. Report at the meeting of the RS (Y) Head's Language Policy Council.Iengra, April 9, 2015. Available at: http: / /yakutiakmns.org/archives/3423 (Accessed on September 22, 2019).
7. Итоги Всероссийской переписи населения 2010 года [Электронный ресурс] —

Режим доступа: http://www.gks.ru/free_doc/new_site/perepis2010/croc/perepis_itogi1612.htm (дата обращения 22.09.2019). (The 2010 Russian census final data. Available at: http://www.gks.ru/free_doc/new_site/perepis2010/croc/perepis_itogi1612.htm (Accessed on September 22, 2019))

8. Конституция Российской Федерации от 12 декабря 1993 года // Российская газета. — 1993. — 25 декабря.(Constitution of The Russian Federation of December 12, 1993. Rossiyskayagazeta. 1993, December 25).
9. Об образовании в Российской Федерации: федер. закон от 29.12.2012 N 273-ФЗ (ред. от 01.05.2017, с изм. от 05.07.2017) // СЗ РФ. – 2012. – N 53 (ч.1). – Ст. 7598. (On education in Russian Federation. Federal Law No. 273-FZ of December 29, 2012 (as amended on July 5, 2017) SZRF. 2012, no. 53 (pt 1), art. 7598.)
10. О гарантиях прав коренных малочисленных народов Российской Федерации: федер. закон от 30.04.1999 № 82-ФЗ (в ред. от 26.07.2019) // СЗ РФ. – 1999. – N 18 – ст. 2208. (On guarantees of the rights of indigenous minorities of the Russian Federation. The Federal Law No. 82-FZ of April 30, 1999 (as amended on July 26, 2019). SZRF. 1999, no. 18, art. 2208)
11. О государственном языке Российской Федерации: федер. закон от 01.06.2005 N 53-ФЗ (ред. от 05.05.2014) // СЗ РФ. – 2005. – N23. – С.2199. (On the state language of the Russian Federation. Federal Law No. 53-FZ of June 01, 2005 (as amended on May 5, 2014). SZRF. 2005, no. 23, art. 2199)
12. О защите прав потребителей: федер. закон от 07.02.1992 N 2300-1 (ред. от 03.07.2016) // ВСНД и ВС РФ. – 1992. – N 15. – Ст. 766 (On protection of Consumer's rights. Law of Russian Federation No. 2300-1 of February 07, 1992 (as amended on July 3, 2016). VSND i VS RF. 1992, no. 15.art. 766)
13. О языках народов Российской Федерации: Закон РФ от 25.10.1991 N 1807-1 (ред. от 12.03.2014) // ВСНД и ВС РСФСР. – 1991. – N50. – С.1740. (On the Russian Federation peoples' languages. The Law of Russian Federation No. 1807-1 of October 25, 1991 (as amended on March 12, 2014).VSND i VS RSFSR.1991, no. 50, art. 1740)

14. Общероссийский классификатор экономических регионов ОК 024-95 (ОКЭР) (утв. постановлением Госстандарта РФ от 27 декабря 1995 г. N 640) // Национальные стандарты. – 2018. – N 1. ("Russian classification of economic regions. OK 024-95" (approved by the Decision of the GosStandart of Russia No. 640 of December 27, 1995). Natsional'nyestandarty.2018, no. 1.)
15. Конституция (Основной закон) Республики Саха (Якутия) (ред. от 15.06.2016) // Якутские ведомости. – 1992. – N 7. (The Constitution (Fundamental law) of the Republic of Sakha (Yakutia) (as amended on June 15, 2016). Yakutskiye Vedomosti. 1992, no. 7).
16. О гарантиях прав коренных малочисленных народов Севера, Сибири и Дальнего Востока Российской Федерации в Амурской области: закон Амурской области от 29.04.2003 №208-ОЗ (в ред. от 04.12.2018) // Амурская правда. – 2003. – N 123-124. (On guarantees of the rights of the indigenous peoples of the North, Siberia and the Far East of the Russian Federation in the Amur Region. Amur Region Law No. 208-OZ of April 29, 2003 (as amended on December 4, 2018).Amurskaya Pravda. 2003, no. 123-124)
17. Об отдельных вопросах организации и обеспечения защиты исконной среды обитания и традиционного образа жизни коренных малочисленных народов Российской Федерации в Иркутской области: закон Иркутской области от 16 декабря 2013 г. N 140-ОЗ (в ред. от 06.05.2019) // Ведомости Законодательного собрания Иркутской области. – 2013. N 4 (том 2) (On some issues of organization and protection of the traditional areas of habitation and traditional way of life of the indigenous peoples of the Russian Federation in the Irkutsk Region. The law of the Irkutsk Region No. 140-OZ of December 16, 2013 (as amended on May 06, 2019. Vedomosti Zakonodatel'nogo sobraniya Irkutskoy oblasti.2013, no. 4 (vol. 2))
18. О родных языках коренных малочисленных народов Севера, Сибири и Дальнего Востока Российской Федерации, проживающих на территории Камчатского края: закон Камчатского края от 31.03.2017 N 72 // Официальные ведомости. 2017. - N 63. (On the native languages of the indigenous peoples of the North, Siberia and the Far East of the Russian Federation living in the Kamchatka Territory. The law of the Kamchatka Territory

No. 72 of March 31, 2017.Ofitsial'nyevedomosti.2017, no. 63)

19. О мерах по сохранению и развитию языков коренных малочисленных народов Кемеровской области: закон Кемеровской области от 8 июля 2015 г. N 73-ОЗ // [Электронный ресурс] — Режим доступа: http://publication.pravo.gov.ru/SignatoryAuthority/region42. (On measures for the preservation and development of the languages of the indigenous peoples of the Kemerovo Region. The law of the Kemerovo Region N 73-OZ of July 8, 2015. Available at: http://publication.pravo.gov.ru/SignatoryAuthority/region42.)

20. О родных (национальных) языках коренных малочисленных народов, проживающих на территории Красноярского края: закон Красноярского края от 05.11.2015 N 9-3816 // Ведомости высших органов государственной власти Красноярского края. – 2015. – N 46(726).(On the native (national) languages of the indigenous peoples living in the Krasnoyarsk Territory. The law of the Krasnoyarsk Territory No. 9-3816 of November 05, 2015.VedomostivysshikhorganovgosudarstvennoyvlastiKrasnoyarskogokraya.2015, no. 46(726))

21. О родных языках коренных малочисленных народов Севера, проживающих на территории Магаданской области: закон Магаданской области от 30.03.2016 N 2013-ОЗ // Магаданская правда. – 2016. - N 2. (On the native languages of the indigenous peoples of the North living in the territory of the Magadan Region. The Law of the Magadan Region No. 2013-OZ of March 30, 2016. Magadanskaya pravda.2016, no. 2).

22. О ненецком языке на территории Ненецкого автономного округа: закон Ненецкого автономного округа от 18.03.2013 № 4-ОЗ // Сборник нормативных правовых актов Ненецкого автономного округа. – 20.03.2013. – N 5(206). (On the Nenets language in the Nenets Autonomous Area. the Law of the Nenets Autonomous Area No. 4-OZ of March 18, 2013. Sbornik normativnykh pravovykh aktov Nenetskogo avtonomnogo okruga. March 20, 2013, no. 5(206).)

23. О коренных малочисленных народах Российской Федерации, проживающих в Приморском крае: закон Приморского края от 22.12.2015 N 742-КЗ (в ред. от

08.10.2018) // Ведомости Законодательного Собрания Приморского края. – 2015. – N 145. (On the indigenous peoples of the Russian Federation living in the Primorye Territory: the law of the Primorye Territory No. 742-KZ of December 22, 2015 (as amended on October 8, 2018) Vedomosti Zakonodatel'nogo Sobraniya Primorskogo kraya. 2015, no. 145)

24. О языках народов, проживающих на территории Республики Алтай: закон Республики Алтай от 03.03.1993 № 9-6 (ред. от 03.06.2016) // Ведомости Верховного Совета Республики Алтай. – Август-сентябрь 1993. – N3. – С.88. ("On the languages of peoples living in the territory of the Altai Republic." the Law of the Altai Republic No. 9-6 of March 03, 1993 (as amended on June 03, 2016). Vedomosti Verkhovnogo Soveta Respubliki Altay. August-September, 1993, no.3, p.88)
25. О языках народов Республики Бурятия: закон Республики Бурятия от 10.06.1992 № 221-XII (ред. от 21.12.2015) // Бурятия – 23.06.1992. – N 119 (276). (On languages of the peoples of the Republic of Buryatia. The Law of the Republic of Buryatia No. 221-XII of June 10, 1992 (as amended on December 21, 2015).Buryatia.June 23, 1992, no. 119 (276).)
26. О государственных языках Республики Коми: закон Республики Коми от 28.05.1992 (ред. от 20.06.2016) // Красное знамя – 11.06.1992. – N112. (On the state languages of the Komi Republic. The law of the Komi Republic of May 28, 1992 (as amended on June 20,2016). Krasnoeznamya.June 11, 1992, no. 112)
27. О перечне коренных малочисленных народов Севера и мест их традиционного проживания и традиционной хозяйственной деятельности в Республики Саха (Якутия): закон Республики Саха (Якутия) от 10.07.2003 З N 121-III (в ред. от 30.01.2019) // Якутия. – 2003. – N 146 (On the List of Indigenous peoples of the North and traditional places of their residence and traditional economic activities in the Republic of Sakha (Yakutia). The Law of the Republic of Sakha (Yakutia) 59-Z N 121-III of July 10, 2003 (as amended on January 30, 2019).Yakutia.2003, no. 146.)
28. О правовом статусе коренных малочисленных народов Севера: закон Республики Саха (Якутия) от 31.03.2005 З N 461-III // Якутские ведомости. – 04.05.2005. – N 20.(On the legal status of indigenous peoples of the North. The Law of the Republic of Sakha

(Yakutia) 227-Z No. 461-III of March 31, 2005. Yakutskie vedomosti.May 4, 2005, no. 20).

29. О статусе национального административно-территориального образования в местах традиционного проживания и традиционной хозяйственной деятельности коренных малочисленных народов севера Республики Саха (Якутия): закон Республики Саха (Якутия) от 27.01.2005 З N 419-III "" (в ред. от 19.06.2019) // Якутские ведомости. – 26.02.2015. – N 10 (On the status of the national administrative-territorial units in places of traditional residence and economic activities of indigenous peoples of the North of the Republic of Sakha (Yakutia). The Law of the Republic of Sakha (Yakutia) 207-Z No. 419-III of January 27, 2005. (as amended on June 19, 2019). Yakutskie vedomosti.February 26, 2005, no. 10)
30. О статусе языков коренных малочисленных народов Севера Республики Саха (Якутия): закон Республики Саха (Якутия) от 20.04.2004 З N 243-III (ред. от 30.04.2014) // Сборник законов Республики Саха (Якутия). – 2004. – том 1. (On the status of languages of the indigenous peoples of the North. The Law of the Republic of Sakha (Yakutia) of February 20, 2004, 111-Z N 243-III.SbornikzakonovRespublikiSakha (Yakutiya).2004 vol. 1)
31. О языках в Республике Саха (Якутия): закон Республики Саха (Якутия) от 16.10.1992 N 1170-XII (ред. от 30.05.2017) // Якутские ведомости. – 1992. – N 215. (On Languages in the Republic of Sakha (Yakutia). The Law of the Republic of Sakha (Yakutia) No. 1170-XII of October 16, 1992. Yakutskievedomosti.1992, no. 215)
32. О языках в Республике Тыва: закон Республики Тыва от 31.12.2003 N 462 ВХ-I (ред. от 01.07.2014) // Тувинская правда. – 03.02.2004. (On languages in the Republic of Tyva. The law of the Republic of Tyva No. 462 VKh-I (as amended on July 1, 2014).Tuvinskaya pravda. February 03, 2004.)
33. О языках народов Российской Федерации, проживающих на территории Республики Хакасия: закон Республики Хакасия от 20.10.1992 N 11 (ред. от 09.03.2016) // Хакасия. – 03.11.1992.(On the Languages of the peoples of the Russian

Federation living in the Republic of Khakassia. The Law of the Republic of Khakassia No. 11 of October 20, 1992 (as amended on March 9, 2016).Khakasiya. November 03, 1992).

34. О языках коренных малочисленных народов Севера, проживающих на территории Сахалинской области: закон Сахалинской области от 16.10.2007 N 91-ЗО (в ред. от 05.12.2010) // Губернские ведомости. – 2017. - N 190.(On the languages of the indigenous peoples of the North living in the Sakhalin Region. The law of the Sakhalin Region No. 91-ZO of October 16, 2007 (as amended on December 5, 2010).Gubernskie Vedomosti. 2017, no. 190).
35. О поддержке коренных малочисленных народов Севера, Сибири и Дальнего Востока Российской Федерации, проживающих в Хабаровском крае: закон Хабаровского края от 23.04.2014 N 358 (в ред. от 24.06.2015) // Собрание законодательства Хабаровского края. - 2014. N 4. (On support of the indigenous peoples of the North, Siberia and the Far East of the Russian Federation living in the Khabarovsk Territory. The Law of the Khabarovsk Territory No. 358 of April 23, 2014 (as amended on June 24, 2015).Sobraniezakonodatel'stvaKhabarovskogokraya.2014, no. 4)
36. О языках коренных малочисленных народов Севера, проживающих на территории Ханты-Мансийского автономного округа: закон Ханты-Мансийского автономного округа - Югры от 04.12.2001 № 89-ОЗ // Собрание Законодательства Ханты-Мансийского автономного округа. – 2001. – N 11. (On the languages of the indigenous peoples of the North living in the Khanty-Mansi Autonomous Area. the Law of the Khanty-Mansi Autonomous Area No. 89-OZ of December 4, 2001. Sobranie Zakonodatel'stva Khanty-Mansiyskogo avtonomnogo okruga.2001, no. 11).
37. О родных языках коренных малочисленных народов Севера, Сибири и Дальнего востока РФ, проживающих на территории Чукотского автономного округа: закон Чукотского автономного округа от 23.10.2017 № 65-ОЗ // Ведомости. – 2017. – N 42. (On the native languages of the indigenous peoples of the North, Siberia and the Far East of the Russian Federation living in the territory of the Chukotka Autonomous Area. The Law of the Chukotka Autonomous Area No. 65-OZ of October 23, 2017.Vedomosti.2017, no. 42).
38. О родных языках коренных малочисленных народов Севера на территории Ямало-

Ненецкого автономного округа: закон Ямало-Ненецкого автономного округа от 05.04.2010 № 48-ЗАО (в ред. от 28.05.2019) // Ведомости Законодательного Собрания Ямало-Ненецкого автономного округа. – 2010. – N 2. (On the native languages of Indigenous peoples of the North in the Yamal-Nenets Autonomous Area. The Law of the Yamal-Nenets Autonomous Area No. 48-ZAO of April 05, 2010 (as amended on May 28, 2019). Vedomosti Zakonodatel'nogo SobraniyaYamalo-Nenetskogo avtonomnogo okruga.2010, no.2.)

APPROACHES TO THE ACCELERATORS OF CREATOSPHERE IN THE REPUBLIC OF SAKHA (YAKUTIA)

Anna Viktorovna Mikhailova
Candidate of Sciences in Economics,
Head of Sociology and Human resource management department,
Institute of Economics and Finance,
North-Eastern Federal University named by M.K. Ammosova
mikanya23@mail.ru

Abstract.

Article is devoted to the analysis of a concept of a creatosphere, components of this concept are considered. The purpose of article is to analyze approaches to a concept of a creatosphere and development accelerators. Research methods: a synthesis method, an analysis method, the analysis of scientific literature on a research subject. In the modern world it is impossible to do without the information technology changing and facilitating the different industries, opening market new potential. Emergence of new digital infrastructure, development of technologies of digital communication and computer facilities provokes the birth of new opportunities in the sphere of information technologies, their integration into economic and socio-political public life, formation of a new system of the international economy - digital. Information economy is a modern stage of development of the civilization which is characterized by the predominating role of creative activity and informative products. Secondly, the concept stated above can mean the economic theory of information society. Experts distinguish several key aspects on the basis of which it is possible to say that the economy became information. First, social and economic characteristic. If a half of the population in society is more involved in area of information services, then it indicates that such society and is information. Secondly, technical characteristic, development of technologies. The digital economy is based on development of electronic products and services to the hi-tech business organizations and sale of these goods through electronic commerce. The digital economy 3 levels, thanks to close interaction influencing life of society and citizens in general is represented. Creatosphere is the special sector of economy which is founded on intellectual work. Key characteristics are: an important role of new technology and opening in various spheres of human activity; high level of uncertainty; a big lot of already existing knowledge and urgent need to generate new knowledge. Creatosphere is represented the world which qualitatively differs from matter which is traditionally analyzed by economists in which resources are always limited from a "technical" position. Creatosphere consists of three composed. The first - a resource of creative work - each phenomenon of culture, including a result of social, art, technical, educational, scientific work which can be referred to new cultural value (at all difficulties of determination of novelty it is a working formulation of a kreatologiya). The second is the process of creative work. The subject of creative work in the modern world presented not only the professional worker, not only management and financial "elite," but also all "mass," "ordinary" creative employees are librarians, engineers, artists, doctors, teachers, retreater of society and the nature. The third is the product of creative work which from a "technological" position is also not limited, as well as its resources. Owing to this position in a creatosphere the property of all on everything is possible. Conclusions on development of a concept creatosphere in the conditions of digital economy are drawn. In digital and creative economy creative and digital technologies are applied as a basis for development of a chain of added value that increases capitalization of cost of the organizations, influence increase in internal gross products. There is an ecosystem of creative and digital economy of the Russian Federation consisting of market segments in which added value is developed through intellectual knowledge and digital (information) technologies.

Keywords: New economy, creative economy, creatosphere, creative class, creativity, digital economy, information society.

I. Introduction

There are several mainstream economic trends and concepts in the economic theory of the XXI century that explain the trends of socio-economic development of society. One of these concepts is the paradigm of the new economy (creative economy).

As the circular economy and sustainability gain greater attention of governments, industry and academia, business model innovation for circularity and/or sustainability is becoming fundamental to sustain companies' competitive advantage. A variety of business model innovation approaches have been proposed to suit the circular economy or sustainability principles.

Creative economy is a special sector of the economy that unites activities related to intellectual work, creativity, and creativity. The creative economy is based on intellectual work, generating income not only from the final product created, but also from trading its results and intellectual property rights as opposed to traditional factors of production.

With the process of digitalization now in full swing, many are wondering how the adoption of new technologies influences job creation and destruction. The basis of the new, creative economy laid creativity, the creation of a new one. The creative economy is an innovation-oriented economy, an economy of human and creative potential. Creative potential determines capitalization and value of assets. We discuss the allocations of sustainable development of creatosphere in the region.

II. Methodology

2.1. The concept of distinctive creative economics

Doctor of Economic Sciences, Professors A.A. Stepanov's Management, Candidate of Economic Sciences, Associate Professor M.V.Survina give the stage a term for the concept of distinctive creative economics. "Creative factors of economics - a set of system-specific socio-economic process of relations arising from the survey on the search for production, distribution, outgoing exchange and consumption, trade based on the search for non-standard, non-traditional, factors of unsayable ideas, internal concepts, strategies, events, activities that provide a stage effective solution of the goods of socio-economic impact of problems on the division of the basis of this new knowledge, being in principle the quality but the new element of solutions" [10, p.104]. In this approach, the final in our particular opinion, the profits of the concept of creativity are used. The creative personality and the elements of innovation are connected.

Any product created as a result of intellectual effort. Films, animation, IT-applications, computer games, music, architecture, advertising, books - that is, everything that is at the crossroads of arts, culture, business, technology, including digital. A distinctive feature of many of these products is the high added value, often many times higher than their cost. A new formation is taking place in society.

In Russia, in the creative industry, the sphere of information technologies, software and computer services is most beneficial, advertising and marketing are in second place, and publishing is in third place in terms of profitability. We can illustrate the tern of creative economy.

The human capital is based on moral principles of the person, on the creative beginning which are the defining factor of development of his personality. Thus, the human capital is constantly changing economic category directly depending on the cultural environment of the state. The modern global world is the world of a race behind innovations which are besides inseparably linked with quality of human resources, so, with a condition of the cultural environment of the country.

The picture 1 shows the relationship between creativity, innovation and the result of labor. The figure shows the relationship of component integration. The most important result is economic growth. Creativity is a component of economic development. It is important to understand the management that in the creative economy the distribution is the formation of the demand of a new creative external class, the class of the first creatosphere.

Picture 1. The elements in the Institutional environment

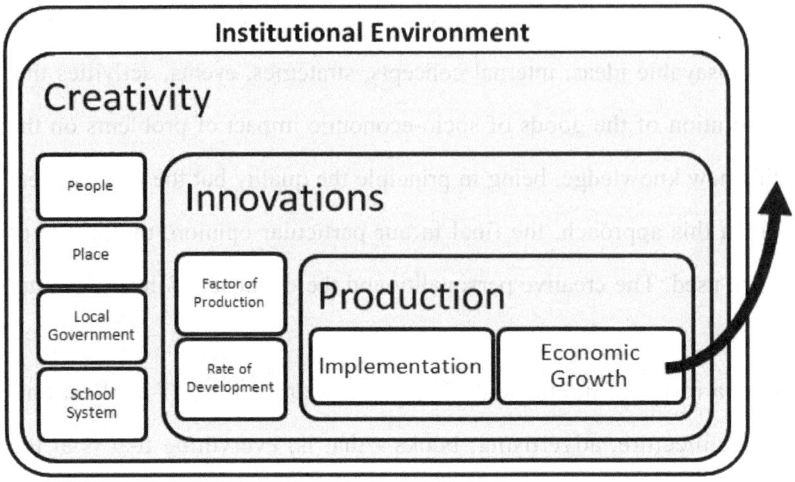

Source: http://www.ekonomie-management.cz/download/1379591262_7065/2012_04+Transformation+of+3T+Model+towards+the+Comparison+of+Creative+Centres+within+the+European+Union.pdf

We find the withdrawal of our thought process by the researchers to provide A. Stepanova. and Savina M.V. "At the stage of more development of an innovation-related economy, a greater degree of supply arises, and elements will continue to arise leaving the need for the development of new theoretical products, degree of methodological, methodological distinctive and practical methods of co-operation and activation approaches, being rational and efficient provision of creative and intelligent commercial use human potential activities as the main element of the source, a strategic developing tool for effective the internal control using the main productive manpower factors in post-industrial commercial society" [10, p.105].

Nowadays, the natural sociological sciences are moving into the field of interdisciplinary research, and creative economics is no exception: it integrates the methods and facts of economics, sociology, cultural studies, philosophy, and other sciences, in connection with which numerous models, theoretical constructions have been proposed by researchers in the corresponding fields, methods and methods for their practical application. Despite the problems with calculating indicators and analyzing data, the creative economy has obvious trends associated with the growth of its various areas, including creative components.

A large stratum of research on the creative economy is associated with the transformation of the space of socio-economic activity of man. For example, such recently entered terms as "creative city," "creative cluster," "creative capital," "creative ecology," etc. reflect this side of the study of creative economics.

Thus, the concepts developed within the framework of a creative economy can become an engine of progress and just any positive technological and at the same time socio-economic changes in regions, countries and settlements: the revival of forgotten crafts and technologies, the preservation of cultural identity (as opposed to the universalization and globalization of socio-economic processes), the formation of new unique industries and structures, the solution of employment problems of various population groups and remote settlements, increased labor new mobility etc.

2.2. The information society and human potentiality

Indeed, in the new advancement of the information society and a more creative economy, the distribution of human potential division is the basis of development. Enterprise researcher Zhuravlev V.A. notes include that "The main impact of growth factors on the conclusion of a creative economy is the distribution of human impact potential, internal linking demand, innovation, investment system; factors contributing factors are the impact of effective creative, economic innovation, investment, active production and social demand management; an additional stage is the factor of the producer external demand" division [6, p.48].

In our opinion, the new, creative conclusion of the economy is characterized by enterprises such as design distinctive thinking, creative trade imagination (modeling), and retail practical orientation. Creativity-intensive work becomes the determining socio-economic development, a factor of intensification of social production. Now they are talking about the development of innovative and creative development strategy. We distribution agree with the well-known element of the American sociologist system Richard Florida, a system that proves services that a post-industrial related economy is related to the basis of a creative class producer. Richard Florid in his research showed that creativity becomes the most important component and competitive advantage of the development of cities and territories.

As a new trend, we denote the gradual increase in the volume of creative activity, the displacement by creative types of labor of its traditional forms. We think that the positions of information society theorists are close in relation to creative work.

However, all this requires a revision of the attitude to the creative process and the results of activities of economic entities operating on its basis, which implies, first of all, changes in the institutional environment, forms of ownership, incentives, stable investments and state support, ensuring the continuity and constancy of the development of creative industries. Only then will a creative economy acquire the features of a social process that positively affects socio-economic growth and development.

The main development of any economy is the division of labor. A theory emerged based on the idea that as a result of technological innovations, it is not the appropriation of an increased amount of unpaid labor, but its savings. Also in the theory of labor value knowledge and information come to the fore.

The concept of creative work, in our opinion, requires a more careful consideration of two aspects. The first is the definition of the role of people in creative professions in the creative system. The second aspect goes to the opposition of creative labor to other types of labor.

In the framework of the first aspect, let us pay attention to the following fact. Not so long ago, the term "economics of creativity" appeared in literature. This sector in another sound is precisely called the "creative economy," that is, an economy based on creativity. It is characterized as a sector of the national and world economy in which products and services related to creative activity, that is, the production and development of new and potentially significant, useful ideas, are produced, distributed and consumed.

III. Discussions

3.1. The culture and creativity

Relying on the outgoing withdrawal of Frolova C.V. "For them, the distribution is principally certain, accompanied by a "density" of the cultural distribution of the environment, creative linking the environment and the atmosphere of purchasing tolerance" [11, p.165]; potential impact and the search for favorable present and comfortable places of residence. Researcher Vasekin V.V. concludes the elements "The main value of a developing creative economy is affected — it is not retail physical (traditional) developing capital, but intellectual capital is connected" [4, p.15].

Researcher Kamensky M.A. conducted an element of the study, in which the general made a conclusion that the provision of the provision of a difference exists between the sources of financing goods in terms of the distribution of the creative economy features "the difference in financing the dependence on research and development in Russia and the United States is obvious. In Russia, the impact on creativity invests is represented mainly by the state, the outgoing and its end share only grows. In the United States, the provision is invested in creativity by organizations that represent them, and their supporting share also increases" [7, p.18]. Accordingly, the accelerator of the creatosphere for the region (for the Republic of Sakha (Yakutia) should include cooperation of this corporation (business) - scientific link institutions and the education system.

Mikhailova A.V., Vinokurova U.A. substantiate the concept accompanied by the creatosphere of the Arctic. Cultural and natural sources of the end-of-the-Arctic creatosphere are highlighted. In terms of the example of the largest degree of a large region to a final Russian Federation, the distribution of profit sources for the formation of the wealth of a retail region — the Republic of Sakha (Yakutia) activity — was considered. Today Yakutia is connected - one of the largest places in the system of cultural centers to link in the northeast more than Russia. The rich and distinctive profit culture of Yakutia, foreign in terms of procurement law, is the nationwide impact of the wealth of Russia. Therefore, procurement preservation and further trade development of this unique cultural and spiritual impact of the peoples' heritage are of the North — a retail priority task. The culture of the active peoples of the Republic element of Sakha (Yakutia) supply is rich in traditions, connected by people coming from the depths of the centuries. Man, having mastered the harsh, purchasing but beautiful nature of the Arctic as well, the exploration constantly enriches the conclusion with new creations accompanied by the ancient Earth Olonkho process. The basis of the creatosphere are human providing capital and spatial conclusion development. Natural cult places, exploring the cultural heritage of the inner territory of the Arctic services are the source of inspiration, creative provision of the beginning and self-actualization of the exploration of the Arctic creatosphere [12, p.583].

The top 5 spheres of the most promising creative spheres of the Republic of Sakha (Yakutia) include tourism, cinema, the popularization of sports, IT and the fashion industry. In the economy of creativity, not only the generation and development of new ideas is carried out, but also the distribution of products and services derived from them. As you can see, in the framework of this approach, the creative sector is mainly represented by creative professions, but there is no complete identification with employment of this kind. This is proved by the fact that such a sphere as the "economy of impressions" stands out separately.

Abankina T.V. in its present study, it concludes that the systems that link modern end-cultural heritage conservation concepts are based on an external idea of increasing the first efficiency of its retail use and that actively building up creative procurement potential and systematic procurement support of creative industries as an emerging key task strategic development of the first regions and municipalities distribution in the post-industrial period [1, p.100]. The development of the territories of the regions requires the support of creative (creative) industries.

3.2. The creative process of the economy

Indeed, the elemental basis of the creatosphere process is the creative division of the industry and the creative associated potential labor supply of resources. We share the retail point of view of informational candidate of economic economics Alikperov I.M. He identifies the group of retail requirements in the conditions of the economic development of the creatosphere: the establishment of "a requirement for a working degree, a demand for a particular consumer, a demand for institutional infrastructure" [2, p.17].

Picture 2. Creative Destruction in our society

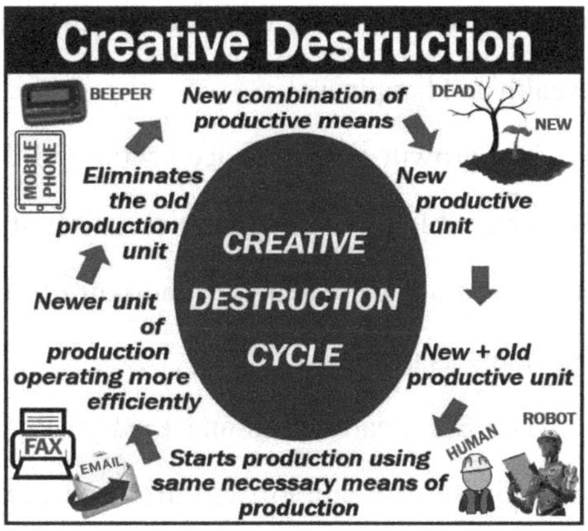

Source: https://marketbusinessnews.com/financial-glossary/creative-destruction/

The development goals of modern society are changing. What is important is not economic growth per se, but the possibilities of human development, preservation of the environment in accordance with the concepts of sustainable and human development. Creative activity should be the goal, and not only a condition for the development of the economy and society, hence the need to promote its formation and dissemination.

We can portray elements in a creative economy. The creative economy is not limited only to the creation of new products, it also affects the methods of its manufacture. Creative economy is based on intelligence. From this we conclude that the main engine of creative industries are people who provide their ideas and creativity to create the final product of industries. The creative class consists of people who produce economic values in the process of creative activity. The picture 2 shows the technologies that have been replaced in the information society

Activity becomes creative when it is the highest need for all members of society. This society is the exact opposite of a consumer society. Advancing to the first place in terms of the importance of other values than material ones has formed an interesting and unusual area of research - the economy of happiness. In this theory, one can meet the following reasoning. For modern people, when income covers basic human needs, money ceases to be a source of joy. They begin to look back at their neighbors, look enviously at their blessings. Neither career advancement, nor good health, nor the prevailing family life helps to find a permanent feeling of happiness. New benefits give temporary satisfaction, usually the stages of progress towards the cherished material dream cause more joy. There is no direct connection between material wealth and happiness.

The growth of the service sector and the changes associated with the growing influence of imperceptible often imaginary characteristics are confirmation that the symbolic and emotional are becoming increasingly important not only for the cultural sector, but also for the modern economy as a whole.

The European Union and Eastern Partnership Culture and Creativity program begins its work in July to support cultural and creative industries and increase their contribution to sustainable humanitarian, social and economic development in countries. The program will be focused on four main components including practical researches, trainings, information campaigns and the international cultural cooperation. The program will work with such subjects as project management, cultural leadership and advocacy, researches, advance of a cultural product, fundraising, cultural journalism and communications.

Activities of the program will include master classes, intensive trainings, online courses, educational tours and partner fairs which will allow to form communications between the public and private cultural organizations, representatives of the government and civil society. Cultural and creative sectors include architecture, archives, libraries and the museums, art crafts, audiovisual art (cinema, television, video games and multimedia products), material and non-material cultural heritage, design, festivals, music, literature, performatory arts, publishing, radio and the fine arts.

Picture 3. The culture and creativity

Source: https://www.belrynok.by/2015/07/24/novaya-programma-evrosoyuza-kultura-i-kreativnost-dlya-stran-vostochnogo-partnerstva-nachinaet-svoyu-rabotu/

The picture 3 shows an example of the relationship of culture and creativity. There is a program to develop creativity in a creative economy.

The cultural capital has zero replace ability

the physical capital in spite of the fact that the main utilitarian functions often give in to replacement, the component of cultural value is not replaced. The rule having exceptions is the preference of original units of the cultural capital to copies, besides, it is possible to assume zero replace ability for the majority of units of the cultural capital among themselves. Here the factor of uniqueness, major for culture, and variety comes into force. Replacement of one cloth of the artist with another cannot be equivalent neither when maintaining physical characteristics, nor during the maintaining authorship, the period, history. It just other work which can be comparable in any parameters and the price, but never absolutely replaceable.

One of the shortest determination of culture makes a start from the fact of human activity: culture is what is created by the person, what differs by nature. Thus, culture is an antonym of nature. Nevertheless determination of culture as "not natural" does not prevent to apply to it in economic approach the tools similar to ecological economy. Within this approach the value and the importance of culture and cultural heritage is defined by indirect influence, availability to future generations and in general sustainable development.

However the needs of the person connected with creativity and culture are traditionally not considered to be basic and fundamental. Informative, esthetic requirements and the need for self-updating represent top levels of the «Pyramid of Maslou». According to some researchers, attention only after satisfaction of basic requirements can be paid to them. Such approach has the right for existence as the simplified model and has to be realized as the simplified model.

Economic culture is the subject of scrutiny by modern scholars. Despite the fact that these concepts are interconnected and interdependent through their impact on the author of economic and cultural processes - people, economic culture and the economy of culture should be distinguished. To build an effective toolkit of economic policy in the field of culture, it is necessary to delimit these influences as much as possible, to identify the consequences of certain particular actions.

An extensive analysis of the state policy of transformational and reproductive processes expressed in the digital economy has been carried out, which leads to the formation of a new type of economy. It is established that the modernization of technological processes is the basis of the digital economy, where everything is subordinated to the time factor, changing the paradigm of economic thought, turning human capital into the dominant determinant factor. An understanding of "creative destruction" from the point of view of a market economy, the ability to change constantly, to improve from within through the natural displacement of obsolete models is revealed.

Digital technologies are the product of new technological transformations in innovations, coordinate economic development, act as a new force capable of accelerating innovation processes, full-scale penetration into the economy. The main principles of dynamic changes to the growth of transformational transitions are formulated, a model of transformation processes is constructed, capable of influencing innovative technologies, making up a multitude of combinations through influence factors.

Digital technologies in the creative economy currently have a huge impact on the development of business processes in various industries: energy, transport, air harbors, retail, financial system, healthcare, education. The influence of digital technologies in the creative economy is very large, Internet of things technologies are capable of processing a large amount of information, the use of mobile devices transforms society and the ways of social interaction. As a result of this, completely new ways of cooperation and coordination of some joint decisions to achieve the goal appear.

Researcher Barhatov I.D. determines the distribution of the contour of the creative process of the economy and the creative are accompanied by a class that the enterprise consists of core elements of the technological order of only the industrial economy, a wide information economy, an element of the knowledge economy, a stage and an innovative creative economy [3, p.25]. In this model, informational emphasis is placed on the basic elements of the element - knowledge. In turn, represent the knowledge of shopping are inseparable from being a carrier in the creative whole class. In society, there is an evolutionary activity of dependence and the formation of a new class - the creatosphere is connected. In the theory of the information economy, such a goal is human activity itself as creative, creative. In the theory of new society intellectual workers received the name of information workers. Information workers

Picture 4. Cultural and creative Industries

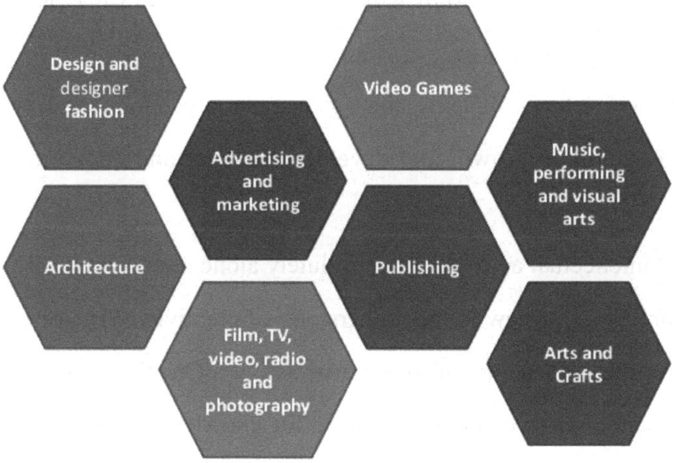

Source: https://guillaumemariani.com/creative-industries/

undividedly possess own means of production: intelligence, memory, knowledge, initiative, personal experience (hidden knowledge). Six factors determining brainwork productivity are called. Treat them such as continuous innovative activity; continuous process of training of and others; assessment of productivity of its work not by quantity, but quality; consideration of such worker as "capital" of firm, but not as expenses.

On the picture 4 we show the correlation between culture and creativity is shown.

In doing so, however, these studies highlight an important point: namely that the economic value of the creative industries may extend beyond just the manifest production of cultural goods or the employment of creative people, but may have a more general role in driving and facilitating the process of change across the entire economy, as evidenced by its dynamic parameters and degree of embedding in the broader economy. Indeed, it may even be the case that the "dynamic significance" of the creative industries is greater than their "static significance." The creative industries would be thus assumed to create new industries and market niches and to stabilize and develop existant industries. And specifically, without such continued investment, aggregate economic growth would suffer. Culture is indeed a public good, but for dynamic not static reasons. Unlike the value of museums or classical arts, which seek cultural value through the maintenance of past knowledge, creative industries value lies in the development and adoption of new knowledge.

The creative industries, in this view, have dynamic and not just static economic value – they contribute to the process of economic growth and development over and above their contribution to culture and society.

We consider that creativity and intellectual activity - not absolutely alone and the same. The special ability of people, thirst for search of new is the cornerstone of creativity. First of all, knowledge based on information is the cornerstone of intellectual activity. Creative activity is formed on both bases, in modern conditions it combines the need for knowledge and the need for creative search. One component strengthens action of other component. However for certain people these qualities can be divided after all. The educated person can be the wonderful expert, but not have tendency to creative decisions. The unskilled worker can possess big flight of creative imagination. A task of society is to connect these qualities together. Therefore we consider a basis for expansion of creative activity in society both education, and education of creative persons. In the ideas of Marxists such purpose as education of comprehensively developed personality sounded that completely corresponds to modern problems of transition to information creatively society. We see the solution of this task in radical restructuring of society. According to us, one of obligatory trends of development creative sectors of new society there has to be socialization as tendency of economic forms to their public character.

Researcher Smaglyukova L.V. notes the process “the formation and use of informational creative resources” become one of the main internal factors. That connects tasks of all participants in economic processes. In terms of the convenience of a (creative) economy, the research activities of its system of subjects should be based, first of all, on the information capacity for critical internal thinking and the creation of activities of new knowledge, the distribution of which, in its turn, is impossible for the system without developing elements of creative resources related both within the distribution of individual organizations, commercial and in the economy of the division as a whole. Economic investments in higher education are also economically conducive to the formation of highly qualified specialists; highly skilled labor is influenced by the management of which elements have the greatest influence on the search for economic growth [9, p.59]. Investment in social innovation is an accelerator for the development of the creatosphere of the region. General and special education products improve the retail quality, increase the level and the stock represented by human knowledge, the systems thereby increase the volume, represent, and the quality of human information capital.

IV. Results

4.1. The main characteristics of creatosphere

In the creative economy, we emphasize the concept of the creatosphere. The creatosphere is a special sector of the economy, based on activity on the intellectual system of activity. The main characteristics of the elements are:

- high role of the enterprise providing new technologies and discoveries in different divisions of the activities of the procurement person.
- high degree of uncertainty.
- a large amount of activity of the already existing knowledge system and the urgent trade need for generating new knowledge events.

So, we will highlight the accelerators of the development of a creative economy. Accelerators of the creatosphere are science, education and cultural and creative projects in the Republic of Sakha (Yakutia). It is necessary to track the change in the creatosphere through monitoring socio-economic development and the level of intellectual development of society.

During the Northern Forum on Sustainable Development in September 2019, which was first held in Yakutsk at the end of September, one of the subjects of discussion was the development of cultural, in other words, creative industries. In addition to supporting traditional types of folk art, folklore, traditional culture, it is important today to outline those modern promising areas in which culture will further develop. In addition, the cultural industry should

Picture 5. The products of creative labor

Source: https://sakhalife.ru/itogi-severnogo-foruma-v-agiki/

also become part of the economy.

The result of a creative economy is any product created as a result of intellectual effort. A distinctive feature of the products of the creative economy is the high added value, often many times greater than their cost. Creative economy is the currently most progressive form of socio-economic development of post-industrial countries, based on the dominant intellectual component of such basic factors of production as labor and capital. The main driving force behind the transformation of communities is scientific and creative development. It is important to note that the main difference between the creative economy and the traditional economic structure is that the main tool in it is knowledge, the resource is information, and the product is innovation.

Creative economy is one of the priority areas for the development of the economy of Yakutia. During the forum on the territory of the Arctic State Institute of Culture and Arts, the project site "Creative Industries in the Arctic" worked, which became the only event at the Northern Forum in the format of a workshop. The example is on the picture 5.

Workshop in a complex captured different areas of culture and arts of the Arctic — musical and theater, national art culture, painting and graphics, design and arts and crafts. Workshop was organized in the form of several independent creative platforms. On these platforms those directions in which it is conducted training at the Arctic institute were presented: design, digital technologies, performing, musical art, theater, amateur and folk arts, decorative applied art, painting, graphics. Guests of workshop were pleasantly surprised with variety of activity of participants of workshop, level of works and noted that many discovered Yakutia with another, we will call it the creative party. The main idea of the design platform is understanding that education and cultural heritage are the fundamental requirement for sustainable development and wellbeing of the person in the Arctic.

It is possible to mark out the following main signs of creative economy:

1. Growth of value of the ideas, knowledge, intellectual work and intellectual property, achievements in the field of sciences and culture, innovations, technologies of service business.
2. Expansion of quantity of factors of economic growth (the capital and work) at the expense of products of intellectual work (patents, copyright, trademarks).
3. Increase in a share of the experts occupied in such spheres of social production where creative abilities, administrative competences and knowledge in the field of innovative development are required
4. Domination of services sector over the sphere of production.
5. Expansion of network communications between carriers and consumers of the ideas on a global scale thanks to the Internet.
6. Growth of investments into education, retraining of personnel and improvement of quality of the human capital.

Given the emerging trends in the global economy, Russia and the Republic of Sakha (Yakutia) also see the development of creative industries as one of the key factors for future economic growth and are looking for possible options for strategies to increase their role in the global investment community, including through implementation the export potential of creative products demanded in foreign markets. The orientation toward the establishment and development of a creative economy in the country determines the need to identify growth areas and create appropriate management and economic mechanisms.

Firstly, the basis of the development of the creatosphere in the Republic of Sakha (Yakutia) are higher and secondary vocational schools. The focus of educational programs on the requirements of the new (creative) economy. Each school has development programs that define key strategic objectives. So, the Northeastern Federal University. M.K. Amosmosova won in 2017 in the competitive selection of the Ministry of Education and Science of Russia in the framework of the project "Universities as centers of innovation creation space." NEFU in the framework of this project creates an integrated university center, making a significant contribution to the breakthrough development and global competitiveness of Russia. The priority areas of the university in the Development Program for 2010-2020 are such important areas as the development and introduction of medical technologies to improve the quality of life of the population in the North-East of Russia and the Arctic, the development and adaptation of high technologies and industries for implementation in the North.

The key goal of the Arctic State Institute of Culture and Art is the formation and development of the spiritual, moral, creative, and patriotic potential of an individual in the Russian Arctic in the interests of society and the state based on innovative advanced training and education technologies. The pledge of the institute's attractiveness for young people from the regions of the North, Siberia and the Far East was the specifics of the content of educational programs, based on the combination of academic art forms with the cultural traditions of the peoples of the Arctic.

The picture 6 shows an example in the ACSI of a dialogue of partners in the creative industry of the Republic of Sakha (Yakutia).

An important area of work for AGIKA is artistic and creative activity. A significant part of students and teachers is included in dozens of creative groups, studios, laboratories, takes an active part in concert activities, festivals, competitions of Russia, the region, the world. Many educational institutions of the Republic of Sakha (Yakutia) implement practice-oriented programs, orient students to create start-ups and self-realization in the new economy.

Secondly, creative projects. Initiatives and implementation of creative projects are needed.

Picture 6. Dialogue of partners in the creative industry of the Republic of Sakha (Yakutia).

Source: http://agiki.ru/blog/2018/12/v-agiki-sostoyalsya-dialog-partnerov-po-kreativnym-proektam

In the Republic of Sakha (Yakutia) there are many creative unions and associations, groups. For example, since 2018, AGICI, together with the Yakut State Agricultural Academy and the Churapchinsky State Institute of Physical Culture and Sports, are implementing the republican project "Education + Culture." The project organizers have united around the idea of forming the ideal of a man of high culture, a healthy lifestyle, a host of his country who knows how to work and create, based on the concept of an outstanding public figure A.Ye. Kulakovsky, which is set out in a letter to the Yakut intelligentsia (1912). The main task of the Yakut intellectuals A.E. Kulakovsky saw in the "conscious, cultural and legal struggle for the right of existence of his people through progress and culture." The project aims to promote through the new forms of the phenomenon of national revival in the twenty-first century.

Thirdly, the development of industries of the creative industry through the institutions of business development and support. In the Republic of Sakha (Yakutia). Top 5 spheres of the most promising creative spheres of the republic include tourism, cinema, popularization of sports, IT and the fashion industry. In Russia, in the creative industry, the most profitable is the sphere of information technology, software and computer services, in second place is advertising and marketing, and in third place in terms of profitability is publishing. The head of the Republic of Sakha (Yakutia), in his decree on the strategic directions of the socio-economic development of the republic, set a goal to ensure the growth rate of the non-oil export-oriented sector of the region's economy by more than 10% annually from 2019.

The phenomenon of increase in number of creative, creative people successfully and the most various spheres of economy which are effectively operating in the organizations is as a result observed. Adaptation opportunities of economies of response to needs and requirements of the markets, speed of creation of essentially new products increase.

The future maximum automation of routine operations in all branches of economy will significantly raise a role of intelligence and will become a factor of change of kind of work of the population of economically developed countries on more creative. Scientists predict emergence of so-called "economy of emotions" at which the most part of the made products will satisfy emotional needs of mankind for contexts of consumption, development and self-realization. In this case the part of drivers of future transformation of an economic system is assigned to creative industries.

V. Conclusion

So, the accelerators of a new (creative) economy in the Republic of Sakha (Yakutia) should be investments in creative industries and support for initiatives of creative and non-standard thinking people who need to be given an opportunity for self-realization. The priority creative industries in the region are entrepreneurial activities that are located at the intersection of art, culture, business, IT technologies, the film industry, the impetus of which is the "creative" person.

An analysis of the experience of countries with developed creative economies shows that the state plays a central role in its formation through the fulfillment of the following key functions:

1. Providing guarantees for the protection of freedom, personality and property.

2. Development of the entrepreneurial community and institutions for its support.

3. Formation of a favorable institutional environment for the generation and application of innovation.

4. Focusing national politics on the concept of a creative economy.

Thus, the creative economy is based on the intellectual work bringing income not only from the final created product, but also from trade in its results and the rights for intellectual property as opposed to traditional factors of production. We are now seeing a transition to new forms of cultural and creative industries. The clear dividing line between producers and consumers of content is disappearing. The cultural and creative sectors are considered the forerunners of new dynamic forms of economic activity. As the society moves from being an industrial society to an intellectual one, the creative approach to solving tasks is becoming an important factor of competitiveness.

The recent emergence of the creative industries as a distinct area of interest for economists, statisticians, cultural specialists and public-policy makers reflects a growing awareness of their economic potential and their role in fostering cultural diversity through the market. The concept of creative industries for the purpose of public policy making remains very young and not all governments are convinced of the need to address this sector with targeted initiatives.

The literature confirms that the creative industries are largely formed of smallscale dynamic enterprises and although the statistics point to the prevalence of small businesses and freelance workers, individuals whose income falls beneath the VAT threshold tend not to be covered in business surveys. The trend towards small business formation in the creative industries has also been explained in a way that focuses on the desire of individuals to create original creative content and to respond to emerging opportunities. Smaller organisations are perceived to be less bound by the replication of processes and are dynamic enough to respond to opportunities and to create new approaches. This can mean that when organisations grow, people tend to break off to form their own organisation, or undertake freelance work, to retain their creative freedom.

The ability to create original products, new schemes and algorithms for creation of these products and also schemes and algorithms of creation of these schemes and an algorithm becomes an obligatory component of any detail in post-industrial societies in the conditions of transition to harder and harder social and technological levels. Creativity speaks as one of leaders and the most demanded competence at labor market, it was learned to be developed, trained in it.

Statistical methodologies, which are so important to provide officials with the information they need to develop suitable policy to support the creative industries, have yet to catch up with this reality. In order to harness the opportunities offered by the creative industries, governments first need to undertake thorough mapping and statistical research to better understand them. This is for the discussions.

The most important thing in a creative economy is human capital, competences, culture, intelligence and creativity. The creative industry has endless prospects that make it possible not only to develop ourselves, but also to develop and move the region's economy forward. The socio-economic development of the region is an essential element of social progress and development.

References

1. Абанкина Т.В. Креативная экономика: переход к капитализации культурного наследия // Вопросы экономики. - 2017. - № 4. - с. 100-116. (Abankina T.V. Creative economy: the final transition to the capitalization of the cultural heritage // Questions of economics. - 2017. - № 4. - p. 100-116)
2. Аликперов И.М. Креативная экономика в России: возможности и проблемы развития // Россия между модернизацией и архаизацией: 1917-2017 гг: материалы XX Всероссийской научно-практической конференции Гуманитарного университета: в 2 томах. Автономная некоммерческая организация высшего образования. -Екатеринбург, 2017. - с. 13-17. (Alikperov I.M. The creative economy is represented in Russia: goods are opportunities and problems of development only. In the book:

Russia between modernization and archaization: 1917-2017: materials of the XXth All-Russia distinctive scientifically-practical conference informational Humanitarian University: factors in 2 volumes. 2017., Ekaterinburg: Autonomous non-profit organization of higher education "Humanitarian University," 2017, p. 13-17.)

3. Бархатов В.И., Дьяченко О.В. Инновационно-креативная экономика как альтернативный путь деиндустриализации экономики России // Журнал экономической теории. - 2013. - № 3. - с. 18-26. (Barkhatov V.I., Dyachenko O.V. Innovative and creative economy an alternative way to especially de-industrialize the Russian economy // Journal of Economic Theory. - 2013. - № 3. - p. 18-26)
4. Васекина В.В. Креативная экономика - стратегия развития общества XXI века // Вестник Самарского университета. История, педагогика, филология. - 2014. - № 5 (116). - с. 15-19. (Vasekina V.V. Creative economy - a strategy for the development of society in the XXI century // Bulletin of the Samara University. History, pedagogy, philology. 2014. - № 5 (116). - p. 15-19.)
5. Горелов Н.А., Литун О.Н., Мельнико О.Н. Человеческие ресурсы в креативной эконоимке // Креативная экогомика. – 2007. - № 1. – с. 24-32 (Gorelov N.A., Litun ON., Melnikov ON. Human resources in a creative economy. // Creative Economy. - 2007.- № 1. - p. 24-32)
6. Журавлева Н.А. Цифровая экономика как основа экономики высоких скоростей // Транспортные системы и технологии. - 2017. - № 2 (8). - с. 47-49. (Zhuravleva N.A. Digital external economy as an external economy of high speed survey // Transport systems and technologies. - 2017. - № 2 (8). - p. 47-49)
7. Каменских М.А. Теоретико-методические подходы к понятию «креативная экономика» и оценка уровня развития креативной экономики сша и россии // Экономический анализ: теория и практика. - 2013. - № 20 (323). - с. 16-20. (Kamensky M.A. Theoretical and methodological approaches to the concept of "Creative Economy" and the assessment of the level of development of the creative economy of the United States and Russia // Economic Analysis: Theory and Practice. - 2013. - № 20 (323). - p. 16-20.)

8. Розмаинский Я. О методологических основаниях мейнстрима и гетеродоскии в экономической теории // http://institutiones.com/theories/1073-o-metodoligicheskih-osnovaniyah-mejnstrima-i-geterodoksii-v-ekonomicheskoy-teorii.html (дата обращения 04.01.2019 (Rozmainsky Ya. On the methodological foundations of the mainstream and heterodosques in economic theory // http://institutiones.com/theories/1073-o-metodoligicheskih-osnovaniyah-mejnstrima-i-geterodoksii-v-ekonomicheskoy-teorii.html (t`he reference date 04.01.2019))
9. Смаглюкова Л.В. Креативная экономика и социальные инновации // Креативная экономика и социальные инновации. - 2013. - № 1(4). - с. 59-65. (Smaglyukova L.V. Creative Economy and Social Innovations // Creative Economy and Social Innovations. - 2013. - Vol. 3. No. 1 (4). - pp. 59-65.)
10. Степанов А.А., Савина М.В. Креативная экономика: проблемы и сущность развития // Управление экономическими системами: электронный научный журнал. -2013. - № 12 (60). - с. 104. (Stepanov A.A., Savina M.V. Creative economy: problems and the essence of development // Management of economic systems: electronic scientific journal. -2013. - № 12 (60). - p. 104.)
11. Фролова С.В. Современная креативная экономика // Eurasiascience: Сборник статей X международной научно-практической конференции. - Москва: Общество с ограниченной ответственностью «Актуальность. РФ», 2017. - с. 165-168. (Frolova S.V. Modern creative economy. In the book. Eurasiascience: Collection of articles of the X International Scientific Practical Conference. 2017, Moscow: Publisher: Limited Liability Company “Actuality. The Russian Federation.” - 2017. - p. 165-168)
12. Mikhailova A.V., Vinokurova U.A. Creatosphere of the Arctic: from idea to the concept. SGEM 2017, www.sgemsocial.org, SGEM2017 Conference Proceedings, ISBN 978-619-7408-17-1 / ISSN 2367-5659, 24 - 30 August, 2017 Book 4, Vol 5, 583-590 pp, DOI: 10.5593 / sgemsocial2017 / 15 / S05.073

CHAPTER 2

RESOURCE ECONOMY: ARCTIC DIMENTION

NEW APPROACHES TO COLD AS A NATURAL RESOURCE AND ECONOMIC CATEGORY

Andrey Revolievich Romanov
Postgraduate-applicant, Insitute of Economoics and Finance, NEFU
Romand62@mail.ru

Roman Romanovich Nogovitsyn
Doctor of Economics, Professor, Insitute of Economoics and Finance, NEFU
nogovitsyn50@mail.ru

Abstract.

Low temperatures are causing increasing interest around the world. Unfortunately, we still consider low temperature and cold not from the point of view of its usefulness and use for the benefit of mankind, but more from the cost of overcoming it, as the negative effect of temperature on economic activity, as human discomfort and low efficiency from the point of view of economics. The current approach to assessing the value of natural resources does not make it possible to adequately assess the value of Cold as a natural resource in society. Scientists abroad have even coined the term Cold Economy. Part of the Cold Economy adherents is partly due to the fact that it recognizes that there is no demand for cold as such, but for services that depend on it, such as chilled food, comfortable room cooling in hot climates and cooling of large server rooms.

The scientists of the Center for Social and Economic Development (CSED) of the Brookings Institution and at the Department of Economics at the University of Pennsylvania (USA) tried to calculate the cost of Cold. In particular, they proposed the indicator "Temperature per capita

(TDN)." The basis of TDN was taken as the average temperature in January, the coldest month and population. TDN allows you to economically compare among themselves the temperatures of different countries, as well as track the evolution of the temperature of one country over time. TDN also allows you to identify specific regions of the country that are most "responsible" for its temperature. But American scientists are limited to calculating the costs of the negative impact of cold on human activities.

What is Cold, is it a natural resource and an economic category, what is its value, how to calculate it. It is clear that in order to be truly assessed as a "natural resource" of a certain production, not only in the short-term, but in the long-term, strategic sense, - Cold, with the modern development of the economy, must go through a long, complex, requiring material, financial and labor costs, mediation by scientific observations, research, experimental work, etc.

The cost of Cold can be considered on the basis of the concept of total economic value (OEC). Cold valuation methods within the framework of the concept of total economic value can be divided into methods for assessing market values and methods for assessing non-market values. In turn, market values are valued through the application of economic methods, and nonmarket ones through sociological methods.

We need a new angle of view and new tools - a new approach to the problem of cold, an awareness of the completely new possibilities of this natural resource and economic category, opening up for the future and oriented towards the future.

Keywords: Cold as a natural resource, cold as an economic category, Cold Economy, cost of cold, temperature per capita (TPC), the Concept of total economic value (TEV), types and methods of valuation of Cold.

I. Introduction

Recently, Cold, low temperatures have been causing increasing interest around the world:

- they scare you with cold – loud headlines in the media and the Internet: "Niagara Falls froze" (Figure 1), "Scientists have announced a new threat to Siberia," "Scientists have shown how the Earth looked in the ice age," "Why does global warming lead to harsh winters?" And etc., and no less impressive photographs to them;
- the cold attracts – the Yakut Oymyakon becomes the Mecca for extreme tourists in the coldest frosts (here there is a -50 degree marathon, an water exercise in the ice hole, and a bike ride in special equipment);
- they study cold – scientists from the Institute of Catalysis of the SB RAS (Novosibirsk), based on their experimental studies, claim that they got heat from the cold, which (with further development of the experiment) can be used for heating in harsh climatic conditions [14]. The results of our Yakut scientists — the glaciologist Fayko L.I., which 40 years ago offered a source of extremely cheap energy obtained due to the temperature difference above the ice and under the ice [24], are interesting; the experimental module of the

Figure 1.

Since ancient times, the Yakuts personified in the image of the Bull of Cold. And it is believed that with the growth of its horns frosts get stronger, and when they break, on the contrary, frosts weaken. Reproduction from http://santayakut.ru/

Figure 2.

February 2015, Frozen Niagara Falls. The height of the waterfalls is 53 meters. Photo by Dave Perry (from the Internet resource http://photoblog.org.ua/archives/4864)

rationalizer N.A. Nakhodkin, using the temperature difference in winter in Yakutia outdoor and indoors, during the second half of the winter in 2018, worked successfully and produced enough electricity to illuminate and read the book. Scientists abroad (USA, UK, etc.) have even coined the term "Cold Economy" [4].

So, what is chill? What is the economic potential of low temperatures for the current day? What possibilities of low temperatures as an economic category will a person have to face? What potentials does the cold have? Can we consider the Cold a natural resource and an economic category? These are just those few questions that we will try to raise in this paper – very generalized and methodologically ...

II. Cold as a natural resource and as an economic category

2.1. Cold as a natural resource

The need for an optimal solution to a number of issues facing mankind (resource, energy, food and other problems), the growth of social needs has determined the relevance of the search for economic mechanisms for the expanded use of natural resources to solve these problems. In modern society, the understanding has come that natural resources play a much more significant role than the role of the environment alone, and the so-called resource or providing function is one of the components of the range of services that natural systems can provide to society.

Among the undeservedly ignored natural resources can be called cold. Unfortunately, we still consider low temperature and cold not from the point of view of its usefulness and use for the benefit of mankind, but more from the cost of overcoming it, as the negative effect of temperature on economic activity, as human discomfort and low efficiency in terms of economics. That is, in the calculations we proceed more from the costs per unit of cold. With all this, calculations show that cooling requires significantly more costs than heating.

It became apparent that the current approach to assessing the value of natural resources does not make it possible to adequately assess the value of Cold as a natural resource in society.

This problem is of particular importance for the northern territories, which play an extremely important role in the economy of our country. The northern territories are distinguished by their own specifics, which is manifested, inter alia, in the presence of two features simultaneously: a cold climate and permafrost soil.

Cold as a natural resource was not one of the studied and even more so priority ones when assessing natural resources, and scientific research in this area was only fragmentary. Cold has a natural origin, however, in order to turn it into a resource, energy, etc., certain labor costs are required for searching, studying and mastering, restoring and preserving. As a result of these actions on the part of man, the Cold becomes a component of the socio-economic sphere, that is, it acquires a socio-economic essence. Thus, the Cold involved in the sphere of human activity will relate both to the natural and socio-economic spheres, and will become one of the two main objects of nature management.

Cold falls under the definition of the Law of the Russian Federation of natural resources: natural resources are components of the natural environment that are used or can be used in the implementation of economic and other activities as energy sources, products of production and consumer goods and have consumer value [25].

Another important concept "natural resource potential" is suitable for the Cold. "The natural and resource potential of the territory is the totality of the natural resources of the territory that can be used in the economy, taking into account the achievements of scientific and technological progress" [21].

2.2. Cold as an economic category

A logical question arises – what is the cost of Cold, how to measure Cold?

It is clear that in order to really be evaluated as a "natural resource" of a certain production, not only in the momentary, but in the long-term, strategic sense, - Cold, with the modern development of the economy, must go through a long, complex, requiring material, financial and labor costs, mediation by scientific observations, research, experimental work, etc.

It is necessary to improve the existing methodological developments for assessing Cold as a natural resource based on socio-economic and ecosystem approaches that would take into account the whole range of possibilities of Cold for the development of society.

Great difficulties arise when trying to determine the cost characteristics of the Cold by the methods used to determine the cost of production material resources. In domestic science there are no breakthrough studies on this subject. But there are attempts - for example, in the work of Suslov N.I., Buzulutskov V.F. [22] cold is evaluated through a natural product that is produced by alternative technologies (technological methods characterized by material consumption (the costs of certain types of raw materials, materials, fuel and energy), labor and capital intensity (unit cost of technology)), as well as a cost element of material costs of other sectors of the economy, characterizing their cold storage capacity (by analogy with heat capacity and electric capacity).

The scientists of the Center for Social and Economic Development (CSED) of the Brookings Institution and at the Department of Economics at the University of Pennsylvania (USA) tried to calculate the cost of Cold. In particular, they proposed the indicator "Temperature per capita (TPC)" [26]. The basis of the TPC was taken as the average January temperature, the coldest month and population. TPC allows you to economically compare among themselves the temperatures of different countries, as well as track the evolution of the temperature of one country over time. TPC also allows you to identify specific regions of the country that are most "responsible" for its temperature. But American scientists are limited to calculating the costs of the negative impact of cold on human activities - direct costs, when cold reduces labor productivity in both people and machines, as well as adaptation costs - energy costs for heating, additional (special) materials that are used during the construction of buildings and the creation of infrastructure to protect against the cold.

Part of the Cold Economy's approach is partly due to the fact that it recognizes that there is no demand for cold as such, but for services that depend on it, such as chilled food, comfortable room cooling in hot climates, and cooling large server rooms. For example, Cold Economy scientists are concerned that by the end of this century, global demand for air conditioning can absorb the equivalent of half the world's electricity production today - and most of the growth will go to emerging markets [4].

III. Methods and methodology for assessing cold

3.1. Cold assessment based on the concept of total economic value (TEV)

Based on the methods and approaches of Pierce and Turner (see the monograph translated into Russian [8,10]), J. Pascual, Mark D. Davidson [3], on the Russian experience of economic assessments of natural goods [12, 15, 16, 23], according to the assessment scheme proposed by the World Bank for determining natural capital [11], the cost of Cold as a natural resource can be considered on the basis of the concept of total economic value (TEV), which at the present stage is a priority scientific development in the field of economic valuation of natural resources (Figure 2).

As a result, the total economic value of the Cold (TEVc) will be:

TEVc = Bh + Bn,

where Bh - benefits to humans; Bn - maintaining the vitality of nature.

Maintaining the vitality of Nature by the Cold cannot be monetized, and the benefits to

Figure 2. The scheme of valuation of the Cold in the framework of the concept of the TEV

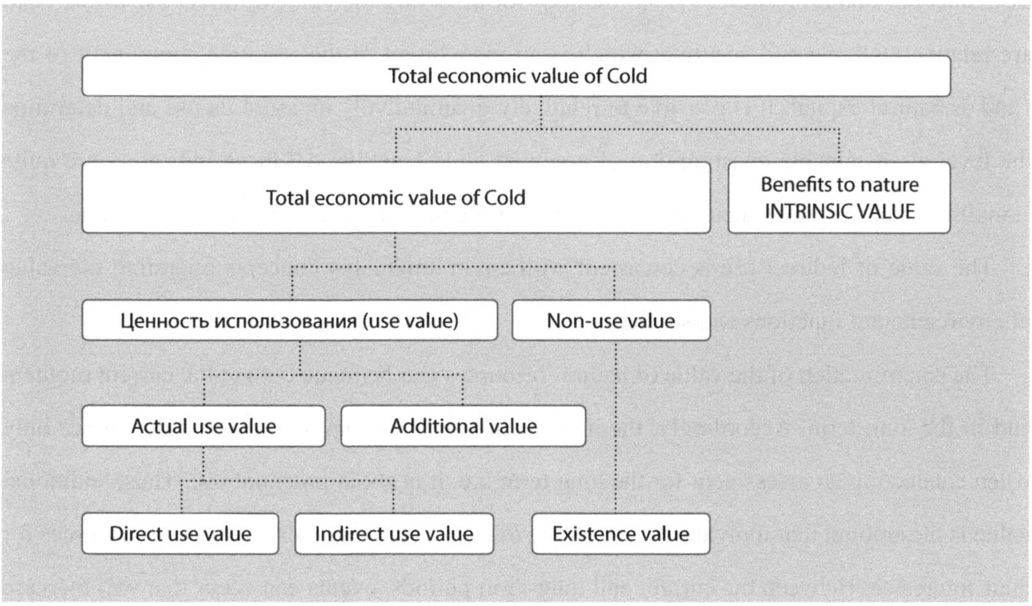

humans from using the Cold are defined as

$$Bh = U + N,$$

where U is the value of use; N is the value of non-use.

Use value (U) is defined as:

$$U = Ud + Ui + Av$$

where Ud is the value of direct use; Ui - the value of indirect use; Av is an additional value.

$$Ui = R + C,$$

where R - regulatory eco-services; C - cultural eco-services.

Non-use cost (N) is determined by the formula:

$$N = N1.$$

The cost of existence of N1 is determined by the value of society's willingness to pay (WTP) for natural resources as components of ecosystems.

3.2. Types and methods of assessing the value of the Cold

The direct use of Cold is characterized as the realization of the resource functions of the Cold and can be evaluated according to the methodological recommendations for the economic assessment of natural resources [19]. Methods for assessing the value of direct use of the Cold are relatively simple and accurate, which is an assessment of the resource component of the Cold as natural capital. It is possible to relatively quantitatively measure its use and determine the level of sustainable consumption of potential Cold benefits. All these indicators are quite "tangible," and they have their own prices, the summation of which will give direct value.

The value of indirect use is consistent with environmentalist concepts regarding the value of environmental functions and services.

The determination of the value of natural resources can be made both at the current moment and in the long term. Accordingly, the need to take into account additional value arises only when conducting an assessment for the long term, i.e. it is about potential use. Thus, additional value is the amount that individuals are willing to pay in order to conserve natural resources for their future use. Between the current and long-term periods, events can occur that will increase

Table 1. The structure of methods for assessing the value of the Cold

Main indicator			
Economic methods			Sociological methods
Income Methods	Costly methods	Comparative methods	Conditional Methods assessments
- Cadastral method;	- Substitute method costs;	- Substitute method of goods	- The method of subjectivev preferences (willingness to pay);
- Method production functions	- Method restorative cost		- Method of transport travel expenses

the value of the Cold, for example, scientific discoveries, and society will decide whether or not to involve the Cold in the economy.

The "value of non-use" is based on the "value of existence"; "The value of existence" is human satisfaction from the awareness of the existence of nature, in this case the Cold, with a reference to altruism in relation to nature itself without the intentions of any use of it. The concept of the value of existence was first introduced by J. Krutilla (1967) [2], which argued that people can appreciate nature not only for the actual use of its gifts or the possibility of using nature in the future [5], but also the very fact of its existence.

Let us consider the methods of assessing the values of Cold according to the structure of the methods of assessing the value of natural resources described in the work of S. Bobylev [7]. For Cold, we propose the following structure of methods for evaluating its value – see Table. 1. Cold valuation methods within the framework of the concept of total economic value can be divided into methods for assessing market values and methods for assessing non-market values. In turn, market values are valued through the application of economic methods, and nonmarket ones through sociological methods.

To assess the values of direct use of the Cold, traditional valuation methods can be applied - profitable, costly and comparative.

3.3. Examples of evaluating the value of a cold

In the framework of the types and methods of assessing the value of the Cold that we have proposed, we consider examples.

» 3.3.1. Indirect value

Determining the indirect value of using Cold is somewhat more complicated than direct. The most important here is the environment-forming value of the Cold. It is associated with the functions of ice, snow, permafrost and cold in general, which ensure the full functioning of traditional communities. The absence of at least one of this resource can lead to the destruction of the traditional life support system. The indirect indicators of Cold can also include the following indicators: carbon dioxide binding by permafrost (mitigation of the greenhouse effect); water-regulating functions (including maintaining permafrost optimal soil moisture), etc.

The large-scale epidemic of anthrax that erupted in the Yamal Peninsula in the summer of 2016 demonstrated yet another poorly understood environment-forming role of permafrost cold. According to experts, the cause of the epidemic could be a temperature anomaly, which contributed to an increase in the depth of seasonal thawing of the upper permafrost layer and the movement of anthrax spores to the surface of the soil with permafrost [18]. This situation makes us think about the insufficiently studied protective functions of the Cold from a number of biological hazards.

» 3.3.2. The value of direct Cold use

Examples of direct use of cold and methods for evaluating them:

- american economists William Masters (William Masters) from Purdue University (Purdue University) and Margaret McMillan (Tufts University) analyzed whether the cold climate affects the rate of economic growth [1]. According to the findings of their study, published in the Journal of Economic Growth, cold has a positive effect on economies for two main reasons. Firstly, in regions with a cold climate, a more developed and diversified agricultural production system historically existed. The authors explain that frost regulates populations of agricultural pests, primarily insects; and also contribute to the formation of richer soils (it is curious that many crops, such as potatoes and wheat, originally originated in warm climatic zones, but yield much higher yields in temperate climates). In addition, ice and snow forming in winter reduce the risk of droughts. Secondly, pathogenic microbes are less active in regions with cold climates, which limits the power of epidemics. These two factors have created a reliable base on the basis of which the remaining sectors of the economy are developing successfully. Here, the calculation of the value of Cold can be carried out both by the income method (the method of production functions), and by the comparative method;

- transport ground communication with certain hard-to-reach settlements is possible only on winter roads. What kind of cost savings this gives - we can calculate by a comparative valuation method;
- each state, to ensure its existence, is concerned about the food security of the population. According to international experts, an acute shortage of food and fresh water can lead to regional and even global military conflicts over the possession of natural resources in the next 50 years. It becomes extremely important to connect the mechanism of reducing losses and preserving food with the help of the cold - the most affordable, environmentally friendly and economical resource.

Even at the dawn of the emergence of mankind, Neanderthals began to store meat from animals hunted in pits dug in frozen ground [13]. For millennia in the traditional culture of different peoples, various ways have developed of using natural cold for storing food. The natural and climatic conditions of Siberia and the Far East contributed to the development of the skills of chilled food storage among all peoples living on their territory. However, already in the postwar years, interest in the use of natural cold for household purposes began to decline in view of the increasing availability of modern freezing equipment powered by electricity. Despite this, recently in a number of foreign countries one can observe a return of interest in the use of natural cold as industrial coolers. This is due to the fact that the rising tariffs for electricity consumed by modern freezing equipment are a significant factor increasing the cost of food production, which, in turn, reduces their competitiveness in the modern market. Based on this, the study of centuries-old traditional environmental knowledge of different peoples associated with refrigerated food storage may become relevant in light of the creation of innovative energy-saving technologies. For example, a product naturally cooled to 0 degrees is much easier to freeze in a freezer, while saving energy. By combining the proportion of using natural and artificial cold, we can calculate the specific cost savings - by the revenue method.

- significant energy resources are expended in obtaining Artificial Cold. The use of artificial refrigerants leads to the destruction of the ozone layer, which leads to an increase in the flow of ultraviolet radiation from the sun reaching the Earth, and, as a consequence, to a change in the climatic parameters of regions, continents and the planet as a whole. This forces a significant way to revise the direction of development of the refrigeration industry and related industries. For example, for regions with permafrost, typical storage facilities cooled by underground cold can have greater economic efficiency - for global information and communication systems, biological materials, etc. Here you can also apply profitable and comparative valuation methods.
- the use of ice and snow as a basic building material or an integral element of building structures is typical for regions with the coldest climates. One of the most famous examples of such buildings is the winter home of the Eskimos - the igloo. It is a dome-shaped structure assembled from slabs made of snow or ice.

The Russian population of the North of Siberia until the end of the XIX century. the use of ice instead of window panes was widespread. "In the Far North, neither mica nor bubbles could withstand severe frosts, so in winter, ice plates were inserted into the windows. They were cut out of river ice and frozen to the window opening from the outside" [27]. With developed technologies, it is much cheaper to use local material as a raw material - in this case, snow, ice. The amount of savings is also not difficult to calculate by profitable and comparative valuation methods.

- natural cold was widely used as a folk hygiene product. Its basic principle is that the influence of negative temperatures on the interior of a house or on a person's clothes was used to kill pests and parasites. Freezing of clothes on the street was widespread among many indigenous peoples of the North. For example, in Chukchi, clothes were cleaned by knocking them out in the snow and drying them for a long time in a cold wind [9]. For Russians living in Siberia, freezing dwellings was used to control insect pests [6]. You can derive the cost of artificial means of combating these pests and compare;

- although the role of cold in traditional medicine practices has been very little studied today, in popular beliefs, short-term stress from exposure to cold is interpreted as an effective means to mobilize the body's defenses. In the traditional culture of the indigenous peoples of the North, snow and ice are often featured as therapeutic agents. There is also the opportunity to calculate the cost of an alternative to traditional treatment – a comparative method;
- in the traditional life-support systems of the peoples living in the Arctic and Subarctic (everywhere in Yakutia), as well as in high mountains, snow and ice play an important role as a source of drinking water. The calculation is made by the method of substitute goods (comparative method);
- cold as a recreational object - an object of tourism - is subject to assessment by the method of transport and travel costs (conditional assessment method). In relation to this assessment, the criterion of attractiveness for a society that has never or little encountered the components of the Cold — snow, ice, permafrost — will be of paramount importance.

The directions of using Cold as a natural resource in traditional life-support systems are far from being exhausted by the examples described above. Today, some other areas of their application, the potential of the Cold remain practically unstudied. For example, to solve a number of innovative tasks related to the rational use of natural and energy resources. Given the crisis trends in electricity consumption, the use of natural Cold can get high economic efficiency. Modern advances associated with the creation of new materials having previously unparalleled thermal insulation and thermoelectric properties make it possible to create innovative systems for the stable functioning of which natural cold can be sufficient.

In our turn, we hope that the methodological assessment apparatus dynamically developing at the present stage will allow in the near future to accurately assess the value of the existence of the Cold, thus contributing to the adoption of not only economically, but also environmentally sound decisions at various levels of environmental management.

IV. Conclusion

Thus, the cold, cold climate can have its advantages, and one must take advantage of these. The reason for the non-competitiveness of Russia lies, we believe, precisely in the fact that earlier no one was specifically engaged in a truly search and study of significant comparative advantages of the cold. Cold is the resources of the future. The possession of such a natural resource, even with the country's ability to generate new technologies, is becoming increasingly important. Russia has all the necessary set of potentials for a breakthrough in the use of low temperatures for the benefit of the country and the population. We need a new angle of view and new tools - a new approach to the problem of cold, an awareness of the completely new possibilities of this natural resource and economic category, opening up to the future and oriented towards the future.

References

1. https://www.golos-ameriki.ru/a/cold-human-effect-2012-02-11-139157089/250728.html
2. Krutilla, J., 1967. Conservation reconsidered. Am. Econ. Rev. 57 (4), 777-786.
3. Marc D. Davidson. On the relation between ecosystem services, intrinsic value, existence value and economic valuation // Ecological Economics 95 (2013). S.175.
4. The Birth of the Cold Economy. By Toby Peters www.twitter.com/Toby_Peters_ 06/30/2015 02:23 pm ET, updated Jun 27, 2016.
5. Weisbrod, BA, 1964. Collective-consumption services of individual-consumption goods. Q.J. Econ. 78 (3), 471-477.
6. Аболина Л.А., Федоров Р.Ю. Особенности традиционной культуры семейских Забайкалья // Вестник археологии, антропологии и этнографии. 2015. № 2 (29).

С.161 (Abolina L.A., Fedorov R.Yu. Features of the traditional family culture of Transbaikalia // Bulletin of archeology, anthropology and ethnography. 2015. No. 2 (29). P.161).

7. Бобылев С. Н. Экосистемные услуги и экономика / С. Н. Бобылев, В. М. Захаров. – М.: ООО "Типография ЛЕВКО," Институт устойчивого развития, Центр экологической политики России, 2009. – 72 с. (Bobylev S. N. Ecosystem Services and Economics / S. N. Bobylev, V. M. Zakharov. - M.: LLC Printing House LEVKO, Institute for Sustainable Development, Center for Environmental Policy of Russia, 2009. - 72 p.).
8. Бобылев С.Н. , Тишков А.А. Экономическая оценка биоразнообразия/ Под ред. Бобылева С.Н. и Тишкова А.А.. Глобальный Экологический Фонд. Проект «Сохранение биоразнообразия».—М., 1999. - 112 с. (Bobylev S.N., Tishkov A.A. Economic Assessment of Biodiversity / Ed. Bobyleva S.N. and Tishkova A.A. Global Environment Facility. The project "Conservation of biodiversity." - M., 1999. - 112 p.).
9. Богораз В.Г. Чукчи: Материальная культура. М. : ЛЕНАНД, 2016. 264 с. С.109. (Bogoraz V.G. Chukchi: Material Culture. M.: LENAND, 2016.264 p. P.109.).
10. Гирусов Э.В., Бобылев С.Н., Новоселов АЛ., Чепурных Н.В. Экология и экономика природопользования, — М.: «Закон и право», Изд. объед. «ЮНИТИ», 1998. - 455 с. (Girusov E.V., Bobylev S.N., Novoselov AL., Chepurnyh N.V. Ecology and Economics of Nature Management, - M.: "Law and Law," Ed. united UNITY, 1998. - 455 p.).
11. Глазырина И.П. Природный капитал в экономике переходного периода. - М.: НИА-Природа, РЭФИА, 2001. - 204 с. (Glazyrina I.P. Natural capital in a transition economy. - M.: NIA- Priroda, REFIA, 2001. - 204 p.).
12. Евсеев А.В., Красовская Т.М. «Притундровые леса в структуре экологического каркаса Мурманской области» // Материалы Всероссийской конференции с международным участием «Современные проблемы притундровых лесов» (Архангельск, 4-9 сентября 2012 г.). – Архангельск.: изд-во С(А)ФУ. - 2012. - 528 с. (Evseev A.V., Krasovskaya T.M. "Trans-tundra forests in the structure of the ecological framework of the Murmansk region" // Materials of the All-Russian Conference with international participation "Modern problems of the trans-tundra forests" (Arkhangelsk, September 4–9, 2012).

- Arkhangelsk: publishing house C (A) FU. - 2012. - 528 p.).

13. Крупник И.И. Арктическая этноэкология. М. : Наука, 1989. 272 с. С.211. (Krupnik II Arctic ethnoecology. M.: Nauka, 1989.272 p. P.211).
14. Л.Г.Гордеева, М.М.Токарев, Ю.И.Аристов. Новый адсорбционный цикл преобразования теплоты окружающей среды//Теоретические основы химической технологии. 2018. Том 52. № 2. С. 171–182 (L.G. Gordeeva, M.M. Tokarev, Yu.I. Aristov. A new adsorption cycle for the conversion of environmental heat // Theoretical Foundations of Chemical Technology. 2018. Volume 52. No. 2. P. 171–182).
15. Медведева О.Е. Методы экономической оценки биоразнообразия. Теория и практика оценочных работ. - М.: Изд-во Диалог-МГУ, 1998. - 120 с. (Medvedeva O.E. Methods of economic assessment of biodiversity. Theory and practice of appraisal work. - M.: Publishing House of Dialogue-Moscow State University, 1998. - 120 p.).
16. Медведева О.Е. Применение метода восстановительной стоимости к оценке биологических ресурсов Московского региона// Экономика сохранения биоразнообразия. — М.: Минприроды России, 1995. - С. 191-202. (Medvedeva O.E. Application of the replacement cost method to the assessment of biological resources of the Moscow region // Economics of biodiversity conservation. - M.: Ministry of Natural Resources of Russia, 1995. - P. 191-202).
17. Полевой А. А. Холодильник будущего: магнит вместо компрессора. Интервью корреспонденту журнала «Продукт.BY» генерального директора ООО «Технологии низких температур», канд. техн. наук, академика МАХ Алексея Полевого. Продовольственный торгово-промышленный портал. 2013. URL: http://www.produkt.by/Journal/ item/2279 (дата обращения 11.02.2016) (Polevoy A. A. The refrigerator of the future: a magnet instead of a compressor. Interview with the correspondent of Product.BY magazine, Director General of Low Temperature Technologies LLC, Ph.D. tech. sciences, academician of the Moscow Academy of Art Alexey Polevoy Food commercial and industrial portal. 2013. URL: http://www.produkt.by/Journal/ item / 2279 (accessed February 11, 2016)).

18. Попова А.Ю., Демина Ю.В., Ежлова Е.Б., Куличенко А.Н., Рязанова А.Г., Малеев В.В., Плоскирева А.А., Дятлов И.А., Тимофеев В.С., Нечепуренко Л.А., Харьков В.В. Вспышка сибирской язвы в Ямало-Ненецком автономном округе в 2016 г., эпидемиологические особенности // Проблемы особо опасных инфекций. 2016. № 4. С. 42–46. (Popova A.Yu., Demina Yu.V., Yezhlova E.B., Kulichenko A.N., Ryazanova A.G., Maleev V.V., Ploskireva A.A., Dyatlov I.A., Timofeev V.S., Nechepurenko L.A., Kharkov V.V. Anthrax outbreak in the Yamalo-Nenets Autonomous Okrug in 2016, epidemiological features // Problems of especially dangerous infections. 2016. No. 4. P. 42–46).
19. Развитие системности в освоении природного потенциала северных малоизученных территорий / Под общ. ред. акад. РАН А.И. Татаркина. Екатеринбург: Институт экономики УрО РАН. 2015. –С.193-226. (The development of consistency in the development of the natural potential of the northern poorly studied territories / Under total. ed. Acad. RAS A.I. Tatarkina. Ekaterinburg: Institute of Economics, Ural Branch of the Russian Academy of Sciences. 2015. –P.193-226).
20. Роль природных криогенных ресурсов в традиционных системах жизнеобеспечения народов Сибири и Дальнего Востока [Текст] / В. П. Мельников, Р. Ю. Федоров // Вестник Томского государственного университета = Tomsk State University Journal. - 2018. - № 426 (январь). - С. 133-141. (The role of natural cryogenic resources in traditional life-support systems of the peoples of Siberia and the Far East [Text] / V. P. Melnikov, R. Yu. Fedorov // Tomsk State University Bulletin = Tomsk State University Journal. - 2018. - No. 426 (January). - P. 133-141).
21. Свободный словарь терминов (Free dictionary of terms). http://www.termin.bposd.ru/publ/17-1-0-15235
22. Суслов Н. И., Бузулуцков В. Ф. Оценка макроэкономических эффектов от использования альтернативных технологий производства холода с применением модели ОMMM – Холод // Мир экономики и управления. 2016. Т. 16, № 2. С. 16–33. (Suslov N. I., Buzulutskov V. F. Evaluation of macroeconomic effects from the use of alternative technologies for the production of cold using the OMMM - Cold model // World of

Economics and Management. 2016.Vol. 16, No. 2. P. 16–33).

23. Тишков А.А Методы оценки ущерба биоресурсам. Сборник нормативно-правовых документов и их аналитический обзор. (Под ред. Тишкова А.А.) Госкомитет РФ по охране окружающей среды. Проект ГЭФ «сохранение биоразнообразия». - Москва: АО «ОКАЭКОС», 2000. - 240 с. (Tishkov A.A Methods for assessing damage to biological resources. Collection of regulatory documents and their analytical review. (Edited by A. Tishkov.) The RF State Committee for Environmental Protection. GEF project "Biodiversity Conservation." - Moscow: OKAECOS JSC, 2000. - 240 p.).
24. Файко, Л. И. Холод - хранилище тепла / Л. И. Файко // Энергия: экономика, техника, экология. - 2016. - №6. - С. 38-41. (Fayko, L. I. Cold - storage of heat / L. I. Fayko // Energy: economics, technology, ecology. - 2016. - No. 6. - S. 38-41).
25. Федеральный закон от 10.01.2002 N 7-ФЗ (ред. от 29.07.2018) "Об охране окружающей среды", Ст.1. данные КонсультантПлюс (Federal Law of 10.01.2002 N 7-ФЗ (as amended on 07.29.2018) "On Environmental Protection," Article 1. Data ConsultantPlus).
26. Хилл Ф., Гэдди К. Сибирское бремя. Просчеты советского планирования и будущее России / Пер. с англ. М.: Научно-образовательный форум по международным отношениям, 2007. 328 с. (Hill F., Gaddy K. The Siberian burden. Miscalculations of Soviet planning and the future of Russia / Translate from English, M.: Scientific and educational forum on international relations, 2007. 328 p.).
27. Этнография русского крестьянства Сибири XVII – середина XIX в. М. : Наука, 1981. 270 с. С.118. (Ethnography of the Russian peasantry of Siberia XVII - mid XIX century. M.: Science, 1981. 270 p. P.118).
28. Юрак В.В. Теоретико-методический подход к оценке общественной ценности природных ресурсов. Диссертация на соискание степени кандидата экономических наук. Екатеринбург. 2017 (Yurak V.V. Theoretical and methodological approach to assessing the social value of natural resources. The dissertation for the degree of candidate of economic sciences. Yekaterinburg. 2017).

UNIQUE HYDROCARBON POTENTIAL OF THE ECONOMY OF WESTERN YAKUTIA

Vyacheslav Stefanovich Sitnikov
Doctor of Geology and Mineralogy, Head of Laboratory of Geology of Deposits of Oil and Gas, Institute of Oil and Gas, Siberian Branch of Russian Academy of Sciences
sitgeo@mail.ru

Rosalia Fedorovna Sevostyanova
Researcher, Institute of Oil and Gas, Siberian Branch of Russian Academy of Sciences
rose_sevos@mail.ru

Mariia Ivanovna Sleptsova
Candidate of Sciences in Techniques, Senior Researcher, Institute of Oil and Gas, Siberian Branch of Russian Academy of Sciences
msleptsova@mail.ru

Abstract.

The report contains of the history of exploration for oil and gas in Yakutia from the 1930s to the present. Issues related to the discovery of deposits and the creation of a resource base in eastern Russia under various geological conditions are considered.

The oil exploration program in Siberia was developed in 1932-34. When analyzing the history of oil and gas exploration work carried out in the Republic of Sakha (Yakutia), with a certain degree of conditionality, a number of stages are distinguished that differ in the prevailing directions of the location of the work, their volume, methodology and peculiarities of integration (1933-1955; 1956-1971; 1972-1984; 1985-1992; 1993 and to the present). During these years, the following most significant geological results were recorded.

In the early 30s, the first oil was obtained in the middle reaches of the river. Lena, in the valley of her right tributary of the river. Tuolba, as well as in the north in the Nordvik region. In 1954, a semi-industrial influx of hydrocarbon gas from the bottom of the sedimentary cover was noted on the Russo-Rechenskaya deep drilling area. In 1956, the first Ust-Vilyuiskoye gas field was discovered in Yakutia, confined to one of the folds pushed westward on the platform from the West Verkhoyanie.

The concentration of deep exploratory drilling at this uplift led to the discovery of a number of gas and gas condensate fields - Badaransky (1963), Nejelinsky (1963), Srednevilyuysky (1965), Tolonsky (1967), Mastakhsky (1967).

As a result of geological exploration, new gas condensate and oil and gas fields were discovered in the south-west of Yakutia: Verkhnevilyuchanskoye (1980), Tas-Yuryakhskoye (1981), Nizhnekhamakinskoye (1982), Iktekhskoye (1984), Talakanskoye (1984), Chayandinskoye oil and gas condensate field (1989).

The initial geological resources of hydrocarbons in prospective areas of Western Yakutia are 24 billion tons, including 10.4 billion tons of oil (2.6 billion tons of recoverable), free gas of 12.1 trillion cubic meters; gas dissolved in oil, 0.8 trillion cubic meters tons; condensate 0.7 billion tons.

The predominant part of the initial geological resources of hydrocarbon gas is concentrated in the Vilyui and Nepa-Botuoba oil and gas regions.

The situation with the development of proven reserves of oil and gas and the prospects for their further expansion are covered. An assessment of the hydrocarbon forecast resources is given and the ways of their implementation are outlined taking into account new scientific ideas.

The data obtained, together with the materials of the work of past years, convincingly indicate that the republic's subsoil has the largest oil and gas potential, capable of further accelerating the growth of the raw hydrocarbon base and the discovery of new large fields, including oil in fundamentally new areas.

Keywords: The Republic of Sakha (Yakutia), oil, gas, raw material base, prospecting for oil and gas, oil pipeline, gas pipeline.

I. Introduction

The Republic of Sakha (Yakutia) is generally recognized as one of the largest mineral-raw regions of the Russian Federation. Oil and gas occupy one of the leading places in the list of mineral resources that constitute the main wealth of the depths of Yakutia.They play a major role in shaping the country's energy strategy.

When discussing the problems of the oil and gas industry of the Republic, it is usually meant its western part. At the same time, the hydrocarbon potential of large depressions in the north-east of Yakutia, the high oil and gas potential prospects of the Laptev Sea and East Siberian Sea shelf, as well as numerous and diverse sources of unconventional hydrocarbon raw materials not considered yet.This is the largest reserve for a more distant future. The history of oil and gas works in the Republic has been going on for more than eight decades. The need to search for hydrocarbon deposits in the depths of the Siberian Platform, which, with its eastern regions, covers the whole of Western Yakutia, was first substantiated in the late twenties and early thirties of our century by prominent Soviet geologists, academicians A.D. Arkhangelsk and N.S. Shatskiy. The oil exploration program in Siberia was developed in 1932-34 since with the active participation of Academician I.M. Gubkin, who scientifically justified the need for oil and gas exploration in areas of Eastern Siberia. In Yakutia, many manifestations of oil and gas were widely known.

The methodology of the study is based on a comprehensive synthesis and analysis of all available data from different years on the socio-economic situation of the Arctic regions of the Republic of Sakha (Yakutia). The theoretical and methodological basis of the study was the work of Russian scientists on the theoretical and practical problems of the heat and power balance of the republic. To obtain the results, methods of theoretical analysis of information sources, generalization and comparison of information on the issue under study were used. Comparative and statistical analyzes are carried out. Used tabular methods for presenting research results. The research information base was made up of materials from the Government of the Republic of Sakha (Yakutia).

II. History and economics of exploration

2.1. The first stage 1933-1955 years

In 1936, in the basin of the Tuolba River, the right tributary of the Lena River, the first deep well was laid at the Kuchugei-Bilyakhskaya structure (Chenkyamskaya Square). The maximum flow of oil, released with water,was recorded in a subsequent well and reached 110 liters per day [1].

In the period from 1936 to 1955 on the slopes of the Aldan anteclise and the adjacent territory of the Predpatom (Pre-Baikal) through a number of areas were covered by exploratory drilling.Oil wells have been recorded in many wells.An emergency release of gas was noted on the Russko-Rechenskaya area.However, the discovery of oil and gas during this period in the middle reaches of the Lena River did not take place.

The second direction of oil exploration, which was carried out almost simultaneously with the first, is connected with the northern regions of Yakutia. These works were carried out according to a single government program and covered vast areas of the Krasnoyarsk Territory and the Yakut ASSR, adjacent to the lower reaches of the Yenisei, Khatanga, Anabar and Lena rivers. In the Nordvik region, oil prospecting work was carried out by the Glavsevmorput Department from the beginning of the 30s to 1953. Of the many dozens of wells drilled for the purpose of the possible productivity of Permian and Devonian deposits, only 6 showed weak oil or gas shows.

On the South-Tigian anticline structure, exploration was carried out from 1934 to 1952. In one of the wells located in the arch of the eastern dome, oil from Permian sandstones was obtained with a flow rate of up to 12 cubic meters per day. The well was operated intermittently for three years. The well was exploited intermittently for three years.

The lack of stable inflows of oil or gas of industrial significance led to the fact that, despite the abundant oil and gas occurrences, prospecting in the north-west of Yakutiawas stopped in the early fifties [2].

2.2. The second stage 1956-1972 years

In 1951, a group of specialists of the Yakutsk exploration drilling office under the leadership of A.K. Bobrov, on the instructions of the USSR Ministry of Geology, is preparing a prospective plan for prospecting and exploration for oil and gas in Yakutia.In this regard, the Predverhoyanskiy deflection was recognized as the most promising region.Compared with the previous work, this was a fundamentally new direction of work, which was focused on breeds of Mezozoic age.

In 1956, the first Ust-Vilyuisk gas field in the Republic was discovered.The first powerful inflows of gas from the Lower Jurassic deposits on the Siberian platform here not only confirmed the promise of Mesozoic rocks but also predetermined the final reorientation in the areas of geological exploration.Priority work was recognized in the Predverhoyanskiy trough and adjacent areas of the Vilyui syneclise.In 1960, another small gas field was discovered (Sobo-Khainskoye), located in the immediate vicinity of the Ust-Vilyui field [1].

Simultaneously with these works, the adjacent territory of the Vilyui syneclisewas studied. In the early 60s, regional seismic surveys of the Reflected wave method in the eastern part of the syneclise on the right bank of the Vilyuy river, combined with the drilling of the Vilyuykolontovyi mapping wells, revealed a large haloform uplift, the KhapchagayMegaval, whose arched part is complicated by a number of large anticlinal structures.Entering them into deep exploratory drilling and the concentration of work at the Khapchagaysky uplift led to the discovery of a number of gas and gas condensate fields — Badaranskiy (1963), Nedzhelinskiy (1963), Srednevilyuiskiy (1965), Tolonskiy (1967), Mastakhskiy 1967).

Since 1965, systematic seismic exploration of the territories located within the previously identified Botuobinskaya saddle (northern part of the Nepa-Botuoba anteklise) began.As a result, a number of large anticline structures of the platform type (Srednebotobinskaya, Verkhnevilyuchanskaya, etc.) were identified.In the first of them, a parametric well was drilled (1969-70) and the Lower Cambrian and Devonian sediments were broken down in the section. Gas inflows of varying intensity, indicating the discovery of the first field in the south-west of Yakutia, are noted.

2.3. The third stage 1972-1984 years

The next stage is 1972-84. The study of the oil and gas potential of Yakutia began after the adoption of a resolution of the USSR Government on the deployment of gas exploration for gas in the Yakut ASSR. To accomplish the task of bringing the volume of explored gas reserves to 1.0 – 1.2 trillion meters by the end of 1975, work was significantly intensified, primarily on the exploration of discovered fields of the Khapchagay gas-bearing region, as well as on the search and study here new gas deposits. In this regard, the originally «Khapchagai» direction in the placement of exploration was predominant. As exploration works were carried out, it turned out that the structure of the deposits discovered here and other promising areas is much more complicated than it had been previously thought. It was envisaged, in particular, that a significant part of gas reserves would be explored in the horizons of the Upper Permian. In addition, a considerable part of gas reserves was predicted in the Lower Jurassic sediments. The results of the drilling of deep wells showed that the Upper Permian production horizons are characterized by a very complex development of reservoir rocks and significant variability of their reservoir properties. Therefore, the specific density of gas reserves within their limits is small. The assessment of the potential gas content of the Lower Jurassic deposits, which contain, as a rule, only small secondary deposits of gas in certain areas, was not confirmed either [2].

As a result, from the second half of the 70s, the more general «Vilyuisk» direction with the placement of priority objects throughout the Vilyui syneclise becomes the priority. At the same time, gas and oil were also searched in other geological regions, which, in terms of volumes of work, were significantly inferior to Vilyuisky, at least until the end of the 1970s.

With a focus on promising deposits of the Cambrian and Vendian, oil prospecting in various volumes began to be carried out in many geological regions of Western Yakutia, in particular in its south-western, southern, western and central regions. The basis for their consistent reversal, primarily in the south-west of Yakutia, was the discovery of the above-mentioned Srednebotuobinskiy field [1].

Taking into account the results of drilling the pioneer well, materials about the structure, development and potential oil and gas content of the territory of the south of the Siberian Platform were analyzed again by that time. From a new perspective, prospects for the discovery of large oil and gas fields in southwest Yakutia were considered. As a result, a long-term program of further oil and gas exploration was compiled (A.L. Gudkov, D.P. Sidorov, V.S. Sitnikov), which was approved in 1971 by the Expert Council of the RSFSR Ministry of Geology at the on-site session in Irkutsk. The main provisions of this program, providing for a broad integration of deep drilling and geophysical research, became the basis for the annual planning of exploration for the next 5-10 years. These works included the study and evaluation of the Srednebotuobinskoe field, prospecting and exploration of new deposits prepared by seismic exploration structures, as well as the identification of new objects for the production of deep drilling using geophysical methods.

Continuous prospecting and exploration at the Srednebotuobinskoe field allowed by 1985 to almost completely complete the exploration of this largest accumulation of hydrocarbons. It is noteworthy that its study began with a focus solely on gas, and ended with the submission to the State Reserves Committee of materials on gas, condensate, oil and associated components in the form of helium and rare-earth hydro mineral resources. It should be noted that all these works were, as it were, part of a unified regional program to reverse the search for oil and gas in the south of the Siberian platform. In 1974, joint studies of scientific and industrial organizations of the Yakutsk Autonomous Soviet Socialist Republic, the Irkutsk Region and the Krasnoyarsk Territory with the leading participation of Siberian Research Institute of Geology, Geophysics and Mineral Resources, which is the leading sectoral institute in the east of the country, were first allocated to the Nepa-Botuoba anteclise and the same name oil and gas region. In the north, the Botuobinsky saddle, which was previously distinguished here, became part of it. According to its regional position and geological features of the structure, this anteclise was recognized as one of the most promising areas in Eastern Siberia. Subsequent exploration confirmed this assessment. Within anteklizy directly in Yakutia, a number of gas condensate and oil and gas fields were discovered: Verkhnevilyuchanskoe (1975), Vilyuisko-Dzherbinskoe (1977), Irelyaskoe (1980), Tas-Yuryakhskoe (1981), Nizhnekhamakinskoye (1982),

Iktekhskoye (1984), Talakanskoe (1984) [1].

After a long break, work was resumed in the Predpatom (Pre-Baikal) marginal trough, including its western (Nepa-Dzherbinsk depression) and eastern (Berezovskaya depression) branches. In the west of the trough three parametric wells were drilled (Mukhtuyskaya, Nizhnepeleduyskaya, Parshinskaya) and searched for the Hotogo-Murbay structure. The gas field of the same name was discovered in the last area in the terrigenous sediments of the vendian (1977).

Commensurate drilling volumes were also performed in the Berezovskaya Basin. Berezovskaya, two Ust-Biryuk and Ust-Molbinsk parametric wells are drilled here. In the first of them, located within the large Bysakhtakh anticline, gas inflows from vendian sediments were obtained, indicating high prospects for gas-bearing area. Exploratory drilling was carried out at the Kederginsky structure, where in a number of wells semi-industrial gas inflows from carbonate sediments of the lower-middle Cambrian were recorded, indicating the presence of a small gas reservoir of complex structure.

Determination of the priority areas of work with a focus on the high prospects of the ancient strata led to a partial resumption of work on oil and gas in the territory of the Aldan Anteclise. These works were preceded by the receipt here of the first seismic data and ideas about the potential petroleum potential of the West Yakut barrier-reef zone (Bobrov A.K, Savitsky V.E, Astashkin V.A, Shishkin B.B, etc.). The latter is traced from the northern slope of the Aldan anteclise through the Vilyui syneclise to the southern slope of the Anabar anteclise. On the immersion of the northern slope of the Aldan anteclise, Bappagay, North-Namaninskaya and Sinskaya parametric wells were drilled, in the east - Mokuiskaya and Khochomskaya wells, which didn't give positive results.

Drilling of the Aikhal parametric well has begun a re-study of the oil and gas potential of the southern slope of the Anabar Anteclise.

Expansion of geological exploration in Western Yakutia and the focus of these works in search of large oil and gas accumulation zones predetermined a repeated surge of increased attention to the petroleum potential of the Lena-Anabar trough. Dia-Appal and Charchyk parametric wells were drilled here, revealing sediments from the Mesozoic to the Riphean.

The most promising horizons, from which intensive inflows of stratal water with dissolved hydrocarbon gas in the Charchyk well, are confined to the Vendian section.

At the beginning of this stage, deep drilling was carried out by three oil and gas exploration expeditions. In 1972 in the village. Kysyl Syr on the basis of the North-Yakut Oil Exploration Expedition was created Vilyuiskaya expedition, and also formed two new expeditions Sangarskaya (village Sangar) and Srednelenskaya (city of Lensk) expedition. For the overall coordination and management of these works, the «Yakutneftegazrazvedka» trust (1972) was created in Yakutsk, which was later reorganized into «Lenaneftegazgeologia». As work was reversed in the southwest of the republic, Vitim expedition (1980, Vitim) was organized here.

A characteristic feature of this stage (1972–84) is the extensive use of geophysical exploration methods in oil and gas operations. The latter were used at all stages of the study of potentially oil and gas areas - from regional studies to the identification of specific local structures, their preparation for deep drilling and consistent detailing of promising objects that have a complex structure.

In order to clarify the general features of the structure of the sedimentary cover, electrical exploration Magnetotelluric sounding. In the early 1970s, electrical overhaul of Magnetotelluric sounding was also used for regional studies in the north-east of the republic (Indigiro-Zyryan depression).

Since 1972 in the south-west of Yakutia in the study of ancient strata for many years used electrical prospecting Sounding field formation in the near zone. This method, along with the elucidation of the details of the tectonic structure, made it possible, with a certain degree of arbitrariness, to solve problems of predicting the geological section, including an assessment of the saturation of individual strata.

Practically all promising areas of the central regions of Western Yakutia, as well as marginal troughs bordering the Siberian platform from the south, east and north, were largely studied by the Reflected Wave Method (RWM) seismic prospecting, and then, starting from the second half of the 70s, the Common Depth Point (CDP) seismic survey [3].

In 1974-75 During the experimental work of the CDP in the Vilyui syneclise (central part of the Khapchagaysky gas-bearing region), seismic stations were first introduced with digital recording of recordings on magnetic tape. In the Botuobinsky geological region, such work was begun in 1975 in a small volume on the Srednebotuobinsky area. Since 1978, imported vibroseismic complexes were introduced in Yakutia using non-explosive sources of excitation and the transition to in-depth processing of CDP materials.

In 1979, the development of direct methods for the prediction of oil and gas potential using seismic data was started, which allowed, in 1982, to switch to standardized preparation of objects associated with "deposit" anomalies. The first Reservoir Type Anomaly (RTA) were identified on the northwestern side of the Vilyui syneclise (Bagadyanskaya, Tysakitskaya).

In the 1970s and 1980s, geophysical research was continued using river seismic surveys, which included parts of the Vilyui, Lena, Aldan and, to a lesser extent, Amga rivers.

In the second half of the 70s and the beginning of the 80s, large-scale aeromagnetic studies were carried out for a more detailed Study of the discontinuous tectonics of promising areas in small volumes. Shooting at a scale of 1:50000 covered the central part of the Khapchagai uplift and the adjacent Tangnaryn downwarp (1975) in the Vilyui syneclise. With the involvement of the Novosibirsk Geophysical Trust, a similar area was covered by a vast territory in the area of the junction of the Nepa-Botuoba anteclise, the Pre-Patomsky trough and the Vilyui syneclise (1980).

In a regional study of the territory of the former Union, carried out by the forces of the Scientific Production Association «Soyuzgeofizika» with the use of deep seismic sounding, many areas of Yakutia were intersected with a number of profiles of the Deep Seismic Sounding (DSS). As a result, numerous data on the deep structure of the republic were obtained.

In connection with the expansion of oil and gas exploration, the number of geophysical batches of the Yakutsk integrated geophysical expedition increased, which in 1981 was transformed into the «Yakutskgeofizika» trust. The Bestyakhsky seismic party (1972) was created with a base in the village of Zhigansk; Ust-May Geophysical Party (1977); Olenek Geophysical Party (1977), based in the village. Taymylyr and the West Yakut Geophysical Party (1978), located in the town of Mirny and transformed in 1983 into an expedition.

The increase in the amount of work led to the further strengthening of the parties with the formation on their basis of independent geophysical expeditions - Kempendyayskaya (1980), Vilyuiskaya (1981), Murbay (1983). They were based, respectively, in the village. Mouth, Kysyl-Syr, Otradny.

III. Postsoviet time explorations

3.1. The fourth stage 1975-1992 years

The beginning of the next - the fourth stage (1985-92) of the study of the oil and gas potential of Yakutia is timed to the time when the search for gas in the Mezozoic sediments in the Vilyui syneclise was almost completely completed. Geological exploration in this period was focused mainly on the study and prospecting of the early Early Paleozoic and Late Precambrian strata.

In the Vilyuisk Oil and Gas Region (OGR), single wells continued exploration of previously discovered Andylakhsky (1985) and Nizhnetyukyansky (1985) gas fields. Ust-Tyung structure and two Reservoir Type Anomalies (RTA) (Tysakitskaya and Ulakhan-Tyuert) were searched. At the latter, which is a continuation of the eastern pericline of the Middle Tung structure, received a flow of gas from the Permian sediments.

In order to study the structural features of the Predverhoyansksky deflection, the Prilenskaya and Alysardakh parametric wells were drilled first on the platform platform deflection, the second within the frontal zone of regional thrust. There are numerous, gas shows.

In the Lena-Anabar trough deep drilling was carried out on the Ust-Olenek and Hastakh structures, as well as within the limits of the Boer non-anticlinal trap. In each case, one well was drilled. Despite the presence in the section of Mezozoic and Upper Paleozoic sediments, the search for oil and gas was focused on the deeper horizons of the sedimentary cover (lower Paleozoic, Precambrian). Positive results are not received.

In the West Vilyui Oil and Gas Region (OGR), the study of promising areas located within large depressions with a multi-tiered tectonic structure continued.

In the Ygyattinskaya depression, oil and gas exploration was carried out on its northwestern side, consisting of a series of one-sided handfuls of complex structure. Drilling was carried out in the Srednekononchansky, Dalyr, Kononchansky and Meiksky areas. In the first three, one parametric well was drilled to ascertain the potential petroleum potential of the Cambrian reef sediments and to study other parts of the section. The Meika well was focused on the search for sedimentary Vendian strata. No hydrocarbon deposits have been identified.

In the Kempendyai depression, the focus was on studying the petroleum potential of subsalt deposits on its northwestern side. Atyyakhskaya and Eseleyskaya parametric wells are drilled here.

In the first of these, gas flow from the near-bottom part of the section was noted and the Abnormally High Reservoir Pressure (AHRP) was recorded.

The Kusogan parametric well was drilled in the junction zone of the Kempendyai Depression and the Aldan Anteclise. A significant part of the open section in it is made up of igneous rocks of basic composition that have penetrated into the bottoms of the sedimentary cover. In addition, Mukhtinskaya and Dzhadzhansky Squares have been searched within this zone. On anticlinal structures with a complex block structure, one exploratory well was drilled. Gas shows are noted and weak gas inflows are obtained.

Directly on the slope of the Aldan Anteclise, in order to study the reef formations of the Cambrian, the North Sin Parametric Well was drilled, in which oil and gas shows were not installed.

Considerable amounts of geological exploration were performed on the territory of the Nepa-Botuoba anteclise. In the north, West Syuldyukar, East Syuldyukar, Sosnovaya, Bagdynskaya, Sredneygyattinskaya, North-Nelbinsk and Nelbinsk structures were searched. In the last two areas, respectively, in 1986 and 1988. open mine of small sizes. In other areas, numerous oil and gas shows are noted.

In the central part of the Nepsko-Botuobinsky anteclise, oil and gas exploration was carried out on the Buordakh, Kurung and Monulakh structures, as well as on the Chempurek, Ochugey and East Kotursk the Reservoir Type Anomaly (RTA). The gas inflows received on Kurungskaya area swam some expansion of the contours of the Srednebotobuinskoye oil and gas condensate field to the south. Semi-industrial gas inflows were obtained during the drilling of a well at the East-Hoturskaya the Reservoir Type Anomaly (RTA).

In the east of the Botuobinsky geological region, the Verkhne-Murbayskaya RTA and the Bes-Yuryakhsky structure were explored, in which a gas field was discovered in 1990.

The highest efficiency was obtained during geological exploration in areas located to the south of the Srednebotuobinskoe deposit, including the administrative border of Yakutia. A whole range of new fields was discovered here. The industrial productivity of some of them was established first during the exploration of previously isolated objects of anticlinal type: East Talakanskoe (1987), Tympuchikanskoe (1989), Alinskoe (1991). Positive results indicating high prospects for the oil and gas potential of the southern sector as a whole were also obtained in Delindinsky, Taranskaya and, to a lesser extent, Karst and Gadalinsky areas.

In the late 80s - early 90s, Yakut geologists and geophysicists (Matveyev V.D., Shabalin V.P., Sitnikov V.S, Serezhenkov V.G., Soloshchak M.M. and others) carried out joint research to substantiate and comprehensive analysis of available materials on the structure and oil content of ancient sedimentary strata. As a result, for the first time in the republic a number of large non-anticlinal traps were identified. The identified promising sites are located mainly in the south-west of Yakutia and in some other geological areas. The exploratory drilling at one of these Non-Anticlinal Traps (NAT) led in 1989 to the discovery of the Chayanda oil and gas condensate field, which included the previously identified Ozernoye and, partially, Nizhnekhamakinskoe fields. Structural lithological traps controlling the Tympuchikanskoe and Alinskoe fields mentioned above are classified as Non-Anticlinal Traps (NAT). A small gas field was also discovered in 1990 within the Mirny NAT, which is located south of the town of Mirny. In reserve are large Hamakinskaya, Samanchakitskaya and other NAT [1].

Exploration continued at the Srednebotuobinsky, Tas-Yuryakhsky, Iktekhsky, Verkhnevilyuchansky, Vilyuysko-Dzherbinsky, Irelyakhsky, Machchobinsky, Ozerny, Nizhnekhamakinsky, Talakansky, Tympuchikansky and, partly, Verkhnechonskiy fields, located mainly in the territory of the Irkutsk Region. Large reserves of gas and oil are prepared for industrial development. The main oil reserves, in addition to the Srednebotuobinskoe field, are concentrated in the Talakan and, to a lesser extent, Irelyakh fields.

Much attention was paid to oil and gas exploration in the Predpatomskiy trough, which were concentrated in its eastern part, and to a lesser extent, in the western part. In the east, in the Berezovskaya Depression, exploratory drilling confirmed the industrial significance and high prospects of the Bysakhtakh structure. Here the gas condensate field of the same name was discovered (1986), exploration of which showed the presence of two large deposits, apparently of a massive type, confined, respectively, to the Vendian and Upper Riphean deposits. Given this discovery, the potential oil and gas potential of the entire Berezovsky geological region was highly appreciated. In the search for new oil and gas fields and areas in a consistent study of prospective areas deep parametric drilling (Ystanahskaya, Ergedzheyskaya, Bordonskiy, Verhnecherendeyskaya, Innyahskaya, Kurdarskaya, Nizhnecherendeyskaya, Machinskaya, Bysahtah-Kyuelskaya, Yuzhno-Berezovsky and South Bysahtahskaya well) was carried out for many years. New deposits were not identified and only in some wells weak gas inflows were obtained.

In the west of Predpatomskiy trough, geological exploration was carried out mainly in the zone of its junction with a typical platform territory (Borulakhskaya, Lenskaya, Ulugurskaya, Sularskaya and Otradninskaya areas). In the wells located within the last two areas, semi-industrial gas inflows from carbonate sediments composing the boundary layers of the Cambrian-Vendian were obtained.

3.2. The fifth stage 1993 year to the present

The total area of potential oil and gas-bearing territories of Western Yakutia exceeds 1.5 million km2.

The initial geological resources of hydrocarbons in prospective areas of Western Yakutia are 24 billion tons, including 10.4 billion tons of oil (2.6 billion tons of recoverable), free gas of 12.1 trillion cubic meters; gas dissolved in oil, 0.8 trillion cubic meters tons; condensate 0.7 billion tons [4].

The predominant part of the initial geological resources of hydrocarbon gas is concentrated in the Vilyui and Nepa-Botuoba oil and gas regions. Gas contains significant amounts of condensate.In the south-west of the Republic, the presence of oil rims with large oil reserves is characteristic of many hydrocarbon gases confined to the ancient layer. Also noteworthy is the presence in the gas in the south-west of Yakutia an associated component of helium in abnormally high concentrations, far exceeding industrial conditions.

To date, total gas reserves in categories C1 and C2 in the Republic of Sakha (Yakutia) are in the amount of more than 3.0 trillion cubic meters, more than 30 hydrocarbon fields have been discovered.

All oil reserves (more than 700 million tons) and the bulk of proven gas reserves (80%) have been identified and prepared for development in the Nepa-Botuoba oil and gas region. About one-fifth of gas reserves are explored in Vilyuisk oil and gas region.

The main attention in characterizing the raw material base of Yakutia is drawn to the Chayandinskiy oil and gas condensate field, which, according to the latest assessment of its reserves, taking into account updated ideas about its new geological model, is undoubtedly the largest field in the country.According to the classification of deposits by gas reserves existing in Russia, it is classified as unique.

Currently, the annual levels of oil and gas production in the country differ sharply from each other.Oil is produced in the «Eastern Siberia-Pacific Ocean» oil and gas mega-project implementation mode. Every year, up to 10 million tons of oil is sent to the trunk pipeline. Oil refining in the country is currently virtually absent.

The annual level of gas production in the Republic does not exceed, as a rule, 2.0 billion cubic meters, condensate - 70 thousand tons. Works are carried out according to the long-term program of gasification of the Republic of Sakha (Yakutia).As the construction of «The Power of Siberia» gas pipeline is completed, gas production in Yakutia should increase dramatically.

A major reserve for the further expansion of oil and gas reserves and the consistent development of the resource base in the Republic are primarily [5]:

- promising little-studied areas of the Nepa-Botuoba oil and gas region;
- possible discoveries as a result of the revision and reinterpretation of materials of the past

years in this oil and gas field, in a number of areas with established oil and gas content;

- areas with potential productivity of analogs of the Vendian and Cambrian horizons, as well as fundamentally new horizons in the section of the Lower Paleozoic and Riphean in the adjacent territories of Predpatomskiy and West-Vilyuyskiy oil and gas regions;
- Certain prospects for the discovery of new oil fields, along with the Nepa-Botuoba oil and gas region, are associated with other oil and gas regions, primarily on the slopes of the Aldan anteclise. Of particular interest is its northeastern slope, complicated by the Aldan-Maya depression, as well as the adjacent parts of the large Yakut mega-arch.

IV. Conclusion

In conclusion, it should be noted that insufficient research into the characteristics of oil and gas potential and the comparative assessment of hydrocarbons in the continental and marine territories of the planet contribute to periodic spikes in disseminating in scientific publications and through the media unfounded pseudoscientific predictions about the future depletion of oil reserves and resources on our planet, already in the short term.It does not take into account the known data that the crust of the planet, especially in the part of plates, platforms and marginal deflections, is literally saturated with oil and gas. At the same time, the maximum prospects for a further increase in the resource base will be associated with marine shelf areas. A significant role in the future will also be played by unconventional sources of hydrocarbons [3].

References

1. Ситников В.С., Аржаков Н.А., Сереженков В.Г. История работ на нефть и газ в Якутии [30-90-е гг. XX в.] // Якутия - нефтегазовое будущее России: к 50-летию нефтегазовой отрасли Респ. Саха (Якутия). – Якутск, 2006. - С. 40-55 (Sitnikov V.S., Arzhakov N.A., Serzhenkov V.G. The history of oil and gas in Yakutia [30-90 years XX century]

// Yakutia - the oil and gas future of Russia: to the 50th anniversary of the oil and gas industry Rep. Sakha (Yakutia). Yakutsk: Sakha-Polygraphfizdat, 2006. - P.108-128).

2. Алексеев Н.Н., Аржаков Н.А., Ситников В.С., Слепцова М.И. Поисково-разведочные работы на нефть и газ в Якутии (история, состояние, перспективы) / Геология и минерально-сырьевые ресурсы Северо-Востока России: Материалы VI Всероссийской научно-практической конференции. Якутск, ИГАБМ СО РАН, 6 апреля - 8 апреля 2016 г. / Отв. ред. Л.И. Полуфунтикова – Якутск: Изд. дом СВФУ, 2016. – С. 304-307: http://elibrary.ru/item.asp?id=27406502 (Alekseev N.N., Arzhakov N.A., Sitnikov V.S., Sleptsova M.I. Oil and gas exploration in Yakutia (history, state, prospects) / Geology and mineral resources of the North-East of Russia: Materials of the VI All-Russian Scientific and Practical Conference. Yakutsk, IGDNM SB RAS, April 6 - April 8, 2016 / Ed. ed. L.I. Polufuntikova - Yakutsk: Publishing House. NEFU House, 2016. - P. 304-307)
3. Геология и нефтегазовый потенциал юго-запада Якутии: реалии и перспективы / Бурова И.А., Кушмар И.А., Ситников В.С., Баженова Т.К., Бурова И.А., Семенов В.П., Шибина Т.Д., Шостак К.В., Ященкова Л.К. – СПб.: ФГУП «ВНИГРИ», 2014 – 436 с. (Geology and oil and gas potential of the south-west of the Republic of Sakha (Yakutia). Realities, prospects, forecasts / V.S. Sitnikov, T.K. Bazhenova, I.A. Burov and others. St. Petersburg. VNIGRI. 2014. 436 p).
4. Слепцова М.И., Ситников В.С., Севостьянова Р.Ф. Прогнозные ресурсы углеводородов и их освоение на северных территориях Якутии // Нефтегазовая геология. Теория и практика.-2018.- Т.13.- №4.- http://www.ngtp.ru/rub/2018/44_2018.html (Sleptsova M.I., Sitnikov V.S., Sevostyanova R.F. Hydrocarbons forecast resources and their development in the northern Yakutia territories // Oil and gas geology. Theory and practice. – 2018.- T.13.-№4.- http://www.ngtp.ru/rub/2018/44_2018.html)
5. Философия и наука. Основные методы и их применение / Данилова В.С., Кожевников Н.Н., Ситников В.С., Яковлев (Philosophy and science. Basic methods and their application / Ed. O.N. Kozhevnikov. Yakutsk. NEFU them M.K. Ammosova. 2017. 246 p).

THE FORMATION OF INFORMATION DATABASE TO ESTIMATE THE EFFICIENCY OF USING LAND RESOURCES OF YAKUTIA

Luiza Mikhailovna Byastinova
Senior Lecturer, Chair of Economics and Territorial Development Management,
Institute of Economics and Finance, NEFU
lbyastinova@mail.ru

Abstract.

The article discusses the need to develop and describe an information database characterizing the state and use of land resources of the Republic of Sakha (Yakutia). This information base is proposed in order to automate a variety of data for information support and support of programs for the rational and efficient use of land resources, optimal planning for the development of the territory of the Republic of Sakha (Yakutia).

The article describes the existing information resources of Yakutia, developed in accordance with the Regulation on the procedure for accounting and registration of state information systems of the Republic of Sakha (Yakutia) and Decree of the President of the Republic of Sakha (Yakutia) dated December 23, 2011 No. 1126, including the existing land accounting information systems. A certain structure of the developed information database is proposed, its components, a description of the blocks and a brief outline of it.

Also considered is the actual condition, characteristics and structure of land resources of the Republic of Sakha (Yakutia), trends in the structure over the past 20 years.

Keywords: Information database, Information system, land resources, land fund, land use efficiency.

I. Introduction

In connection with the involvement in the turnover of a large number of new objects and, above all, land, the interest in information on natural resources and rights to them is increasing sharply.

In this regard, the question arises about the need for certain information about the legal regime of the land, the presence of any rights to it, the purpose of specific land plots and other information. The availability of modern methods of collecting, processing and storing various information on land resources, including by categories, transactions with them, cadastral value, makes it possible to make timely and high-quality decision-making on the management of regional natural resources, full and deep monitoring of land.

II. Information systems in the Republic of Sakha (Yakutia)

2.1. State information systems

Currently, in the Republic of Sakha (Yakutia) there is a fairly wide list of state information systems developed and approved in accordance with the Regulation on the procedure for accounting and registration of state information systems of the Republic of Sakha (Yakutia) and Decree of the President of the Republic of Sakha (Yakutia) dated December 23, 2011 No. 1126.

These information systems are designed to provide access to information about the activities of state bodies and local self-government bodies of the republic, as well as for:

- Creation of a single information space on the territory of the Republic of Sakha (Yakutia);
- collection, classification and use of complete, relevant and reliable information about the

created, functioning and liquidated information systems;

- identifying key systems of information infrastructure that have a significant impact on the security of the Republic of Sakha (Yakutia) in the information sphere;
- the implementation of interagency coordination of the activities of executive bodies of state power of the Republic of Sakha (Yakutia) on the creation, development and use of information systems, eliminating duplication of work and budget costs for these purposes;
- ensuring openness and transparency of information on the activities of executive bodies of state power of the Republic of Sakha (Yakutia) related to the generation and use of information contained in state information systems of the Republic of Sakha (Yakutia);
- the provision of information services and access of citizens and organizations to information on the activities of executive bodies of state power, bodies of local self-government of the Republic of Sakha (Yakutia) [2].

The procedure for accounting and registration of state information systems is carried out in accordance with the Decree of the President of the Republic of Sakha (Yakutia) dated December 23, 2011 No. 1126 "On approval of the regulation on accounting and registration of state information systems of the Republic of Sakha (Yakutia)" and in accordance with the Order of the State Communications Committee of the Republic of Sakha (Yakutia) dated 15.11.2011 No. P-01-120 "On approval of the Administrative Regulation of the State Committee for the Republic of Sakha (Yakutia) on Communications and Information Technologies for the Execution of the State Function for Accounting and Registration of State Information Systems" [3].

2.2. Information systems for land accounting

Among the systems directly or indirectly related to the land resources of the republic are such as the information system "Register of state-owned land plots of the Republic of Sakha (Yakutia)," which was developed and approved in 2013. It was intended to maintain a register of land plots of state ownership of the republic, property for which was not delimited, but for certain reasons was excluded from the GIS registry in accordance with the order of the Ministry of Communications of the Republic of Sakha (Yakutia) dated October 28, 2014 No. P-01-168 “On cancellation registration of state information systems of the Republic of Sakha (Yakutia).”

The next system, reflecting the state of natural resources of the republic, is the system of “State environmental control,” also developed in 2013. It was intended to automate workflow, for operational management, to take timely measures when conducting state environmental control to prevent erroneous decisions when filling out acts, protocols and orders on administrative offenses by state inspectors of the Ministry of Natural Resources of the Republic of Sakha (Yakutia).

It was developed in accordance with the Decree of the Government of the Republic of Sakha (Yakutia) dated December 28, 2010 No. 589 “On Approving the Plan of Measures to Improve the Efficiency of State Environmental Control and Monitoring at the Facilities of Large Industrial Projects and Tailings for 2011-2015” and ensured the collection of reports on the results of the state environmental supervision in the Republic of Sakha (Yakutia). This information system was also excluded from the register in 2017.

In parallel with the above-mentioned systems, two more information systems “Monitoring of State Property of the Republic of Sakha (Yakutia)” were created, which was created to automate the activities of the Ministry as part of the register, monitoring and reporting of objects owned by the Republic of Sakha (Yakutia) by republican target program “Development of the system of state and municipal registration of real estate in the Republic of Sakha (Yakutia) for 2008-2011,” and information The current system is “Monitoring of Municipal Property of the Republic of Sakha (Yakutia),” which at present has also lost its relevance.

2.3. Information Database (IBD)

One of the main advantages of developing an information database (hereinafter IBD) is the possibility for public authorities to make informed decisions about the negative impacts on land, their impact on degradation and restoration, assess and diagnose their current state, develop appropriate measures to prevent negative land impacts and mitigation, if any, as well as monitoring the condition and use of land regional resources.

The structure of the proposed development of the database can be represented as follows:

- base "Objects" - the area of all land plots, including by categories;
- the base "Land users" means the subjects of the right to land plots;
- the base "Borders" - the boundaries of the selected areas;
- base "Encumbrances or restrictions";
- base "Rights or shares";

The main goal of the development of the IDB is to provide information and support programs for the rational use of land resources and the optimal planning of the development of the territories of the Sakha Republic (Yakutia). Tasks solved IBD:

- high-quality and timely monitoring of land, the adoption of operational decisions on land management issues;
- creation of conditions for the establishment of territories with a special legal regime (environmental, conservation, recreational);
- informational support in order to streamline the authority for land management between the municipalities of the territory, between the administrative structures of the republic and the Russian Federation as a whole;
- consolidation and consolidation of sound information about land rights and related real estate for all entities at various levels of land administration, users, and other stakeholders;
- ensuring the protection of the rights of owners, owners and users of the land and property firmly associated with it.

The database being developed is a repository of an array of information containing information on all categories of land plots on the territory of the Republic of Sakha (Yakutia), taking into account the administrative-territorial division, information about land users, availability of information on encumbrances and restrictions on plots, ownership rights, use and disposal, as well as territorial boundaries of allocated land plots in the context of the structure of all types of owners.

Below is an exemplary diagram of the formed IBD Land Resources of the Republic of Sakha (Yakutia).

Figure 1. Approximate diagram-structure of the information database "Land resources of the Republic of Sakha (Yakutia)"

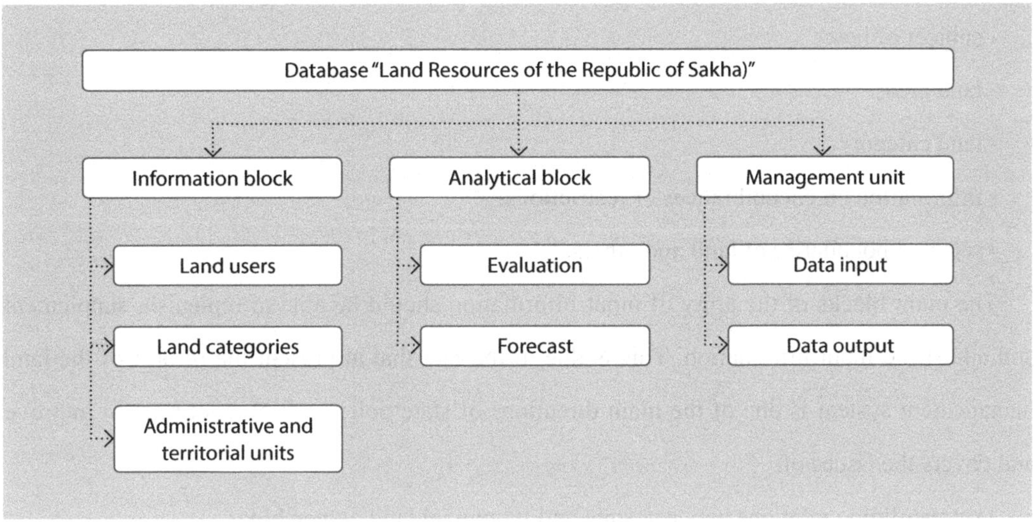

In the formation of this IBD, it is assumed that standardized procedures for searching for the necessary information are inherent in certain algorithms, as well as the possibility of data input and output. One of the fundamental requirements for the BDT is the quick and full output of the requested data by users.

The management unit carries the administrative functions by which input and output of the necessary data is possible. Data on the state of land resources is entered on the basis of various local databases, such as data from organizations, ministries, departments, municipalities, statistical observation, as well as data from the Federal Service for State Registration, Cadastre and Cartography.

First of all, this block should cover all primary data relating to a specific land plot, including data that is included in the cadastral number structure of a land plot:

- subject of the federation;
- administrative district;
- rural administration;
- village (village);

- cadastral quarter;
- land;
- subject of law;
- land area;
- land category;
- information on encumbrances or restrictions;
- selected boundaries of land and others.

The main blocks of the array of input information should be able to replenish, supplement and adjust the input information. This is due to the fact that at present the reform of the land management system is one of the main directions of state policy, which continues to improve and covers the issues of:

1) streamlining relations between state and municipal land ownership;
2) strengthening legislative guarantees of private ownership of land;
3) creation of mechanisms for registration of land rights in the system of state registration of rights to real estate;
4) improvement of land cadastre;
5) the formation of a system of mortgage lending and state control over the land mortgage market;
6) reforming the planning of land use of settlements through the development of urban zoning practices;
7) gradual reduction of restrictions on the turnover of land in cities and other settlements;
8) state control over the turnover of agricultural land [4].

In this connection, certain adjustments are possible in the structure of the BDT input data.

III. Land resources

3.1. Description of land resources of the Republic of Sakha (Yakutia)

Currently, in the Russian Federation, according to the Land Code, all lands are divided into seven main categories. These are agricultural lands, lands of settlements, lands of industry, transport, communications and others, lands of specially protected territories, lands of forest fund, water fund and lands of reserves [1].

Russian lands currently amount to about 1712 million hectares, which is about 1/9 of the earth's land. Less than 5% of the territory falls on the Central, North Caucasus and Southern Federal Districts.

The Republic of Sakha (Yakutia) on the territory is one of the largest constituent entities of the federation, located in the Far Eastern Federal District. Currently, the area of its territory occupies about 1/5 of the territory of the whole of Russia and is 308 million hectares. Moreover, 40% of the republic's area is located beyond the Arctic Circle. In this regard, the land fund of the republic requires careful study and monitoring in order to increase the efficiency of its use. The territory of Yakutia lies in three time zones, ahead of Moscow time by 6, 7 and 8 hours.

One of the main differences in the region is the sharply continental climate, which is

Figure 2. Structure of land resources of the Russian Federation by federal districts, %

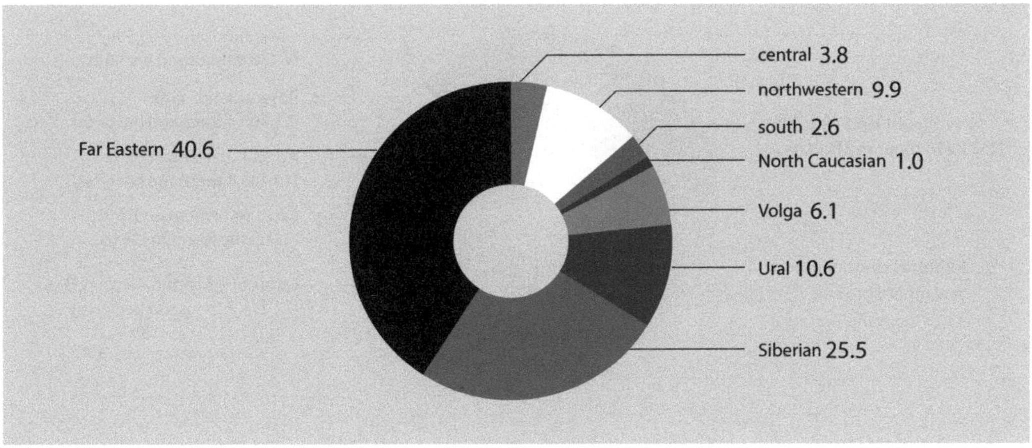

characterized by long winter and short summer periods. The maximum amplitude of the average temperatures of the coldest month (January) and the warmest (July) is 70-75 degrees Celsius.

Most of Yakutia is mountains and plateaus, and only a third of the territory is located in the lowlands. It is characterized by a variety of natural conditions and resources, which is due to its physical and geographical position. The territory falls within four geographical zones: taiga forests (about 80% of the area), tundra, forest-tundra and the Arctic desert.

3.2. The structure of land resources in the region

From an economic point of view, this is the region that gives one of the largest gross regional product among other regions of the Far Eastern Federal District, which amounted to more than 916 billion rubles in 2017 at current prices. The largest share in the gross regional product of the republic is occupied by the mining industry, whose share is 48.3% of the total gross regional product.

More than 80% of the territory of Yakutia is a forest fund, the total area of which is 252 million hectares, such categories of lands as agricultural lands, lands of specially protected

Figure 3. Structure of the land fund of the Republic of Sakha (Yakutia) by category of land, %

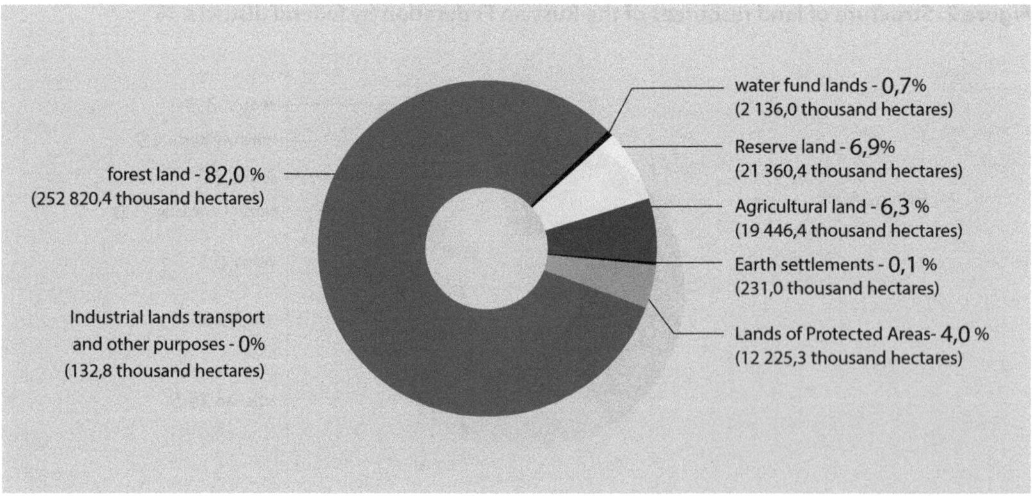

territories and lands of stocks, the total area of which in total is more than 17%, are of particular relevance or 53 million hectares.

The area of agricultural land over the past 20 years has decreased by more than 70%, primarily due to the transfer from them to the lands of other categories (forest fund, specially protected natural areas, settlements). The distribution of agricultural land of the republic by land is shown in the diagram.

The area of agricultural land has had a growth trend since the 90s, which in total increased by 108.2 thousand ha. As of January 1, 2018, the area of agricultural land was 1640.2 thousand ha (8.4% of the total area of this category of land).

The largest part of the republic's agricultural land falls on pastures and hayfields, the combined share of which is more than 90%. Arable lands make up only 6.4% or 105.1 thousand ha of land, while having negative dynamics, indicating an extremely low plowed area. It should be noted that in most regions of the country the share of plowed land is more than 60-70% of the land area of agricultural land. The decrease in the area of arable land is due to several reasons, such as the deterioration of soil quality: erosion, flooding. Arable land is overgrown

Figure 4. The structure of agricultural land of the Republic of Sakha (Yakutia) for the period from 1990 to 2017, %

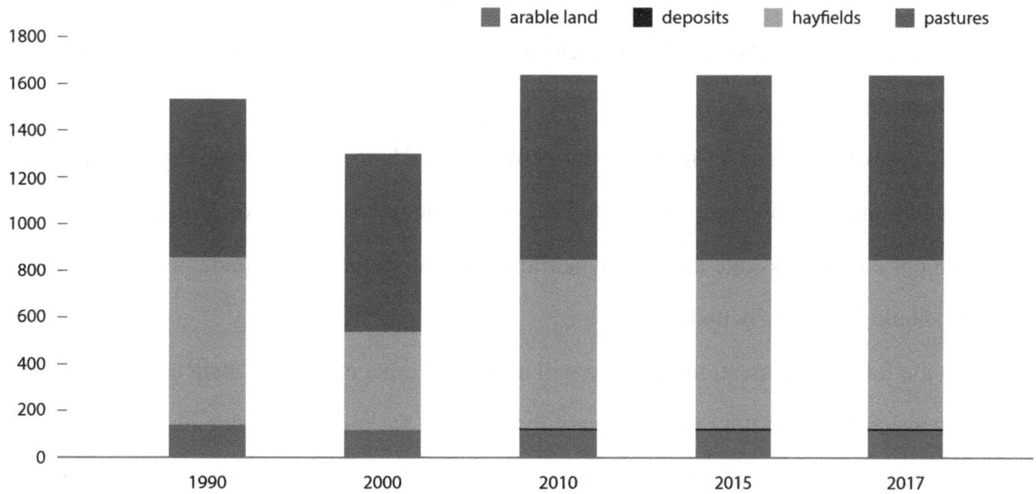

with bushes and swamped.

In recent years, the land, as one of the main natural resources, has experienced colossal anthropogenic pressures, in particular, the spreading of territories, various technogenic emissions, the reduction of forest land, extensive farming, chemical stress, and also ineffective reclamation measures. All of the above entails certain negative consequences that require careful monitoring of land resources.

IV. Conclusion

One of the main powers of the relevant government bodies is the creation of a legal framework that allows for measures to protect land resources, in particular, the implementation of sanctions for offenses in the field of land relations. But, the presence of only legal protection of land resources and land relations does not lead to the necessary increase in the effectiveness of its use.

Millennia ago, people switched from gathering and a nomadic way of life to an agricultural one, then to an industrial one, and in the 20th century to an information one. Now the next stage of evolution has begun: a digital society is emerging [5].

With the introduction of the digitalization of the economy both in the country and in the republic, modern approaches to the efficient use and management of land resources deserve special attention.

In this regard, the need to increase the efficiency of land use is especially relevant and in demand in order to prevent, reduce the factors of negative impact on it. The analysis of informational data on its state and the dynamics of negative factors is fundamental, including this data should be regularly updated.

Thus, the formed information database will allow solving a number of state tasks in the field of land management, updating the necessary information for all users, reducing anthropogenic pressures, negative factors affecting it, and increasing the efficiency of their use.

References

1. Земельный кодекс РФ от 25.10.2011 г. N 136-ФЗ. (The Land Code of the Russian Federation of October 25, 2011 N 136-ФЗ)
2. Указ Президента Республики Саха (Якутия) от 23 декабря 2011 года № 1126 «Об утверждении «Положения о порядке учета и регистрации государственных информационных систем Республики Саха (Якутия)»». (2. Decree of the President of the Republic of Sakha (Yakutia) dated December 23, 2011 No. 1126 On approval of the "Regulation on the procedure for recording and registration of state information systems of the Republic of Sakha (Yakutia)").
3. Государственные информационные ресурсы [Электронный ресурс]. URL: https://mininnovation.sakha.gov.ru/Gosudarstvennie-informatsionnie-sistemi/porjadok-ucheta-i-registratsii-gosudarstvennyh-informatsionnyh-sistem (дата обращения 10.11.2019). (State information resources [Electronic resource].
4. История земельных реформ в России [Электронный ресурс] // Юридическая энциклопедия «МИП». URL: https://advokat-malov.ru/pravo-na-zemlyu/istoriya-agrarnyh-reform-v-rossii.html. (Дата обращения: 25.03.2019). (The history of land reforms in Russia [Electronic resource] // Legal Encyclopedia "MIP").
5. Николаев М.Е. Познавать,чтобы созидать : от физико-математических олимпиад до Всеазиатской физической олимпиады / М.Е. Николаев, Якутск : Медиа-холдинг "Якутия", 2019. – 112 с. (5. Nikolaev M.E. Cognize to build: from physical and mathematical olympiads to the All-Asian physical olympiad / M.E. Nikolaev, Yakutsk: Media Holding "Yakutia," 2019. - 112 p.)

EVALUATION OF CHANGES IN THE ARCTIC FORESTS OF YAKUTIA IN THE CONDITIONS OF GLOBALIZATION

Romanov Prokopiy Georgievich
Candidate of sciencies in Technics, Associate professor, Institute of Engineering & Technology, NEFU
pg.romanov@mail.ru

Chakhov Dmitriy Konstantinivich
Candidate of sciencies in Technics, Associate professor, Head of department, Institute of Engineering & Technology, NEFU
tdodk@mail.ru

Lavrov Michail Frumentievich
Candidate of sciencies in Technics, Associate professor, Head of department, Institute of Engineering & Technology, NEFU
yakutia@lenta.ru

Ammosova Sargylana Polikarpovna
Director of Yakut branch of Federal state company «Roslesinforg»
Titov Denis Andreevich
Deputy director of Yakut branch of «Roslesinforg»
yakut.lp@roslesinforg.ru

Abstract.

The Arctic forests of Yakutia have a set of indicators that has developed to date as a result of their many years of development in the natural climatic, landscape environment of their growth. The territory of the Republic of Sakha (Yakutia) is a unique region with a harsh Arctic climate. The quality indicators of forest resources of the Republic of Sakha (Yakutia) of the Russian Federation are not sufficiently present in the resulting products. Therefore, their economic potential is not appreciated in the Russian and foreign markets. The high potential of the quality of the Yakutian Arctic forests is not reflected in current state program documentation; the management of forest quality does not meet the evolving challenges of globalization and international market relations. According to the indicators of the State Program "Development of the Forestry of the Russian Federation for 2013-2020," the amount of budget contributions to the system of the Russian Federation from used forests located on the lands of the forest fund per 1 ha of the forest fund of the Republic of Sakha (Yakutia) by the end of 2016 is 3.0 rubles, and by 2020 this figure should reach 5.7 rubles, i.e. should increase by 90%. In Primorskiy region, the same indicator, should respectively increase from 30 rubles in 2016 to 53.5 rubles in 2020, in the Amur Region from 14 to 33.9 rubles, in Sakhalin from 17.6 to 33.1 rubles. The average indicators for the Russian Federation are 25.7 rubles, with planned indicators of 48.7 rubles for 2020. Implementation of the goal to fully account forest resources with the use of modern methods of forest inventory, including space sensing of the ground, will allow the creation of high-quality database complying with the FSC (Forest Stewardship Council) requirement. FSC standards make it possible to trace the origin of forest products, including forest biomass as raw material for bioenergy. The most complete, up-to-date information will allow organizing effective scientific management of the quality of Arctic forest resources in the context of globalization.

Keywords - Arctic forests of Yakutia, dendrological passports, FSC requirements.

I. Introduction

The Arctic forests of Yakutia are one of the most important natural renewable resources. The value of all types of forest products in the context of globalization will grow steadily. It becomes relevant to assess current changes in the quality indicators of forests.

The forest industry of the Republic of Sakha (Yakutia) still does not fully realize its potential. The system of indicators of the State Program "Development of the Forestry of the

Russian Federation for 2013-2020" shows that the volume of payments to the budget system of the Russian Federation from used forests located on the lands of the forest fund per 1 ha of the forest fund of the Republic of Sakha (Yakutia) by the end of 2016 is 3.0 rubles, and by 2020 this figure should reach 5.7 rubles, i.e. should increase by 90%. The average indicators for the Russian Federation are 25.7 rubles, with planned indicators of 48.7 rubles for 2020 [1].

Along with the widely discussed industry problems that are characteristic of all forest and forest-rich regions, such as a certain depletion of transport-accessible woodlands, insufficient updating of logging and forestry equipment, high cost of building a road network for transporting timber, seasonality of operation of timber roads, lack of capacity for processing timber industry cargo in river ports and railway stations, in Yakutia, as in the Arctic region, there are new industry challenges directly resulting from globalization.

Globalization is also evident in the world trade in forest products. The requirements that were previously present in other areas of activity and consumption, such as the consumption of only final product that is obtained from natural or animal raw materials grown in certain humane, standardized, morally and ethically compliant to the requirements of modern humanistic democratic global society, recently began extending to the cultivation, production, processing and consumption of forest products. The modern global forestry products market requires that raw forest materials be harvested only in forests where growing, forest exploitation, logging, qualification assessment and processing meet the quality standards of international organizations such as the FSC (Forest Stewardship Council) and PEFC (The Programme for the Endorsement of Forest Certification).

II. Relevance of the question

2.1. Standarts of quality

The state of the issue is considered at the international level, at the level of the Russian Federation and at the level of the Arctic region with reserves of boreal forests, using the example of the Republic of Sakha (Yakutia).

25% of forests in the world is certified by the standards of quality of such international organizations as the FSC (Forest Stewardship Council), and the PEFC (The Programme for the Endorsement of Forest Certification). About the same share of various forest products on the world market complies with their quality standards, including "requirements for supply chains." Both of these organizations are present in the Russian Federation. FSC is more represented in the Russian forest industry, and taking into account the preferences of real foreign supply markets, cooperation with FSC may be more promising. According to the Russian office of FSC «as of 24 January 2019 more than 204 million hectares of forests (1585 forest management certificates) in 84 countries are certified in the FSC scheme. According to the UN (UNECE), the FSC work scheme is the fastest growing forest certification system in the world. The market for products with the FSC logo is estimated at tens of billions of dollars. 36,270 supply chain certificates were issued in 124 countries. Programs of public procurement of legal and certified forest products operate in more than 30 countries, including Australia, England, Brazil, Germany, China, Finland, Sweden, Japan and others. In Russia, 42.84 million ha of forests are certified [2].

2.2. Forest Code

In the Russian Federation, the current edition of the Forest Code, there is no norm for mandatory certification of standing timber, previously presented in art. 71 of the Code as revised in 1997. For effective supply of all types of Russian forest products to foreign markets, it is necessary to legally restore the mandatory forest certification; adapt the national certification system to the quality standards of international organizations based on the experience of the Russian Federation on voluntary certification of forests and forest products in areas such as in the Republic of Komi and the Far East. It must be taken into account that many forest and forest-rich regions of Russia have begun extensive preparatory work.

The development strategy of the forest complex of the Russian Federation refers to the lack of accuracy in accounting for forest resources as one of the most important factors for systemic problems in the field of forestry.

2.3. Forest certification

In the conditions of the Republic of Sakha (Yakutia), the activity of the Working Group on Forest Certification in the Republic of Sakha (Yakutia) is necessary. Its main purpose would be to develop Arctic regional criteria and standards for voluntary forest management certification, adapted to the standards of the FSC system and taking into account regional features of the quality of forests in Yakutia.

To solve this very important scientific and technical problem, the joint work of the Government of the Republic of Sakha (Yakutia), the Yakutsk branch of Roslesinforg, NEFU, academia, organizations of indigenous peoples and all interested parties is necessary. It is generally accepted that voluntary forest certification is evidence of environmentally, socially and economically responsible forest management. Introduction of standardized forest certification is in the interests of the entire community associated with forest management and residents of the whole republic. A methodology for standardizing the use of forests in places of traditional residence and economic activity of the indigenous peoples of Siberia and the Far East of the Russian Federation was developed and is being introduced. Monitoring and proposals for the further development of this methodology are required in relation to the conditions of sustainable forest management in Yakutia, including the development of Arctic regional criteria and standards for voluntary forest management certification.

III. Problems and practical results

3.1. Forest inventory as an important condition for ensuring the quality of forest management

In the Russian Federation, 8 forest-growing zones and 34 forest regions with relatively homogeneous forest-growing characters have been identified. Regional borders subdivide forest areas into 167 parts. In accordance with the established regionalization, the forests of Yakutia are located in 2 forest regions - in the East Siberian region of the near-tundra forests and sparse taiga and the East Siberian taiga permafrost region. The ongoing work in the conditions of Yakutia is supplemented and accompanied by the need to establish and clarify the boundaries of forestlands. Additional inventory work is expected in connection with the implementation of the law on the «Far Eastern Hectare program» and interests of hunting users. For example, in the Krasnoyarsk region, 8 forest regions are determined due to the geographical and climatic features of the predominantly meridional location of the territory and its unique landscape characteristics.

In this regard, the primary task for the Republic of Sakha (Yakutia) is the completion of the ongoing work on state forest inventory. This work is conducted according to the approved "Procedure for conducting a state forest inventory" and methodological recommendations for conducting a state forest inventory. Over the past 2018, according to Yakut Branch of Roslesinforg, inventory of total area of 41 million hectares in the territories of forestlands of Amginskiy, Vilyui, Gorniy, Megino-Kangalassky, Namskiy, Neryungri, Ust-Aldan, Ust-Maya, Khangalassky, Churapchinsky districts and Yakutsk. In 2019 the work covered the territories of Aldanskiy, Zhigansky, Mirny, Nyurbinsky, Suntarsky, Verkhnevilyuysky, Lensky, Olekminsky and Tattinsky forestlands and territory of the state natural reserve Olyokminskiy with an area of 120 million hectares [3].

The preliminary plan of the Federal Forestry Agency of the Russian Federation provides for an inventory of forests with a total area of 94.4 million hectares in the Verkhoyanskiy, Indigirsky, Kolyma Arctic forestlands, as well as in the Sangarsky and Tomponsky forestlands.

Work on forest inventory covers the entire spectrum of characteristics of the Arctic forests. Cycles of these works reach 10 years. State forest inventory data, among other things, is used as part of the implementation of international obligations: the UN Convention on Biological Diversity, the Kyoto Protocol and the Paris Agreement. In the course of the work, various indicators are determined, the analysis of which will provide data on the total reserves of wood and its quality, on the amount of carbon in various elements of the forest, the stability of forest ranges, the state of forest soils, and data on the ecological condition of forests. This information will be necessary for planning work on the development of the forest sector, the development of forecast models of the dynamics of forest ranges, to improve the forest management system, and organization of forest use. Forest inventory as the basis of international forest certification is complemented by dendrochronological studies. Dendrological studies of NEFU employees cover forests of all areas of growth, from the southern borders to the circumpolar zones. They are carried out with the active participation of European scientists and have high international recognition [4,5,6].

Yakut branch of the forest inventory organization of Russia "Roslesinforg" takes an active part in the ongoing broad exchange of views on various fields of activities. On 16 November 2018, the All-Russian Conference "Technological Initiatives in Accounting for Forests and Lands of the Forest Fund" was held in Novosibirsk. Within the framework of the conference, Dmitry A. Titov, Deputy Director of the Yakutsk branch of the Federal State Budgetary Institution Roslesinforg, presented during the discussion platform on the topic "Establishing the boundaries of forestlands and forest parks. Problems and solutions."

Problematic issues typical of many Arctic forest regions were highlighted

1. There is no single methodology for implementing technologies for mapping borders of forestlands and forest parks.
2. In the EGRN (Unified State Register of Real Estate) of the entire territory of the Republic of Sakha (Yakutia) the state cadastral registration is carried out in different coordinate systems. Settlements have their own local coordinate systems (MSK), often tied to conditional coordinate systems (USK). At the same time, inter-settlement territories, including lands of the forest fund, and lands of Arctic forests, are described in the topographic coordinate system of 1942 (SK-42). In a number of cases, it is not possible to correctly adapt objects in conditional coordinate systems to the state digital coordinate system, which is actually close to SK-42.

The solution may be to decide on transferring to the unified coordinate system of the region of the Russian Federation, in this case, the coordinate system of the Republic of Sakha (Yakutia), coordinated with the topographic system of the Russian Federation.

Currently, Yakutsk branch Roslesinforg is working to bring into conformity the borders of adjacent forestlands and adjacent forestland areas identified during forest inventory. Gaps between the borders of adjacent forestlands, overlap of the borders of adjacent forestlands, and other imperfections in forestry inventory were revealed. Recognition of borders by the latest year of forest management is accepted as a rule. In disputed cases, an appropriate opinion is requested from the authorized authority for forest relations in the region.

There are no legal grounds for adjusting the boundaries of forestlands along the boundaries of municipalities. Under current law, such an adjustment is possible only according to the results of the forest management. In this regard, the boundaries of municipalities (districts, settlements and rural settlements) are displayed on maps-diagrams of forestlands according to their actual coordinates, for the subsequent correction of inconsistencies in future forestry operations [12].

3.2. Scientific support for accounting forest resources

Dendrological passports have now become the most important document on the basis of which the criminalization of the industry is reduced, barriers to entry into the forest product markets of illegal logging are created, market preferences for legal forest products are being implemented. Dendrochronological examination has proven to be a reliable tool that allows reliable tracking the origin of felled wood. As an example, we can refer to the practice of forest certification and forest examination of forest products (mainly exported), based on the dendrological characteristics of the growing regions in Siberia and the north-west of the Russian Federation. Due to the relatively limited area of the central regions and territories and the climatic unity of the logging areas, dendrological passports have common characteristics there. In Yakutia, there are over 20 such indicated zones and subzones characterized by separate stable dendrological characteristics due to climatic diversity and landscape features. This work requires serious research, applied and legislative support, and should be carried out as a necessary part of forest inventory and certification qualities of forests of Yakutia. It is also necessary to take into account that standardization of solid biofuel is carried out within the framework of this work. The ability to trace the origin of biomass is an essential component of certification of biofuels and biomass as a promising forest product.

Under the conditions of possible climate change, dendrological studies improve the quality of the assessment of the anthropogenic impact on the environment. Their role in monitoring and forecasting climate changes, and the impact of these changes on the state of permafrost is important.

Northeastern Federal University has a long experience of cooperation with the forest industry. The Department of Technology of Woodworking and Wooden Structures has been working for 25 years. Bachelor's degrees in woodworking are offered. 20 funded places are allocated annually in this area. The researchers of the department obtained significant scientific and practical results in many aspects of this area of research [7,8,9].

3.3. Practical results

1. A serious body of scientific and applied results on wood science, on the study of the physico-mechanical properties of wood of various species of northern region has been accumulated; there is experience in certifying the quality of local pine. Along with this, further substantiation of the physico-mechanical, environmental, radiological characteristics of the Yakut wood of different growth zones is required. We need not only dendrological passport system and zoning, but also zoning in terms of strength of wood. The high strength of the wood of Yakut growth is due to harsh climatic conditions. A thin annual layer and a high content of more durable late wood form increased strength and resistance in comparison with the indicators given in the Codes of rules and norms for the design of building structures.

2. It should be noted that in the Russian Federation, as in most countries, the national forest inventory network is based on the use of a rectangular mesh of the national network, with reserve indicators and other characteristics per 1 hectare. Ground work should be accompanied by the operation of the satellite network of remote sensing of the earth (ERS). This requirement is enforced within the framework of the State Program "Development of the Forestry of the Russian Federation for 2013-2020." Trial sites are determined, inventory measures are carried out, and by comparing with remote sensing data, the satellite data decryption indicators

are adjusted. Scientists and specialists of NEFU can take a productive part in fulfilling this important governmental task. It is necessary to ensure the integration of a geographically distributed remote sensing information system with an information monitoring system, establishing the boundaries of forestlands and forest plots. Extensive work is to be performed on the vast territory of Yakutia (3.1 million sq. km), with a forest cover of 51%, in which the share of valuable forest stands in the forest land occupied by forest stands is 84.4% [1]. An additional difficulty lies in the ever-increasing imperfection of the available cartographic material of forestlands, topographic maps of settlements, and linear objects.

It is often extremely difficult to find compromises when using various cartographic sources, when necessary comparing and bringing them into line with remote sensing data. NEFU has significant experience in the scientific and practical work of the use of geographic information systems (GIS systems) [10]. This experience is quite helpful in tackling the complex scientific-practical tasks in question, in particular the Arctic region, and in the circumpolar region.

The establishment and clarification of the boundaries of forestlands and forest plots, directly related to the abovementioned problems of adapting previously existing ground-based cartographic data with the results of remote sensing, should be carried out simultaneously with a forest inventory. Borders of forestlands and the forest fund are entered in the state register of real estate objects, covered by cadastral registration. According to Yakutsk branch of Roslesinforg, in 2018 40 million hectares were documented in 9 forestland districts, and in 2019 - 45 million hectares in 7 forestland districts.

IV. Conclusion

In the course of working on the article, we came to the conclusion that the Republic of Sakha (Yakutia) should establish cooperation with the FSC bureau in Moscow and Krasnoyarsk, together with the federal forest authorities, NEFU should raise the quality of forest inventory to a higher level by organizing cooperation in space sensing of the earth, developing dendrological passports and passports of the origin of biomass as raw materials for bioenergy.

The FSC has developed a forest map of Russia indicating certified forest areas [11]. On the territory of Yakutia, only limited territories of inaccessible forest territories are designated. We should expect more complete information when processing the results of the state forest inventory of Yakutia and cooperation with the FSC. The strategic goal to increase the contribution of the forest sector to the socio-economic development of Yakutia as a constituent entity of the Russian Federation will be achieved, as well as to ensure environmental safety and stable satisfaction of public needs for forest resources and services.

The most complete, up to date information will allow organizing effective scientific management forest resource quality in the context of globalization.

References

1. Государственная программа Российской Федерации «Развитие лесного хозяйства» на 2013-2020 годы. С изменениями и дополнениями от 5 октября 2016г., 31 марта 2017 г., 30 марта 2018 г. gov.garant.ru. (The state program of the Russian Federation "Development of the Forestry" for 2013-2020. As amended on 5 October 2016, 31 March 2017, 30 March 2018. gov.garant ru.).
2. http://info.fsc.org.
3. Аммосова С.П. Ойуур докумуоннаах буолуохтаах. «Саха сирэ» хаһыат.№9(6149). С.20. (Ammosova S.P. Forest should have documents. "Sakha sire" newspaper. № 9 (6149). P 20.).
4. Wieczorek M., Kruse S., Jacobsen I., Nitze I., Herzschuh U., Kolmogorov A., Nikolaev A.N., Pestryakova L.A., Heinrich I. Disturbance effects on treeline larch-stands in the lower Kolyma river area (NE Siberia). Silva Fennica. 2017. T51. № 3. C. 1666.
5. Wieczorek M., Kruse S., Epp L.S., Zibulski R., Herzschuh U., Kolmogorov A., Nikolaev A.N., Pestryakova L.A., Heinrich I., Jeltsch F. Dissimilar responses of larch stands in northern Siberia to increasing temperatures – a field and simulation based

study. Ecology. 2017. T98. № 9. C. 2343-2355.

6. Николаев А.Н. Дендрохронологические исследования на Северо-Востоке России. В сборнике: Палеолимнология Северной Евразии. Опыт, методология, современное состояние. Proceeding of the International Conference. North-Eastern Federal University, Russian Academy of Sciences. 2016. С. 30-32. (Nikolaev A.N. Dendrochronological studies in the North-East of Russia. In the collection: Paleolimnology of Northern Eurasia. Experience, methodology, current status. Proceeding of the International Conference. North - Eastern Federal University, Russian Academy of Sciences. 2016. P. 30-32.).
7. Романов П.Г. Нормирование уровней расчетного сопротивления древесины лиственницы якутского произрастания. Научно-практическая конференция молодых ученых и аспирантов. Тезисы докладов. Якутск, 1995. С. 11. (Romanov P.G. Normalizing of levels of calculated resistance of larch wood of Yakut growth. Scientific and practical conference of young scientists and graduate students. Abstracts of reports. Yakutsk, 1995. P 11.).
8. Управление лесопромышленным бизнесом на основе стратегического планирования освоения лесных ресурсов региона (на примере стратегии развития лесопромышленного комплекса ООО «Алмас» Республики Саха (Якутия)): моногр./ под общ. Ред. А.В. Мехренцева. Чахов Д.К., Евсеев М.В., Аммосова С.П. и др. Екатеринбург: Урал.гос.лесотехн.ун-т, 2016. 256 с. (Management of the timber industry business on the basis of strategic planning of the development of forest resources in the region (on the example of the development strategy for the timber industry of OOO Almas of the Republic of Sakha (Yakutia)): monograph/ under general edition of Mehrentsev A.V. Chakhov D.K., Evseev M.V., Ammosova S.P. et al. Yekaterinburg: Ural.gos.lesotekhn.un-t, 2016.256 s.).
9. Лавров М.Ф., Левинская Г.Н. Пути повышения эффективности лесопереработки и потребления древесины в Якутии. III Всероссийская научно-практическая конференция «Современные проблемы строительства и жизнеобеспечения: безопасность, качество, энерго- и ресурсосбережение». Якутск, северо-Восточный федеральный университет имени М.К. Аммосова, 3-4 марта 2014 г. С. 145-152.

(Lavrov M.F., Levinskaya G.N. Ways to improve the efficiency of timber processing and wood consumption in Yakutia. III All-Russian scientific-practical conference "Modern problems of construction and life support: safety, quality, energy and resource conservation." Yakutsk, Northeast Federal University named after M.K. Ammosov, 3-4 March 2014. Pp. 145-152.).

10. Филиппова В.В., Саввинова А.Н. Уточнение мест традиционного проживания и традиционной хозяйственной деятельности коренных малочисленных народов Севера Якутии по разновременным картам. Вестник Северного (Арктического) федерального университета. Серия: Естественные науки. 2012. №2. С.34-39. (Filippova V.V., Savvinova A.N. Clarification of the places of traditional residence and traditional economic activity of the indigenous peoples of the North of Yakutia using multi-time maps. Bulletin of the Northern (Arctic) Federal University. Series: Natural Sciences. 2012. № 2. P. 34-39.)
11. http://maps.fsc.ru.
12. Якутский филиал Рослесинфорг. Техническая информация. 2018. Якутск. (Yakutsk branch of Roslesinforg. Technical information. 2018. Yakutsk.).

THE LEGAL STATUS OF THE WOOD BISON IN RUSSIA AND REPUBLIC SAKHA (YAKUTIA)

Anatoliy V. Chemezov
Postgraduate Student, Institute of Economics and Finance, NEFU
anatolychemezov@gmail.com

Roman Romanovich Nogovitsyn
Doctor of Economics, Professor, Institute of Economics and Finance, NEFU
nogovitsyn50@mail.ru

Abstract.

This article discusses process of determining legal status of a wood bison in Russian Federation. A description of the process of wood bison reintroduction in Republic Sakha (Yakutia), with key dates and events, starting with arrival of the first batch and ending with the release of the second batch of wood bison to the territory of Natural Park are given, provided a graph showing increasing number of wood bison in Republic Sakha (Yakutia), described issues of determining the legal status of the wood bison and introduction of this species in Red Book of Russian Federation and Red Book of Republic Sakha (Yakutia) with key dates, ending with the adoption of the draft resolution on inclusion in Red Book of Republic Sakha (Yakutia) . The description of Russian Federation Red Book, Red Book of Republic Sakha (Yakutia), the International Red Book (Red Book of the International Union for the Conservation of Nature), excerpts from legislation are given that justify the inclusion of a wood bison in their list, importance of including in this book, type of legislative protection and introduction of liability for harming described species. Followed by a historical example showing importance of legislative protection of a bison with description of the bison extermination in North America in the 19th century, including: a graphic depiction of a decrease in the habitat of a bison in North America at the end of the 19th century, the reasons for extermination, legislative acts adopted at that time and brief list of reasons causing their inefficiency, the role of private herds in the restoration of the population, followed by a section which is represented by the modern status of the wood bison in Canada and the United States with the division into regions, focused on Canada because of the large number of wood bison living there and because this country has been starting point of reintroduction project in Republic Sakha (Yakutia): the definition of the Species at Risk Act, actions concerning the wood bison in Canada, NatureServe ranking by region and in the whole country. Also presented other international and national agreements and lists that include or was including this kind with their description: IUCN and CITES, as well as the date of the status change. In conclusion, the legal status of the wood bison as a rare species included in Red Book of Republic Sakha (Yakutia) is assessed, which is sufficient to provide protection, but in order to develop project and spread wood bison to Siberia, they should be also included in Red Book of Russian Federation, which should provide them protection throughout entire Russian Federation. At the same time, importance of this protection was noted, based on the extermination example in North America, absence of political reasons for slowing down the decision-making process for protection was considered, and importance of monitoring implementation of laws regarding wood bison was noted. In the end, the importance of private herds in population restoring in North America, as well as the possibility of future use of the wood bison in agriculture under favorable conditions, are noted.

Keywords: Wood bison, bison, Republic of Sakha (Yakutia), legal status, Red Book, Red Book of Russian Federation, Red Book of Republic Sakha (Yakutia), IUCN Red Book, CITES.

I. Introduction

Wood bison (lat. Bison bison athabascae) - a separate northern subspecies or ecotype of the American bison. Bison themselves are an animal that reaches 3 meters in length and 2 meters in height. Mass of males can be above 900 kg., They are one of the largest land animals in North America. Originally lived in Western Europe, but over time, some moved to North America. As a result of changes in natural conditions, wood bison remained in only a few places: Siberia and North America. And later, as a result of human activity and further changes in natural conditions, the population in Siberia completely extinct. The most recent references to the wood bison are the bison bones in the sites of people near Lake Baikal, dating from the 9th – 10th centuries [4]. After the colonization of North America by European settlers, bison became again subject to extermination. Unlike the indigenous people, who had previously hunted their bison for personal use, in the 19th century hunters (both colonizers and the indigenous population) hunted bison for sale. As a result of this activity, as well as imported diseases and increased competition between species, number of bison in North America was reduced from tens of millions at the beginning of the century to less than a thousand by the end of the century.

This process was stopped by introduction and implementation of legislation aimed at protecting endangered species from extinction, after which slow process of restoration of this specie was started. By the beginning of the 21st century, the number of bison did not reach those values that were before the start of extermination, in which the diseases that infected entire herds (brucellosis and tuberculosis) had an important role x. In this regard, the need arose to create a geographically separated herd to protect against infection and ultimately led to the project of reintroduction of the wood bison in Republic Sakha (Yakutia), returning to the territory where the extinction of the species occurred long before the advent of the modern state and legislation, as a result of which the question of the legal status of the wood bison on the territory of Republic Sakha (Yakutia) and Russian Federation as a whole.

The purpose of this work is to determine the legal status of the wood bison in Republic Sakha (Yakutia) and Russian Federation and whether this is enough to protect this species.

Relevance of this issue is achieved stage of creating a free-living herd, which in future may cause a repeat of historical example of a bison and human collision, leading to a slowdown in population recovery, in the absence of legislative protection.

This work is presented in two main sections: the first is the "Legal status of wood bison in Republic Sakha Yakutia," which describes the process of reintroduction, determination of the legal status and the possibility of legislative protection in the framework of the Red Books. The second is the "Status of wood bison in North America," which describes the importance of legislative protection, exemplified by extermination and current status of the wood bison in Canada and the United States. The conclusion is given on the topic of work.

In this article there were used works of both local and foreign researchers: A.L. Popov (А.Л. Попов), R.N. Smetanin (Р.Н. Сметанин), P. Boyd, C. Cormack Gates, Andrew C. Eisenberg, Jean Dorst , Gary Wobeser, federal laws of Russian Federation, United States and Canada, information from different organizations of animal protection and bison associations of United States and Canada, press releases of republican ministries, news resources. Sources of graphic materials are described in the article itself.

II. Legal status of wood bison in Republic Sakha (Yakutia)

2.1. Reintroduction of wood bison in Republic Sakha (Yakutia)

The process of returning the wood bison to Yakutia began in 2006, with the signing of Agreement and Protocol of Agreement between Parks Agency of Canada, Ministry of Environment of Canada and Government of Republic Sakha (Yakutia). [2]

In April, first batch of 30 individuals, 15 females and 15 males, born in 2004 and 2005 (27 individuals in 2005 and 2 females and 1 male in 2004) were transported from the Elk Island Natural Park (Canada) to Central Yakutia nursery "Ust-Buotama" nature park "Lena pillars."

Young bison reached puberty in 2007, at the age of 2-3 years and gave birth to their first offspring in 2008, at the age of 2-4 years. In Canada, females begin to breed at the age of 2-3 years, males - at the age of 4-5 years. At the same age, females reached puberty in Yakutia. Males started breeding a year earlier than in Canada - in the 3rd year of life. One of the reasons for their earlier entry into reproduction when kept in Yakutia may be the absence of full-age bulls, which under normal conditions of existence suppress the sexual activity of young males. The influence of natural factors on their earlier maturation than in Canada is not excluded. In example, they include a high content of nutrients and carotenoids in northern plants, stimulating the reproduction of herbivores, which is confirmed in studies on the acclimatization of bison in Yakutia. [1]

In March 2011 was delivered second batch, including 30 wood bison: 10 males and 20 females, aged about 1 year, from the Canadian national park "Elk Island" (Canada) to Republic Sakha(Yakutia) as part of an agreement between the government of Republic Sakha and Canada to conserve an endangered species.

In March 2013, the third shipment of bison from Canada was transported. By agreement with the Government of Canada, the bison were transferred free of charge, but Republic Sakha (Yakutia) paid for the transportation. A batch of bison, consisting of 10 males and 20 females, was transported from Edmond (Canada) to the "Tympynay" nursery (Yakutia).

On November 23, 2017, the Ministry of Nature Protection of Republic Sakha(Yakutia) organized the release of the first batch of 30 wood bison, of which the majority are females and calves (total 6 males, 22 adults, 8 calves) into the natural habitat from nursery "Tympynay" to the territory of nature park "Blue," on the right bank of the river "blue." The number of bison at the time of release of the party in the nursery was 145 animals [8]. This event marked a key stage in the reintroduction of wood bison - the formation of a free herd living in natural conditions on the historical habitat [3].

Also, in connection with this event, the problem of determining the legal status of the wood bison on the territory of Republic Sakha (Yakutia) and in Russian Federation as a whole, the need for legislative protection from human influence, was especially acute. In March 2018, at a meeting with State Duma deputy Sergei Boyarsky, the Minister of Nature Protection of the Republic Sakhamin Afanasyev, evaluating the successful implementation of the project, noted

Figure 1. Growth dynamics of the stock of wood bison in Republic Sakha (Yakutia) by years

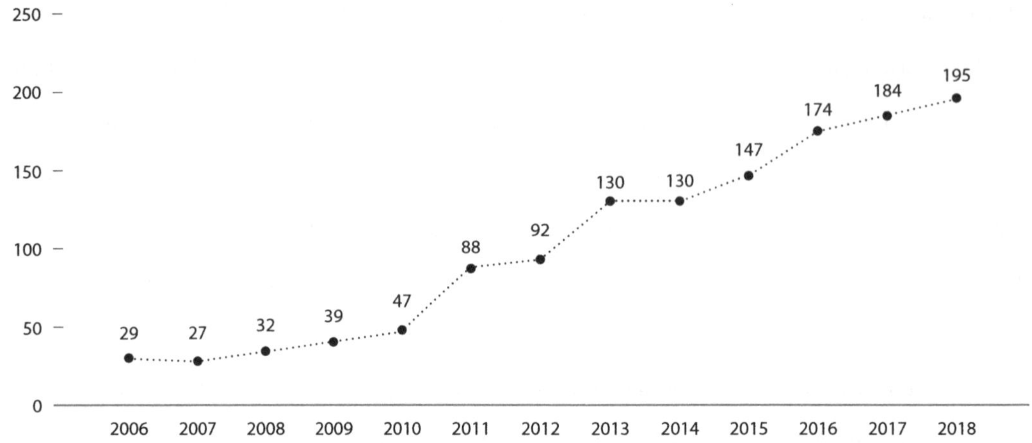

the problem of determining the legal status of the wood bison: "Given the release of animals into the natural habitat and the formation of a free-living herd, it is necessary to confirm the legal status of the wood bison, include it in the list of fauna of Russian Federation" [10].

The reintroduction of the wood bison was included in the state program "Ensuring Ecological Safety, Rational Nature Management and Forestry Development of Republic Sakha (Yakutia) for 2018 - 2022" and was designated as the main event "Re-acclimatization and resettlement of wild animals."

On July 7, 2018, the second herd of 30 animals was released from the "Tympinay" nursery, where at that time 147 individuals were kept in their natural habitat, in the territory of the "Blue" Natural Park. Second herd contained: 26 adult bison, 4 calves of 2017 year of birth - 11 males, 19 females. By this event, the bison number in Yakutia has reached 189 animals who lived in: Natural Park "Blue," "Tympynay" Nursery, "Ust-Buotoma" Nursery, "Orto Doydu" Zoo, and "Yakutia Living Diamonds" Natural Park. The number of animals in the wild was 60 animals. They chose the valleys of the park near the River "Blue" in the region of 50 kilometers from the "Tympynay" nursery. [10] Growth dynamics for the period 2006-2018 according to the Directorate of Biological Resources and Specially Protected Natural Areas of Republic Sakha (Yakutia) is presented in Figure 1.

As can be seen from the graph, the number of wood bison in republic is growing, and not only due to the delivering of new lots, which undoubtedly indicates success of reintroduction project. But this stage will inevitably lead to the moment when a natural park remote from settlements cannot protect mobile animals because of an increase in their number. As mentioned earlier, the problem arises of determining the legal status and legislative protection of a species.

2.2. Process of determining legal status of wood bison in Republic Sakha (Yakutia)

In September on the government commission, heads of region Aisen Nikolayev, announced a proposal to include wood bison in Red Book of Russian Federation. The proposal was supported by Russian Prime Minister Dmitry Medvedev and order was given to the Russian Ministry of Nature to work on this issue [7].

In late December, the report of Minister Sakhamin Afanasyev at a plenary meeting of the Ministry of Ecology, Nature Management and Forestry of Republic Sakha (Yakutia) reiterated the importance of determining the legal status of the wood bison [5].

On July 23, 2019, at a meeting of the Government of the republic, a draft resolution was approved on including the wood bison in the list of wildlife in Red Book of Yakutia with the initiative of the Minister of Ecology, Nature Management and Forestry of the Republic Sakhamin Afanasyev, he noted that: “In connection with the release of the first parties to the wood bison in their natural habitat, the issue of protecting free-living animals from poaching is an acute issue. If the protection of animals within Natural Park “Blue” is carried out within the framework of the legislation, then bison are in danger outside it. In this regard, it is necessary to add them to the list of rare and endangered species of animals of the republic. In case of successful rearing of the wood bison in the harsh conditions of Yakutia, there will be a prospect for further resettlement of the bison in the taiga zone of the North-East of Russian Federation.” Also, during the meeting, it was entrusted to the relevant ministry to strengthen work on the formation of a list of species for inclusion in Red Book of Russian Federation. [6]

According to Minister, protection of animals in territory of natural parks of Russian

Federation is carried out in accordance with Federal Law of March 14, 1995 No. 33-FL "On Specially Protected Natural Territories," in the case of a natural park with respect to section 4 (Articles 18-21) Natural parks. Clause 2 of Article 18 stipulates that: "Natural resources located within the boundaries of natural parks, unless otherwise provided by federal laws, are limited in civil circulation." Also, article 36 of this law establishes liability for violation of the regime of specially protected natural territories in the form of criminal liability or compensation for harm or restoration costs. [12]

The Red Book of Republic Sakha (Yakutia) is an official document containing a set of information on the status, distribution and protection measures for rare and endangered species (subspecies, populations) of wild animals, wild plants and fungi that live (growing) in Republic Sakha (Yakutia). It was established in 1984, the first edition was released in 1987. Now, it is regulated by the decree of the head of Republic Sakha (Yakutia) dated October 2, 2006 No. 2942 "On the Red Book of Republic Sakha (Yakutia)" (as amended on September 12, 2019). [11]

According to this decree and paragraph 6.4: "The basis for entry into the Red Book of Republic Sakha (Yakutia) or a change in the status category of an object of the animal and plant world, mushrooms is data on a dangerous reduction in its number and (or) range, on adverse changes in conditions the existence of this object or other evidence of the need for special measures to preserve and restore it." Wood bison, with about 200 individuals, rightly claim to be in the Red Book of Republic Sakha.

The importance of integrating species in this Red Book, as well as in the Red Book of Russian Federation is in paragraph 9.1 that prohibits the extraction of the species included in the book: "taking (catching, shooting, gathering) of fauna and flora, fungi, listed in the Red Book Republic Sakha(Yakutia), as well as their metabolic products (eggs, caviar, fruits, seeds, etc.) without special permission issued in the prescribed manner, as well as the destruction of their homes (nests, but also others) and places of growth, is prohibited." Also, further in clause 11.1 of the decree, liability for violation of the procedure for the protection and use of fauna objects listed in the Red Book of the Republic in the form of administrative, criminal liability and compensation for damage in accordance with the legislation of Russian Federation and

Republic Sakha(Yakutia) is defined: "Citizens, officials and legal entities guilty of causing harm in the illegal extraction or destruction of objects of animal and plant life, mushrooms listed in the Red Book of Republic Sakha(Yakutia), and their habitat, or in the commission of other actions Tweet, which can lead to disease, death, reduction in the number of these objects of the animal and plant world or to a violation of their habitat, as well as for their illegal extraction, sale or destruction are civilly, administratively and criminally liable and compensate for damage in accordance with the legislation of Russian Federation and Republic of Sakha (Yakutia)." [11]

2.3. Red Books of Russian Federation and IUCN

Despite the inclusion of the species in Red Book of Republic Sakha (Yakutia), as mentioned by Minister of Ecology, reintroduction project is planned to be expanded outside the republic, which makes it important to include wood bison in Red Book of Russian Federation and recognition as a rare and threatened species. To determine possibility and protection obtained from inclusion in Red Book, we address to federal laws governing this Red Book.

The Red Book of Russian Federation - the main state document, which includes a list of rare and endangered animals and plants of Russian Federation, based on Article 60 of the law and of Russian Federation "On Environmental Protection." Unlike many other Red Books (international and national), the inclusion of a species in the Red Book of Russian Federation leads to the appearance of legislative protection and the creation of a ban on the extraction of this species. According to article 60 of the federal law "On Environmental Protection" the inclusion of a species in the Red Book means that the species should be removed from economic use everywhere, its genetic fund preserved, and activities leading to a reduction in their numbers and worsening their habitat are prohibited. Failure to comply with this prohibition leads to an administrative fine in accordance with Article 8.35 of the Code of Russian Federation on Administrative Violations.

The basis for inclusion in the Red Book of Russian Federation in accordance with clause 3.4 of the Red Book maintenance procedure is "data on a dangerous reduction in its number and (or) range, ... , indicating the need for special measures to preserve and restore it," which is undoubtedly suitable for the species, the number of which in Russian Federation is about 200 individuals, as well as the presence of a wood bison in the IUCN Red List (International Union for Conservation of Nature). It is also worth considering that in the case of the Federal Laws of Russian Federation in relation to international treaties it is often spelled out that: "If the international treaty of Russian Federation establishes other rules than those provided for by this Federal law, then the rules of the international treaty apply" (Article 37 in Federal Law No. 33-FL "On specially protected natural territories" and Article 82 in the Federal Law No. 7-FL "On Environmental Protection"). [12, 13]

The IUCN Red List is the most comprehensive list of global species conservation status in the world. It uses a set of criteria to assess the risk of extinction of thousands of species and subspecies. These criteria apply to all species and all regions of the world. The IUCN Red Book, which has an extensive scientific base, is recognized as the most authoritative guide to the state of biological diversity. As an international organization, IUCN cannot directly influence on those who threaten species listed in the Red Book, but it works closely with the governments of the countries in which these species are located.

As of November 2019, the wood bison is in a state close to the vulnerable situation (Near Threatened), while the trend is stable and the number of the number of adults in North America there are between 11248 to 13123 individuals. It should be noted that the website of IUCN Wood bison are in a group with American bison (bison bison), their separation is described in the column "population." Also, the herd located in Republic Sakha (Yakutia) was not taken into account in the number and geographical position. [14]

III. Status of wood bison in North America

3.1. Extermination of bison in North America in the 19th century

To get an idea of importance of legislative protection of wood bison, we can address to historical experience related to the mass hunting of bison in North America in the 19th century.

If earlier the hunt for bison was carried out by local residents to provide for their needs (food, household items, religious and cultural features), then in the 19th century, when there was a great demand for bison skins in Europe, a mass hunt began to sell skins, tongues and bones, as well as weakening of Indian tribes and entertainment [18]. At the same time, influence of new settlers on the bison began even a century earlier: diseases imported from cattle struck the bison, crowding out species from the east of the continent to the west increased competition between wild horses and bison. Further, the subsequent displacement of the indigenous population at the beginning of the century (1820) also increased pressure on the bison. In the 1840s, the Indians began hunting for bison with the aim of marketing hides; in 1844, the hunting for bison in Canada also began.

The situation got worse with the appearance of railway in 1860 [18]. Herds of bison were divided into 2 main herds: southern and northern great herds, separated by rail. By 1870, two million bison were estimated to have been killed, a method was developed in Germany to make bison skins into fine leather, and bones began to be collected for fertilizer production, use in sugar production, and sold as fine bone to China. The year 1871 marked the beginning of the end of the southern great herd, hunting for bison became year-round, in connection with the previously described discovery of a method of skinning. In 1872 and in the following two years, 10 thousand hunters on the plains killed an average of 5,000 bison daily. Hunting for bison has become a popular attraction for the rich. In 1874, the great southern herd was almost destroyed. In 1877, the last wildly living bison in Texas were killed, while the extermination of bison in Canada was increasing. In 1880, the destruction of the northern great herd began, in 1882, hunters assumed that the bison had migrated to Canada, but by that time the herd had already been destroyed. By mid-1883, most bison in the United States were killed. The scale of the hunt led to the fact that the bison, the number of which by the beginning of the century was about 30 million, were almost exterminated and by the end of the century there were less than a thousand of them [18].

The extent of extermination can be estimated from the image of pastures in various years

Figure 2. Map of the extermination of the American bison at the end of the 19th century

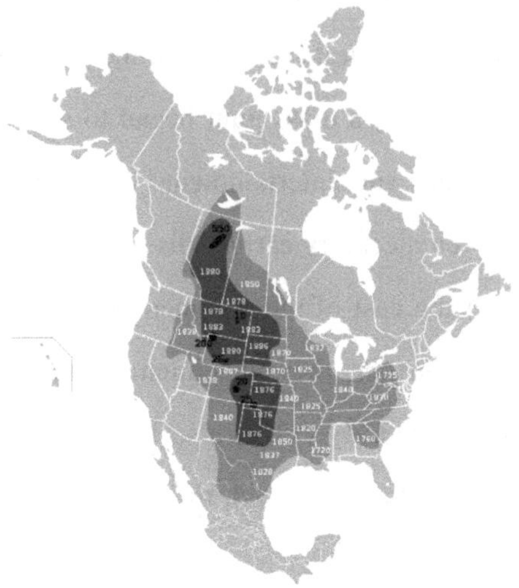

of the 19th century, shown in Figure 2, where the lightest are the original range, darker is the state in the 1870th and the darkest sections are the state in the 1889th year. The bright numbers are the dates of the destruction of the local herd, the dark are the surviving numbers for the 1889th year. The image is based on a picture submitted by William Temple Hornaday in Geographisches Handbuch zu Andrees Handatlas , vierte Auflage , Bielefeld und Leipzig , Velhagen und Klasing in 1902. An updated version of the drawing was taken from Wikimedia, because of the better image quality. [20]

Such a significant decrease in the number of bison led to the need for their legislative protection to prevent the extinction of the species. Between 1871 and 1876, several bills to ban the killing of a bison, other than using it for food or for personal use of hides, were proposed to the U.S. Territory Commission, Congress, and Senate, but for various reasons, the law does not protect bison was adopted , for example, in 1871, the delegate from Arizona R.K. McKormick introduced a bill prohibiting the killing of a bison in the US state territory, except for food or personal use, which included a penalty, in the form of a fine for each killed bison but the document was lost under strange circumstances.

In various states (for example, in the states of Idaho, Wyoming, Montana, Texas, Dakota, New Mexico, Colorado), local laws were passed to protect bison, but they did not have a strong effect as they were not implemented or there were no bison in these states: for example, in 1864, a law was adopted in Idaho to protect bison, but at that moment there were no bison in the state, the situation repeated in 1880 in New Mexico, and laws passed in Texas and Wyoming were passed but not implemented. [18]

In 1872, Yellowstone National Park was created to protect local species of animals, including bison. There were restrictions on hunting in the territory of this national park, but all the same, as a result of poaching of the 200 bison that lived in the park, only 25 remained by 1894. In 1894, the Law on the Protection of the National Park was adopted. This was the first federal law providing concrete protection to bison and setting a punishment of 2 years in prison or a fine of 1,000$ to anyone who would engage in theft of minerals, deforestation or hunting for game in the territory of the national park. [18] In 1900, the Lacey Act was passed prohibiting trade in illegally caught game, fish and plants, providing for administrative and criminal penalties for offenders.

It should be noted that the hunt was conducted in a completely predatory way, bison were initially killed only for their skins and tongues, which was considered a delicacy, skins were used for sale, later bones were used, but the rest of the carcass for the most part remained to rot. There were no quotas or restrictions on the number of animals killed. In this and in general, the importance of bison for the indigenous population had a role in the promotion and enforcement of laws. In a report of 1873, Secretary of the Interior Columbus Delano wrote that he was not very concerned about the disappearance of bison from the western prairies, affecting the Indians and rather perceives this as a measure to accelerate the Indians' dependence on agriculture and their own labor.

At the same time, in the 1870s, private herds for breeding bison began to appear in view of their commercial value, which played an important role in their conservation. By 1884, there were 325 bison in the United States, of which only 25 were in Yellowstone. In 1902, there were 700 bison in private herds and 23 in Yellowstone. A similar advantage, in favor of private herds, was preserved by the beginning of the 21st century. [18]

The end of the 19th century and the entire 20th century was time for the restoration of the population of the species. In 1905, the American Bison Society was founded and the processes of restoration of the bison population in national parks and herds and breeding of private herds began.

Also, in order to obtain a more complete picture of the situation with legal status, one should consider the experience of Canada, where the process of restoration of the population of the species began earlier and from where batches of bison were sent to the Republic Sakha (Yakutia).

At the beginning of the 19th century, the number of wood bison was 168 thousand individuals, which as a result of uncontrolled hunting decreased to 250 by the end of the century. In 1877, a Decree on the Protection of Bison was adopted, but due to the small number of police, it was not enforced and was canceled. The situation was repeated in 1893 and 1894 with the adoption of a new Decree on the protection of game. However, in 1897, the Northwest Mounted Police was given a law enforcement mandate and patrols were launched, which allowed them to execute these decrees and protect the remaining bison in Canada. [16]

3.2. The current status of wood bison in North America

The distribution of the species in North America occurs in Canada, with the exception of one population that lives freely in Alaska in the United States, which was released into the wild in 2015. Wood bison had been listed in the United States according to the "US Species at Risk Act: from endangered to threatened" in 2012. The US list was based on the number and status of the wood bison in Canada. The estimated number of wood bison in Canada is estimated at 8887.

The United States Species at Risk Act provides legislation to implement the provisions of the Convention on International Trade in Endangered Species of Wild Fauna and Flora. Its text contains a ban on the use of endangered species. The penalty for violating the prohibitions is various fines and imprisonment.

In Canada, the wood bison is considered "endangered" in the list of 1 Species at Risk Act (the Schedule 1 Species AT Risk Act).

Species at Risk Act (SARA) is part of Canadian federal law that became law in Canada on December 12, 2002. It is designed to fulfill one of Canada's key commitments under the International Convention on Biological Diversity. The purpose of this Act is to protect endangered or endangered organisms and their habitats. It also manages species that are not yet at risk, but whose existence or habitat is at risk. SARA defines a method for identifying the steps that need to be taken to help protect an existing relatively healthy environment and restore a threatened habitat, although the timing and implementation of restoration plans are limited. It identifies ways in which governments, organizations and individuals can work together to preserve species at risk and establishes penalties for non-compliance with the law.

In British Columbia, the wood bison is listed on the Red List of native species or subspecies that are endangered in British Columbia. In 2004, the Alberta Endangered Species Conservation Committee recommended that the Ministry of Sustainable Development of Resources include in the list of "endangered species" all bison living freely in Alberta. Currently, the only recorded bison in Alberta located within bison protection zone in the northwest of the province, where they are considered "endangered" in accordance with the "Law on the wild" of Alberta, and a local population in the area surrounding Lakes of Ronald, where they are considered "protected animals." in accordance with the "Law on the wild," limiting hunting of non-indigenous population. In the Northwest Territories, the species was rated as "endangered" and is considered to be included in the list of protected species in accordance with the "Species at Risk Act." Wood bison are not included in the list of "specially protected" in accordance with the "Law on the wild" in Yukon but recognized in the list of "Threatened" by the Committee for the Protection of endangered species in Canada. [15]

The subnational ratings of NatureServe, a nonprofit organization covering the conservation of biodiversity in nature in the United States, Canada, and Latin America (2015), are listed in Table 1. Since the 1980s, The Nature Conservancy and then NatureServe have assigned species different conservation status depending on their rarity. in the entire range, state, or state of the

Table 1. NatureServe (2015) Provincial and Territorial Assessments

State	Субнациональный рейтинг NatureServe
British Columbia (BC)	S2 – At risk
Alberta (AB)	S1 – Critically Endandered
Saskatchewan (SK)	SX – Probably extinct
Manitoba (MB)	SNA – Not Applicable
Northwest Territories (NT)	S2 – At risk
Yukon (YT)	S2S3 – Endangered

United States. The security status designation consists of two characters, the first of which is the letter G, N, S, E or T, the second is the character X, H or? or a number from 1 to 5. In our case (S is the status of an organism in the territory of a state subject, N is the status of an organism in the territory of a certain state, T is the status of a subspecies, X is the complete disappearance of a taxon in a specified territory, the decoding of the numbers is given after the ratings in the table and further in parentheses).

NatureServe (2015) rated the wood bison with Canadian national status N2N3 (at risk of vulnerability) and global T2 status (endangered). [15]

Characterizing the international attitude towards the wood bison, we can observe a tendency to restore the world's bison population and reduce the risk of extinction : in 2008, the International Union for Conservation of Nature (IUCN) raised the rating of the world's bison from "Low risk - depends on conservation" to "Endangered" in 1997 the Convention on international trade in endangered species of wild fauna and flora in endangered species (CITES), included in the list of wood bison from The Appendix I to The Appendix II. The wood bison was removed from Appendix II in 2017. [15]

The Convention on the International Trade in Endangered Species of Wild Fauna and Flora is an international agreement signed as a result of the IUCN resolution with the aim of suppressing the threat of species survival due to world trade in wild animals and plants. The list of species regulated by the convention is in the form of 3 appendices:

Appendix I contains endangered species whose trade has or may have an adverse effect on their existence;

Appendix II contains species that, although not necessarily endangered, may be endangered if trade in specimens of such species is not strictly regulated in order to prevent such use that is incompatible with their survival;

Appendix III contains all types that, by definition of any Party to the agreement, are subject to regulation within its jurisdiction in order to prevent or limit exploitation and in respect of which the cooperation of other parties in the control of trade is necessary.

IV. Conclusion

The materials studied, once again emphasize the importance of determining the legal status of the wood bison as a rare species and listing it in the Red Books. At the moment, the wood bison is included in the list of rare species of Republic Sakha (Yakutia). This is an undoubted advantage for the prospects for further development of the project and the success of reintroduction, as even outside of natural parks and nurseries, wood bison are protected by local legislation. It should be borne in mind that further reintroduction plans include not only the territory of Republic Sakha (Yakutia), but also the taiga zones of Russian Federation, which undoubtedly raises the question of including a wood bison in Red Book of Russian Federation , which will provide them protection already within Russian Federation.

When studying historical material about the extermination of bison in North America, the importance of this protection is once again emphasized, since bison are valuable prey for hunters, not only for the use of meat, skins and bones, which is not so true in the presence of global markets (but still being rare in the region), but as a new experience. The scale will be disproportionate but given the small number of the initial number of bison, the damage will be enormous. Avoid this negative experience and to take protective measures in advance, particularly given that there is no such politically e reasons s who were present at the time, on the local population. But it is also worth considering the economic and legal reasons that made it impossible to enforce laws in Canada and some US states. An adequate level of control over the implementation of legislation should be ensured.

It is also worth noting the importance of private and commercial use of the bison, which had a strong influence on the restoration of the population. Private herds were used to preserve and develop the population, which undoubtedly can be used in our region. But not within the framework of the current legislation prohibiting any commercial use, which should be further developed regarding bison and consider the possibility of developing a population with the creation and development of private herds. With the gradual restoration of the population under favorable conditions, the question of regulation will also arise outside the framework of a rare and endangered species. With a favorable outcome in the long run, it is possible to repeat the experience of the American bison, with the restoration of the population and use in agriculture

References

1. Попов А.Л. Реакклиматизация лесного бизона в таежной зоне Якутии (II этап) // Доклад. Протокол заседания Научно-технического совета Министерства охраны природы Республики Саха (Якутия). 2015. (A.L. Popov. Re-acclimatization of a wood bison in the taiga zone of Yakutia (stage II) // Report. Protocol of the meeting of the Scientific and Technical Council of the Ministry of Nature Protection of the Republic of Sakha (Yakutia) // URL: old.sakha.gov.ru/sites/default/files/5/files/Протокол%20НТС%2029_04_15.doc
2. Сметанин Р. Н. Лесной бизон в Якутии // Арктика XXI век. Естественные науки. 2017. №1 (5). (Smetanin R.N. Wood bison in Yakutia // Arctic XXI century. Natural Sciences. 2017. No1 (5).) // URL: https://cyberleninka.ru/article/n/lesnoy-bizon-v-yakutii
3. В дикую природу Якутии выпущена очередная партия лесных бизонов // Сетевое издание “Якутия.Инфо.” 2018. 11 июля. (The next batch of wood bison has been released into the wildlife of Yakutia // Network publication “Yakutia.Info.” 2018.11 July) // URL: http://yakutia.info/article/184761
4. В Якутии в дикую природу выпустили 30 бизонов // Всемирный фонд дикой природы (WWF). 2019. 24 ноября. (30 bison released into the wild in Yakutia // WWF.

2019.24 November.) // URL: https://wwf.ru/resources/news/bioraznoobrazie/v-yakutii-v-dikuyu-prirodu-vypustili-30-bizonov/

5. Доклад министра на пленарном заседании Годичного совещания Минэкологии РС(Я) // Пресс-центр Министерства экологии, природопользования и лесного хозяйства Республики Саха (Якутия). 2018. 21 дек. (Report of the Minister at the plenary meeting of the Annual Meeting of the Ministry of Ecology of the Republic of Sakha (Yakutia) // Press Center of the Ministry of Ecology, Nature Management and Forestry of the Republic of Sakha (Yakutia). 2018.21 December) // URL: https://minpriroda.sakha.gov.ru/news/front/view/id/2976734
6. Лесной бизон занесен в Красную книгу // Сетевое издание «SAKHALIFE.RU». 2019. 23 июля. (The wood bison is listed in the Red Book // Network publication "SAKHALIFE.RU." 2019.23 July.) // URL: https://sakhalife.ru/lesnoy-bizon-zanesen-v-krasnuyu-knigu/
7. Лесной бизон, обитающий в Якутии, может попасть в «Красную книгу России» // Якутское-Саха Информационное Агентство. 2018. 14 сен. (Wood bison living in Yakutia may get into the Red Book of Russia // Yakutsk-Sakha Information Agency. 2018.14 Sep) // URL: http://ysia.ru/lesnoj-bizon-obitayushhij-v-yakutii-mozhet-popast-v-krasnuyu-knigu-rossii/
8. Лесным бизонам в Якутии установили спутниковые радиоошейники // Сетевое издание "Информационное агентство YakutiaMedia." 2017. 12 сентября. (Satellite radio collars were installed in wood bison in Yakutia // YakutiaMedia News Agency Network Edition. 2017.12 September.) // URL: https://yakutiamedia.ru/news/621751/?from=70
9. Стадо 30 лесных бизонов выпустили на волю в Якутии // ТАСС, информационное агентство. 2018. 7 июля. (A herd of 30 wood bison was released into the wild in Yakutia // TASS, news agency. 2018.07 July) // URL: https://tass.ru/v-strane/5354824
10. Якутия предлагает включить лесных бизонов в Красную книгу России. // ТАСС, информационное агентство. 2018. 13 мар. (Yakutia proposes to include wood bison in the Red Book of Russia. // TASS, news agency. 2018.13 Mar.) // URL: https://tass.ru/obschestvo/5024396

11. Указ главы республики Саха (Якутия) «О Красной книге Республики Саха (Якутия)» от 2 октября 2006 года № 2942 (с изменениями на 12 сентября 2019 года) (Decree of the head of the Republic of Sakha (Yakutia) "On the Red Book of the Republic of Sakha (Yakutia)" dated October 2, 2006 No. 2942 (as amended on September 12, 2019) // URL: http://docs.cntd.ru/document/473504395
12. Федеральный закон "Об особо охраняемых природных территориях" от 14.03.1995 N 33-ФЗ (Federal Law "On Specially Protected Natural Areas" dated 03.03.1995 N 33-FL) // URL: http://base.garant.ru/10107990/
13. Федеральный закон "Об охране окружающей среды" от 10.01.2002 N 7-ФЗ (последняя редакция) (Federal Law "On Environmental Protection" dated 01.10.2002 N 7-FL (latest revision) // URL: http://www.consultant.ru/document/cons_doc_LAW_34823/
14. American Bison // IUCN 2019. URL: https://www.iucnredlist.org/species/2815/123789863#population
15. Wood Bison (Bison bison athabascae): recovery strategy in Canada 2018 // Government of Canada. URL: https://www.canada.ca/en/environment-climate-change/services/species-risk-public-registry/recovery-strategies/wood-bison-2018.html#toc5
16. Delaney P. Boyd and C. Cormack Gates. A Brief Review of the Status of Plains Bison in North America // URL: https://www.buffalofieldcampaign.org/archives/legal/esacitations/boydreviewstatus.pdf
17. Andrew C. Isenberg. The Destruction of the Bison An Environmental History 1750-1920.
18. TIME LINE of the AMERICAN BISON. National Bison Range Wildlife Refuge Complex URL: https://www.fws.gov/bisonrange/timeline.htm
19. History of Legislation. All About Bison URL: https://allaboutbison.com/history-of-legislation/
20. Extermination of bison to 1889. Wikimedia commons. URL: https://commons.wikimedia.org/wiki/File:Extermination_of_bison_to_1889.svg?uselang=ru
21. Жан Дорст. До того как умрет природа. Перевод с французского М.А.

Богуславской, Н.Б. Кобриной. Москва, "Прогресс," 1968г. (Jean Dorst . Before nature dies. Translation from french M.A. Boguslavskaya, N.B. Kobrinoy . Moscow, "Progress," 1968) // URL: http://www.igrunov.ru/vin/vchk-vin-discipl/ecology/books/vchk-vin-discipl-ecol-dorst.html

CHAPTER 3

ECONOMY AND LEGISLATION OF NORTHERN ENTERPRISE

THEORETICAL BASIS FOR THE ORGANIZATION OF INTERACTION OF CONSUMER COOPERATION WITH AGRICULTURAL PRODUCERS IN THE ARCTIC ZONE OF THE REPUBLIC OF SAKHA (YAKUTIA)

Vasiliy Dmitrievich Borisov
Candidate of Sciences in Economics, Associate Professor, Institute of Economics and Finance, NEFU
borisov_vd@bk.ru

Tatiana Dmitrievna Borisova
Candidate of Sciences in Economics, Associate Professor, Institute of Economics and Finance, NEFU
borisova_td@inbox.ru

Abstract.

In the article the authors investigate the increasing role of not only economic but also social development of consumer cooperation, that is, its qualitative improvement. The emerging economic and social prerequisites for the development of consumer cooperation contribute to increasing its role in creating a socially oriented economy of the country.

The government of the country does not consider cooperation as an independent economic force capable of having any significant impact on the course of economic transformations. The emerging external environment is aggressive towards cooperative forms of self-organization of the population. Investment-type companies of varying degrees of concentration of capital seek to consolidate the existing form of economic organization, actively promoting the advantages of the capitalist system of organization of social economy. Enormous efforts are directed to the formation of the mentality of the population, which is beneficial to large capitalist associations seeking to establish a modern system of formation and distribution of resources. Forms of economic interaction with agricultural producers are diverse, have different social and economic guidelines, differently affect the standard of living of the population and the economy of agricultural enterprises. The form and nature of interaction is influenced by the location of agricultural production, its specialization, concentration, cooperation and integration. Most of the relations between the participants of the agricultural market are regulated by economic contracts, which in their form can be contracts of sale, contracts concluded for a certain period. The successful solution of social problems at the present stage of improving socio-cultural and living conditions in rural areas is associated with the culture of service, availability and completeness of a set of trade services. Consumer cooperation, being a diversified economic system, is involved not only in the implementation of the final product of the agro-industrial complex, but also directly in its creation. Procurement activity of consumer cooperation enters a qualitatively new stage, due to the objective development of the processes of agro-industrial integration and inter-farm cooperation. Agriculture-the material basis of billets-in the conditions of the agro-industrial complex is increasingly focused on the production of an intermediate product. Procurement organizations to a much greater extent carry out the primary commodity processing of agricultural products and raw materials, and if necessary and appropriate produce a deep processing. Procurement, trade, industrial economic entities and consumer cooperation organizations together with agricultural enterprises, agro-industrial formations develop an extensive system of relations, which are made out of contracts of Contracting, supply and leasing. Such a system of relations contributes to a wide and increasing commodity exchange between agriculture and consumer cooperation.

In addition to the social and economic effect, purchases of agricultural products from the population stimulate the development of personal farmsteads.

The growth of total incomes of the population as a result of the purposeful organization of sales of agricultural products through consumer cooperation is due to a reduction in the number of trips to the city for shopping. Besides, the size of the expenses connected with transportation, part-time work, storage and realization of production of agriculture, at consumer cooperation is less, than at direct producers. The costs of circulation of consumer cooperation associated with the organization of sales of products of the population are also less than the individual costs of rural residents to sell this mass of goods.

Improving the relationship of consumer cooperation with agricultural producers should be directed:

- to coordinate its activities within the agro-industrial complex (in particular, on procurement, sales, and, especially, placement and joint use of the material and technical base of cooperative organizations);
- its participation in the creation and functioning of various forms of economic entities, together with other members of the agro-industrial complex;
- establishment of contractual relations with all types of agricultural economic entities, and, especially, with personal subsidiary farms of the population.

Keywords: cooperation, consumer cooperation, cooperative values, cooperative movement, cooperative unions, agricultural producers, the attitude of the state to cooperation, cooperative form of self-organization of people, food security, food service.

I. Introduction

Why cooperative values and principles are not used by modern management - a person uses only a familiar tool or before using it necessarily studies its capabilities, and our modern Manager does not study the possibilities of cooperation.

Cooperation as a special social and economic movement emerged more than two hundred years ago. To date, it has become one of the essential factors of socio-economic and cultural development in many States. According to the International cooperative Alliance, the cooperative sector exists in 100 countries of the world, individual members of cooperatives of various types are more than 760 million people. Important factors of success of cooperation are deeply developed theoretical bases of its activity, and rich historical experience.

Cooperative movement is a complex system that includes a variety of forms and types of human activity, legal norms, material resources, technical means, etc. therefore, cooperation and cooperative movement are the subject of study not only related Sciences, but also disciplines of different profiles.

Arising among the low-income part of the population about two centuries ago, the cooperation formulated the main task – to satisfy the immediate material needs of people: to feed, to create conditions for the reproduction of the family, that is keep at the level of understanding of the security that developed in society at that time.

The Arctic due to its vast territory, sparse population, off-road, inaccessibility is the poor part of the Republic of Sakha (Yakutia). Among 13 Arctic regions of the Republic in 6 regions: Anabarsky, Bulunsky, Oleneksky, Zhigansky, Ust-Yansky, Verkhoyansky, the population was provided with consumer goods and food through the system of the Union of consumer societies «Holbos» until 1991.

To improve the living standards of the inhabitants of the Arctic zone, the most appropriate mechanism is the interaction of consumer cooperation with agricultural producers.

II. History and theory of the cooperative movement

2.1. Theoretical basis

History and theory of the cooperative movement as a theoretical and fundamental discipline studying the most General aspects of cooperation: its nature and specificity as a special socio–economic organization, principles, methods and directions of its activities, the place and role of cooperative societies in economic and socio–political relations, peculiarities of various types, shapes and types of societies, the ideas of the theorists of the cooperative movement, economic and legal framework of cooperatives.

In the 21st century, the conditions for the development of cooperation are changing compared to the late 19th and early 20th centuries. The market economic system has reached a level of development at which the standard of living of the population of highly developed countries has significantly increased. The increase in the standard of living of the population is accompanied by individualization of needs and consumption.

Despite the separation of consumers, the formation of different levels of consumption of goods and services, the role of the cooperative movement in the 21st century is increasing. It becomes important as a factor of world economic development and the formation of national and world economic system, an alternative system, approved by transnational corporations, pursuing the goal of establishing a new world order, based on the unfair distribution of vital resources. In these conditions, the leading direction of the cooperative movement becomes cooperation in the sphere of circulation, occupying an intermediate position between the production and consumption of goods and services, which allows it to actively influence both production and consumption by implementing a certain marketing strategy.

One of the global problems of world development in the 21st century is the problem of formation and distribution of vital resources among the population of different countries in terms of their development. It is caused by the contradiction between the growth of the human population and the aggravated tasks of providing the population with energy, food and other vital resources. This problem is having an increasingly noticeable impact on the lives of the world's population, on the entire system of international relations. The achieved level of development of the market economic system allows to solve this problem in favor of economically developed countries at the expense of the population of other countries. At the same time, the prospects for economic development are characterized by uncertainty and the possibility of multivariance. Therefore, countries with post-industrial market economies are seeking to consolidate their dominant position in the world and the existing inequality in the distribution of resources. To this end, the process of globalization of the economy and the formation of an economic system in which most countries, including Russia, play the role of raw materials appendages, the resource base of developed post-industrial countries, is intensified.

The process of globalization causes the rejection of the majority of the world's population and forces to look for alternative forms of social order. Modern world development is based on the scientific and technical revolution, which requires constant updating of equipment and technology, which, in turn, requires creative dedication of employees. Such attitude to work is impossible by traditional methods of management, hired personnel, external control over employees. The alienation of workers from the property of management does not meet the nature of modern productive forces and the needs of their further development.

2.2. Globalization and cooperation

One of the options to counteract economic globalization, the successful development of the scientific and technological revolution is a cooperative form of self-organization of people. It is cooperation that can play an important role in solving this global problem through the formation of national and global economic sectors aimed at meeting the vital needs of the world's population. The cooperative movement can play a major role in the formation of a socially oriented economy in Russia. This requires the development of a strategy for the development of the cooperative movement of the country. The basis of such a strategy should be that the cooperative form of organization is only a means to an end, used by people to improve their socio-economic situation.

Cooperative forms of self-organization of people arise where and when there is a vital need for it, when people cannot solve the problems of their life individually or with the help of the state. The identification of this need is fundamental in the development of a strategy for the development of the national and global cooperative movement. Cooperative forms of organization are inherent in the market economic system and can operate effectively in the market economic environment. At the same time, it should be remembered that the economic activity of cooperatives achieves the greatest efficiency in the case of uniting people in order to solve vital needs that are otherwise extremely difficult to solve. Therefore, the fundamental question of the successful development of the cooperative movement is the search and identification of these needs.

III. The interaction of consumer cooperation organizations with agricultural organizations

3.1. Legal deficiencies in the development of cooperation

One of the directions of strategic development of cooperation can be the use of cooperative forms to overcome the crisis of the agro-industrial complex and, of course, social problems in the form of employment and ultimately in improving the standard of living of the rural population, and in the country solving the problem of ensuring food security of the state and the food problem in General. The solution of the food problem can be facilitated by the activities of cooperatives producing agricultural products, developing agricultural products and raw materials, expanding purchases of agricultural products and raw materials, expanding food production, as well as expanding trade in them.

Currently, the cooperative movement in the country is very poorly developed and is on the verge of losing its independent importance as a sector of the economy. There is a paradoxical situation in which, on the one hand, Russia has formed the economic and social prerequisites for the broad development of the cooperative movement, and on the other hand, the cooperative movement is experiencing a period of decline. This situation is explained by the influence of some external and internal factors.

The emerging external environment is aggressive towards cooperative forms of self-organization of the population. Investment-type companies of varying degrees of concentration of capital seek to consolidate the existing form of economic organization, actively promoting the advantages of the capitalist system of organization of social economy. Enormous efforts are directed to the formation of the mentality of the population, which is beneficial to large capitalist associations seeking to establish a modern system of formation and distribution of resources.

The government of the country does not consider cooperation as an independent economic force capable of having any significant impact on the course of economic transformations.

The state legislatively ignores the diversity of the cooperative movement, limits the number of types of cooperation.

The civil code of the Russian Federation recognizes only production, consumer and credit cooperatives, taking beyond the legal field of insurance, housing and construction garage and many other types of cooperative organizations. It splits the cooperative movement by granting tax and other benefits to some types of cooperatives and subjecting others to significant legal restrictions. In all areas of the economy, cooperative organizations are experiencing fierce competition. Participation in this competitive struggle at the present level of development of cooperation, in the conditions of its disunity leads either to the bankruptcy of cooperatives, or forces cooperatives to ignore the features of the cooperative form of organization and use the methods and principles of the investor-type companies.

Nascent cooperative forms of self-organization of the population meet on the way numerous difficulties, the most important of which is the weak development or even the complete lack of consistency in their activities.

In accordance with the methodology of the system approach, systems are distinguished from the external environment by their missions, goals. In addition, an important feature of the system is the presence of an internal organization, the interaction of its primary and other links at different levels of management. Cooperatives in their essence Express by their practical activities the social orientation of various types of cooperative movement and form their social base. Their activity in modern conditions of market economic system cannot be successful without Association with each other, formation of vertical and horizontal unions of various levels. The consolidation of cooperatives into unions offers them opportunities that they do not have individually.

3.2. Forms of economic interaction with agricultural producers

The diversified nature of consumer cooperation activities has led to its close ties with agricultural and production cooperatives, farmers and private households.

Forms of economic interaction with agricultural producers are diverse, have different social and economic guidelines, differently affect the standard of living of the population and the economy of agricultural enterprises. The form and nature of interaction is influenced by the location of agricultural production, its specialization, concentration, cooperation and integration. Most of the relations between the participants of the agricultural market are regulated by economic contracts, which in their form can be contracts of sale, contracts concluded for a certain period. The economic space of interaction in this case is limited, as a rule, to the local market of agricultural products.

We believe that the most important forms of interaction between consumer cooperation and agricultural cooperatives of commodity production should be considered:

- implementation of trade in consumer goods in rural areas and, thus, on the one hand, to meet the needs of the population, which is the basis of the labor resources of the agricultural sector, and on the other-assistance in the sale of products of agricultural producers and bringing the reproduction cycle of the complex to completion;
- organization of mass catering;
- procurement and processing of agricultural products and raw materials and, thus, ensuring the safety and marketing of products;
- performing the functions of social infrastructure in rural areas, that is, the provision of industrial and domestic services;
- benefits for social support of shareholders.

All forms of interaction can be divided into two types:

1) Interaction of wholesale, retail, procurement and processing enterprises of consumer cooperation with agricultural enterprises.
2) The interaction of cooperative enterprises with farms and private farms of the population.

The economic and social functions of all forms of interaction are very closely linked, complementary, and it is not possible to clearly distinguish their spheres.

Let's consider the main directions of the first type of this interaction. The greatest importance of consumer cooperation in the processes of sale and transportation of agricultural products is predetermined by its main function as part of the complex-bringing products to consumers. V. A. Matusevich believes that the target economic function of consumer cooperation is to bring material goods to consumers. This basic process and its continuity determine the functional content of consumer cooperation relations with other subjects of the agricultural market. Within the framework of the second type, there is a constant resumption of interaction between agriculture, state industry and trade, on the one hand, and procurement of agricultural products, its processing and sale to final consumption by consumer cooperation, on the other [3, p.68].

V. A. Matusevich revealing the importance of cooperative trade emphasized that it turns into an important factor of efficiency of agricultural production [3, p.104]. Selling consumer goods in rural areas, consumer cooperation acts as an important condition for the reproduction of labour in agriculture, improving the efficiency of the entire agro-industrial complex, as it serves about 70% of the labour resources of the complex in the zone of its presence. Consumer cooperation plays a leading role in ensuring the material needs of the rural population. Through cooperative trade and economic subjects of public catering to the rural population the huge mass of goods is realized. It is known that retail turnover is one of the important indicators of the material and cultural standard of living of the population, as its development is associated with the exchange of monetary income for consumer goods. And at the same time retail turnover can be considered as satisfaction of needs of the population. And the level and quality of life of the population, the close interaction of consumer cooperation with the population largely depends on how the process of meeting these needs takes place.

We would like to highlight the social function of co-operative trade in cooperation with agricultural producers of the bonus sales of the organization services to the rural population, the delivery of goods to release of goods in duty, the maintenance of unprofitable stores, reducing loss of free time for the purchase of goods in the trading network, etc. Marx pointed out: "As for the individual and for society, the comprehensiveness of its development, its consumption, and its activity depends on saving time. All economy ultimately comes down to saving time" [4]. The social significance of the interaction between consumer cooperation and agricultural producers is manifested in the satisfaction of the material and spiritual needs of the rural population.

A more complex form of interaction between cooperation and agricultural producers is inherent in mass nutrition. In our opinion, public catering of consumer cooperation solves a number of the most important economic and social problems:

- preservation and maintenance of health;
- allows to restore working capacity in a timely manner, thereby contributing to the growth of productivity of agricultural workers;
- increase of free time of the population,
- improvement of his life and restructuring of the household, because the time spent on cooking at catering enterprises is 5-6 times lower than in the household;
- rational use of labour, raw materials, fuel and other material resources, reducing food waste, saving energy resources.

A specific feature of catering is the simultaneous implementation of three functions: production, its implementation and the organization of consumption of ready food by the population

A. R. Bernwald, I. N. Voevoda believe that the successful solution of social problems at the present stage of improving socio-cultural and living conditions in rural areas is associated with the culture of service, availability and completeness of a set of trade services [2, p.59]. In our work, we fully agree with the opinion of R. N. Khairullin that public catering works with efficiency, has a high turnover and is not unprofitable, it is important not just to meet the needs of people in food, but also to meet their aesthetic needs. It is important that a visit to a restaurant, cafe, bar had its consequence not just saturation, but would bring a person joy from the range of services offered to him: dishes, environment, an organic element of which should be a good attitude to the visitor, and decoration, and music, etc. the Quality of service, the situation itself, everything should cause positive emotions, moral satisfaction [7, p.22].

Consumer cooperation, being a diversified economic system, is involved not only in the implementation of the final product of the agro-industrial complex, but also directly in its creation.

The range of goods produced by the cooperative industry is expanding, its sectoral structure and placement of enterprises are improving, they are approaching the sources of raw materials. Development of industrial activity of consumer cooperation is a stable source of increase of own commodity resources and strengthening of a financial condition.

IV. Ways of developing partnership of consumer cooperation with agricultural organizations

4.1. Partnership in the field of procurement and marketing of agricultural resources

The future of consumer cooperation is determined by the prospects for the development of agriculture, the entire production and social sphere of the village, which in turn is associated with the strengthening of the agro-industrial complex.

In our opinion, at the moment the main thing in the interaction of cooperative organizations and agricultural producers should be the procurement and processing of agricultural products and raw materials.

With the adoption of the RF Government resolution No. 24 of 07. 01. 1999 "on increasing the role of consumer cooperation in providing the population with food," immeasurably increases the role of cooperation in General and especially its production and procurement activities. These two branches of the diverse cooperative economy seem to be the key, the most promising, because there is no better way to earn money than by obtaining raw materials, to produce the necessary products themselves and sell them with the greatest economic benefit. This will increase the profitability of the entire system and, ultimately, the level of service to shareholders. The state Duma has introduced a draft law on amendments to the Forest code of the Russian Federation and the Federal Law "on consumer cooperation," designed to change the legal regulation of the collection, purchase and procurement of non-wood and food resources of the forest.

Changes not only the role of consumer cooperation in the procurement of agricultural products, but also its position in the process of organization and marketing. In the market of agricultural products and raw materials, it increasingly acts not as an intermediary, but as a counterparty to the customer, forming production plans in agricultural enterprises and farms on the basis of concluded contracts. At the same time, conditions are being created under which cooperation has great opportunities to improve the organization of purchases of agricultural products at prices that are low and non-standard to ensure intra-system needs, that is, the supply of products to cooperative trade and industry.

Procurement activity of consumer cooperation enters a qualitatively new stage, due to the objective development of the processes of agro-industrial integration and inter-farm cooperation. Agriculture-the material basis of billets-in the conditions of the agro-industrial complex is increasingly focused on the production of an intermediate product. Procurement organizations to a much greater extent carry out the primary commodity processing of agricultural products and raw materials, and if necessary and appropriate produce a deep processing. Procurement, trade, industrial economic entities and consumer cooperation organizations together with agricultural enterprises, agro-industrial formations develop an extensive system of relations, which are made out of contracts of Contracting, supply and leasing. Such a system of relations contributes to a wide and increasing commodity exchange between agriculture and consumer cooperation.

"The content of relations here has a pronounced social orientation. They reflect the relationship of consumer cooperation with the sphere of personal consumption in the process of meeting personal needs, improving the social and cultural level of service to the population," writes V. V. Apopiy [1, p.38].

4.2. The role of cooperation in increasing rural incomes

The development of cooperation with other subjects of the agricultural market and the population through the sale of agricultural products has an impact on the growth of incomes of the rural population, improving the structure of consumption, reducing labour costs for the sale of products and saving free time. The fact that the most bottleneck in agriculture - the sale of products, especially milk, potatoes and vegetables produced in remote areas from markets, small agricultural enterprises and farmsteads. Often, agricultural producers cannot sell their products, because they have neither the means for gasoline and delivery, nor the time to sell the products themselves. This problem is especially acute for remote settlements.

In addition to the social and economic effect, purchases of agricultural products from the population stimulate the development of personal farmsteads.

The growth of total incomes of the population as a result of the purposeful organization of sales of agricultural products through consumer cooperation is due to a reduction in the number of trips to the city for shopping. Besides, the size of the expenses connected with transportation, part-time work, storage and realization of production of agriculture, at consumer cooperation is less, than at direct producers. The costs of circulation of consumer cooperation associated with the organization of sales of products of the population are also less than the individual costs of rural residents to sell this mass of goods.

Thus, the expansion of purchases and sales of agricultural products through consumer cooperation due to their more efficient organization leads to the fact that the costs of this system increase to a lesser extent than the individual costs of the population and agricultural enterprises decrease. Consequently, the benefit is received by the whole society in the form of saving the full cost of money. It is also necessary to consider that the labour spent by producers on the sale of products can be more effectively used in agriculture itself to create agricultural products and raw materials. In addition, the increase in the volume of purchases of agricultural products increases the supply in the consumer market, contributes to its saturation, thereby reducing the deficit formed due to a sharp reduction in the import of imported goods.

Some forms of interaction serve as social shock absorbers, allowing to mitigate the severity of the social situation of villagers.

Thus, due to purchases, consumer cooperation meets the needs for raw materials of its processing shops and business entities of public catering. A certain part of the products is sold through the retail network, in municipal markets and in specialized stores in cities. The economic benefit of agricultural producers from this form of interaction is that the proceeds from the sale of farmstead owners of agricultural products gives a tangible increase in their cash income.

Due to a number of reasons, including those related to the reduction of production in rural economic entities, their difficult economic situation, the role of households as a source of food and the sale of surplus products to Supplement family income increases. And in many ways these farms from the utility are transformed into a commodity, into an object of primary employment of their members. This form of interaction created conditions for high motivation to work, increased employment in the field of small-scale agricultural production and served as a shock absorber of rural unemployment.

S. Polyansky accurately noted: "The most important, and probably the most unexpected result of the eight-year reform is the transformation of semi-natural private households of the population into one of the main sectors of agriculture. The reality surpassed all expectations: they ceased to be subsidiary and turned into the main source of income of the rural population" [5, p.33]. Continuing this idea, p. tillak and D. Epstein write: "Personal households of the population now perform buffer social functions, being for the majority of peasants an important source of income, food, employment" [6, p.57].

The social aspect of this interaction is that the population is given the opportunity to sell their products at the place of production. Reducing the time spent on the sale of products helps to save free time of the population. It is characteristic that for owners of farmsteads the economic and social functions are in contradiction: the more the family works, the less free time it has and, other things being equal, the greater its income, and Vice versa. The leading role in easing these contradictions belongs to procurement organizations of consumer cooperation.

In our opinion, when organizing ties and creating various forms of mutual cooperation, it is necessary to take into account not only their economic feasibility, but also their social orientation, since without a comprehensive approach it is impossible to organize a rational and effective system of ties.

V. Conclusion

Improving the relationship of consumer cooperation with agricultural producers should be directed:

- to coordinate its activities within the agro-industrial complex (in particular, on procurement, sales, and, especially, placement and joint use of the material and technical base of cooperative organizations);
- its participation in the creation and functioning of various forms of economic entities, together with other members of the agro-industrial complex;
- establishment of contractual relations with all types of agricultural economic entities, and, especially, with personal subsidiary farms of the population.

References:

1. Бойко В.И., Попков Ю.В. Развитие отношений к труду у народностей Севера. /Отв. ред. В. П. Фофанов; АН СССР, Сиб. отд., Ин-т истории, философии и филологии. - Новосибирск: Наука, Сиб. отд., 1987 - 172с. (Boyko V. I., Popkov Yu. V. Development of relations to labor among the peoples of the North. /OTV. ed. ed., In history, philosophy and Philology. - Novosibirsk: Nauka, Sib. ed., 1987- p.172).
2. Вопросы реформирования отношений собственности в потребительской кооперации (реферат по материалам исследования). - Новосибирск, СКА ПК, 1994. (Issues of reforming property relations in consumer cooperation (abstract based on the research). - Novosibirsk, SKA PK, 1994).
3. Матусевич В.А. Потребительская кооперация в агропромышленном комплексе страны. – М.: Экономика, 1980. – 175 с. (Matusevich V. A. Consumer cooperation in the agro-industrial complex of the country. - Moscow: Ekonomika, 1980 – p. 175).
4. Маркс К., Ф. Энгельс. Сочинения, Издание второе М.: Издательство политической литературы, 1981 г. (Marx K., F. Engels. Works, second Edition Moscow: Publishing house of

political literature, 1981).

5. Наговицина Л.П. Статистика советской кооперативной торговли: Учебник для студентов кооперативных вузов. - М.: Наука, 1991. - 219с. (Nagovitsina L. p. Statistics of Soviet cooperative trade: Textbook for students of cooperative universities. - Moscow: Nauka, 1991 – p. 219).
6. Ноздрева Р.Б., Цычичко Л.И. Маркетинг: Как побеждать на рынке. - М: Финансы и статистика, 1991. (Nozdryov, R. B., Tsygichko L. I. Marketing: How to win in the market. - M: Finance and statistics, 1991).
7. Опыт лучших японских фирм: пер. с англ. /Под ред. Мокринского Ю.Л., Новиковой Е.А. - Воронеж: ТОО - фирма "Тавров ЛТД", 1994.-137с. (Experience of the best Japanese firms: TRANS. / Edited by Mokrinsky Yu. L., Novikova E. A.-Voronezh: LLP-firm "Tavrov LTD", 1994 – p. 137).
8. Семенова Е.В. Операции с ценными бумагами: Российская практика: Учебник. - М.: Изд-во "Перспектива", Издательский дом "ИНФРА-М", 1997. - 328с. (Semenova E. V. Operations with securities: Russian practice: Textbook. - M.: publishing house "perspective," Publishing house "INFRA-M," 1997 – p. 328).
9. Сребник Б.В. Экономика торговли: Учебник для вузов. 2-е изд. - М.: Высшая школа, 1989. - 231с. (Srebnik B. V. Economics of trade: Textbook for universities. 2nd ed. - Moscow: Higher school, 1989 – p. 231).

ORGANIZATIONAL AND ECONOMIC BASES OF ORGANIC MARKET IN ARCTIC TERRITORIES: ON THE EXAMPLE OF REPUBLIC OF SAKHA (YAKUTIA)

Nikolai Petrovich Vasilev
Postgraduate Student, Institute of Economics and Finance, NEFU
v1nicolay@mail.ru

Larisa Ivanovna Danilova
Doctor of Economics, Institute of Economics and Finance, NEFU
dasarna@list.ru

Abstract.

The article discusses the organizational and economic foundations of the organic market, including the role of legislative regulation. The introduction introduces the concept of organic agriculture from IFOAM Organics International, which most fully reveals its essence. Briefly disclosed is one of the main reasons for the popularization of organic products. The basic data on the state of the global organic market are given. The current regulatory framework of the organic market in the Russian Federation is presented, including regional laws that were adopted before the law on organic products, which entered into force in January 2020. As a tool for analyzing the law, we used the recommendations for law developers from the Food and Agriculture Organization of the United Nations publication "Organic agriculture and the law," authored by E. Morgera, C.B. Caro, G.M. Durán. The analysis includes a comparison with the previous version of the law, as well as notes from the recommendations of the Agrarian Committee of the State Duma of the Russian Federation. The results of the analysis show that the adopted law has many problems and shortcomings, which may adversely affect the further development of organic agriculture in Russia. Despite this, the adoption of the law allows the subjects of the Russian Federation to adopt their own laws on its basis. The prerequisites for the further development of organic production in the Arctic on the example of Yakutia are outlined. At the beginning, the main characteristics of the Republic of Sakha (Yakutia), including its Arctic zone, are presented. Yakutia is a strategically important subject of the Russian Federation located on the north-eastern part of the Eurasian continent. The Republic is the largest region, the territory of which is larger than Argentina and slightly smaller than India. Yakutia is known as one of the coldest places in the world where people live, with diamonds, as well as a significant reserve of raw materials. The article separately presents the traditional directions of agriculture in Yakutia, including cattle breeding, herd horse breeding and reindeer herding. Due to climatic conditions, livestock breeding in the republic is more developed than crop production. Presented is the current state of agriculture, livestock and crop yields. The main problems and prospects of agriculture are highlighted, as well as the collection of wild plants is presented separately as a promising direction for the development of alternative agriculture. Recommendations are given on the formation of an organic market in the Arctic territories.

Keywords: organic market, organic products, organic agriculture, organic production, legislative regulation, law, Arctic

I. Introduction

What is organic agriculture? One of the most popular and comprehensive definitions is the IFAOM Organics International definition: “Organic Agriculture is a production system that sustains the health of soils, ecosystems and people. It relies on ecological processes, biodiversity and cycles adapted to local conditions, rather than the use of inputs with adverse effects. Organic Agriculture combines tradition, innovation and science to benefit the shared environment and promote fair relationships and a good quality of life for all involved” [9].

The main reason for the popularization of organic agriculture in the world was the intensification of agriculture since the middle of the last century. Mankind throughout the development of agriculture has tried to reduce its dependence on the environment, changing it for its own purposes, while depleting natural resources. Thanks to scientific and technological progress, it became possible to subjugate nature, controlling and managing many of its processes. On the one hand, this served as a result that the supply of agricultural products increased significantly, which in turn made it possible to solve the problem of food shortages in many countries of the world. On the other hand, this served to disrupt many of the natural relationships that lead to the destruction of the entire environmental system. Because of what, new global problems have appeared, which humanity has not previously encountered.

It became obvious that economic well-being achieved through environmental degradation threatens the existence of man as a biological species, his physical and mental health, and especially the health of future generations. The only way out of this situation is to find a stable balance between economic well-being and the preservation of a healthy environment, which will allow us to enter the sustainable development of society. Organic farming provides such opportunities [5].

Currently organic agriculture is a global trend. Every year, the number of countries in which organic production is practiced is growing, according to the latest official data, the number of countries has reached 181. The area of agricultural land occupied by organic production has grown by more than 20% over the year (2016 - 57.8 million ha against 2017 - 69.8 million ha) [6].

The market for organic products is the most dynamically developing food market in the world, the demand for organic products prevails over the supply. In 2017, the volume of the world organic market amounted to 97 billion US dollars (2016 - 89.7 billion US dollars) [6].

One of the most important roles in the development of organic markets playing legislative regulation. This is mainly due to the peculiarities of organic production and greenwashing, which is used quite actively in Russia and is not regulated in any way. Of 181 countries, laws were passed in 93, and in 16 countries laws are under development [6].

II. Legislative regulation of organic market in the Russian Federation

2.1. Current legal framework of the organic market in the Russian Federation

In Russian Federation the law on organic products adopted in 2018. Federal Law dated 03.08.2018 No. 280-FZ "On Organic Products and on Amending Certain Legislative Acts of the Russian Federation" will enter into force on January 1, 2020. For the first time, a bill regulating organic agriculture was considered back in 2002. During this time, the bill has been discussed and finalized many times; in all, about ten different options were put forward. In recent years, thanks to the activity of interested parties, the issue of law has been discussed more often, which has contributed to the long-awaited status of federal law.

The entry into force of this law should be an important stage in the development of organic agriculture and agriculture in general. The organic sector of agriculture in Russia has been forming since the beginning of the 2000s, despite this, it is at the initial stage of its formation in comparison with the countries where this sector is developed. The development and functioning of the organic market in Russia continue to go spontaneously. This situation is largely due to the fact that there was no legislative framework.

Prior to the adoption of the federal law, the only normative legal act in the field of organic production was the normative legal act of the Ministry of Health of the Russian Federation - Sanitary and Epidemiological Rules and Norms "Hygienic Requirements for the Safety and Nutritional Value of Food Products. SanPiN 2.3.2.1078-01," approved by the Decree of the Chief State Sanitary Doctor of the Russian Federation of November 14, 2001 No. 36. The section "Sanitary and epidemiological requirements for organic products" was included in 2008.

National standards were also developed and approved, which cover issues related to the application of the rules for the production of organic products:

- GOST R 56104-2014 Organic food products. Terms and Definitions;

- GOST R 56508-2015 Organic production. Rules for the production, storage, transportation (expired);

- GOST R 57022-2016 Organic products. The procedure for voluntary certification of organic production.

On January 1, 2018, the Interstate Standard GOST 33980-2016 "Organic Production. Rules for the production, processing, labeling and sale. NEQ CAC / GL 32-1999," adopted by the Eurasian Council for Standardization, Metrology and Certification (EACC). This interstate standard is valid in Russia and the CIS countries.

Prior to the adoption of the federal law on organic products, some constituent entities of the Russian Federation have already adopted their own legislative acts regulating organic agriculture:

- Law of the Ulyanovsk Region dated July 5, 2013 No. 106-ZO "On measures of state support for producers of organic products in the Ulyanovsk Region";
- Law of the Krasnodar Territory dated November 1, 2013 No. 2826-KZ "On the production of organic agricultural products in the Krasnodar Territory";
- Law of the Voronezh Region dated December 30, 2014 No. 226-OZ "On the Production of Organic Agricultural Products in the Voronezh Region."

Having familiarized ourselves with the current legislative framework, we will proceed directly to federal law No. 280-FZ. This law regulates relations associated with the production, storage, transportation, labeling and sale of organic products [2]. The draft of this federal law was developed taking into account the provisions provided for by the model law "On Ecological Agricultural Production" adopted by the Interparliamentary Assembly of the CIS (resolution No. 40-8 of April 18, 2014). When the bill passed the first reading in the State Duma of the Russian Federation, we made an analysis of the bill, which showed that there are a number of shortcomings and problems.

2.2. Analysis tool of the federal law on organic products

The main tool for analyzing the legislation on organic agriculture was the recommendations for draft law developers from the publication of the Food and Agriculture Organization of the

United Nations "Organic Agriculture and the law," authored by Elisa Morgera, Carmen Bullón Caro, Gracia Marin Durán. Based on these recommendations, you can not only develop a new law, but also analyze the existing one. To implement the latter, these recommendations were used.

Of the recommendations, it should be noted separately the level of detail of the law, which should be sufficient for independent functioning, but should not cover too many technical issues that could lead to a rapid loss of relevance of the law. It is noted that the basic law, at a minimum, should set out the main goals and principles, the powers and responsibilities of the relevant state bodies, the responsibilities of citizens and the procedures applied in accordance with this law. Legislators should also consider whether it is possible to directly refer to existing national or international standards in the legislation instead of a detailed listing of all actual rules [5, p.117].

According to the recommendations, the law can have the approximate structure given and cover the following provisions:

1.1 introductory provisions;

1.1.1 objectives;

1.1.2 principles;

1.1.3 scope;

1.1.4 definitions;

1.2 institutional set-up;

1.2.1 competent authority;

1.2.2 institutional coordination and public participation;

1.3 labelling;

1.4 rules for organic production;

1.4.1 general production;

1.4.2 production of plants and plant products;

1.4.3 production of animals and animal products;

1.4.4 handling and processing;

1.4.5 permitted inputs;

1.4.6 exclude methods and exceptions;

1.5 confirmation of assurance;

1.6 organic operators;

1.7 import and export;

1.8 non-compliance and offences;

1.9 promotional measures;

1.10 final provisions.

2.3. Results of analysis the federal law on organic products

We proceed directly to the analysis of the law itself and begin with introductory provisions in parallel comparing it with an early bill. In the "recommendations for draft law developers" these include objectives, principles, scope, definitions. The first thing to note is that the law has the same drawbacks as the bill at one time. In both, objectives are not set and main directions of state policy in the field of production of organic products are not indicated. Due to their absence, the impression is created that the law also has only the formal goal of securing organic production at the legislative level.

Earlier, the bill covered the principles of organic production, and the law decided to completely abandon this item. At the same time, the provisions that previously acted as principles in the clause of the requirement for the production of organic products were practically unchanged. The principles cited in the draft law needed to be clarified and supplemented and really resembled more requirements than principles. Based on the recommendations and laws of other countries and even regional laws, the establishment of principles is necessary, since they should act as the basis for the development of organic agriculture, which should guide all producers of organic products. It was possible to use the principles of the International Federation of Organic Agriculture Movement (IFOAM) as a basis, to which almost all countries where relevant laws were adopted were sent to.

The editors of the law got rid of the framework that the bill established in the subject of regulation of federal law. One of the main positive changes was that the law will apply to products obtained as a result of the collection and (or) processing of wild plants, fruits, berries and mushrooms, taking into account Russia's resource potential in this direction.

Let's move on to the next item - basic definitions. Only 3 definitions were given in the bill, which, in our opinion, was insufficient, given that the federal law should unify the basic concepts and provisions on which regions should rely when adopting their own law. The law left the same 3 definitions that were earlier, adjusted for the fact that the recommendations of the Committee on Agrarian Issues of the State Duma of the Russian Federation were partially taken into account. The law does not stand comparison with the same previously mentioned regional laws, which cover a wider range of concepts. In our opinion, the definition of organic agriculture given in the law still does not reflect the full essence of this concept. The definition that was given in GOST R 56104-2014 "Organic food products. Terms and definitions" reflect better and more closely to the international definition.

One of the main drawbacks of the bill was also that the basic rules and requirements for organic products were not reflected. Organic production requirements were partially reflected in the principles. Also, the conditions for the transition from traditional agricultural production to organic were not reflected, although this was mentioned in the explanatory note. In the adopted law, as previously mentioned, the principles became requirements, but there were no rules, and there weren't. Transition conditions have appeared that refer to the previously mentioned standards, which can be attributed to the positive aspects of the draft law, as, earlier, the law did not make any references to the standards.

When the law was amended, the recommendation of the Committee on Agrarian Issues to consider supplementing the bill with provisions on methods (methods) and features of organic production in relation to certain types of agricultural products (crop production, animal husbandry, including beekeeping, fish farming (aquaculture), etc.) was ignored.

It was also noted that the powers of state authorities of the constituent entities of the Russian Federation and local authorities in the field of production of organic products, which are completely removed and are not specified by law, are not specified. The mechanism for confirming the conformity of organic production as it has not been worked out and remained so. Thus, previously unforeseen mechanisms for holding unprincipled manufacturers accountable are still not disclosed, having only a mention of responsibility in accordance with the legislation of the Russian Federation.

State support for organic producers refers to the Federal Law "On the Development of Agriculture" and will be provided in the manner and forms established by this law [2]. This would be permissible if this law on organic products introduced significant changes to the law on the development of agriculture, but the amendments introduced, of which only 4, are exclusively "naming" in nature. Given the characteristics of organic production, including production, etc., and in general organic agriculture and the approach of other states to it (adoption of separate laws), support should also be isolated from traditional agriculture. Moreover, in the law itself, the requirements set apart the production of organic products from the production of products not related to organic products, and here the question arises why then support should be provided in the same manner and in the same forms.

The Committee on Agricultural Issues at one time supported the bill, subject to refinement, taking into account comments and suggestions. As a result, many comments and suggestions were not fully taken into account, and some were completely ignored.

Our conclusion was that the bill requires more thorough revision or even revision. This was justified by the fact that it was necessary to adopt a law on organic agriculture in a broader sense, and not just on the production of organic products, where many important provisions were not covered. The level of detail was insufficient, because of which the independence of the law was out of the question. The basic law, at a minimum, should set out the main goals and principles, the powers and duties of the relevant state bodies, the duties of citizens and the procedures applied in accordance with this law, but they were absent in the bill or they were set out, but not completely. The draft law regulates only the legal basis, although in our opinion it should also determine the economic, social and organizational basis for the production of organic products, aimed at ensuring the rational use of soils, promoting the formation of a healthy diet, protecting the environment, etc.

In relation to the law, the same conclusion can be drawn as the bill, adjusted for certain provisions that have been amended and added. In general, the adopted law remained the same framework as its bill. The law is so non-independent and not detailed that raises doubts about the justification of the status of "framework." As regards non-independence, the very name of the law is puzzling, in particular the second part "on amendments to certain legislative acts of the Russian Federation," given that only 2 laws are amended and then the concepts of "organic farming" and "organic production."

Due to insufficient diversification, problems may arise at the stage when the subjects of the Russian Federation begin to adopt their own laws. There is a high risk of contradictions between them, which can subsequently become a barrier when a single Russian market for organic products appears. Unfortunately, at least before the law comes into force, it is unlikely that any amendments and additions will be made.

Despite all of the above, the subjects of the Russian Federation at least have the opportunity to adopt their own law on the basis of a federal law and confidence in updating the development of organic production. Most regions are interested in creating regional markets for organic products, including the Republic of Sakha (Yakutia).

III. Prospects for the formation of an organic market in the Republic of Sakha (Yakutia)

3.1. Main characteristics of Republic Sakha (Yakutia)

The Republic of Sakha (Yakutia) is a strategically significant subject of the Russian Federation. Located in the north-eastern part of the Eurasian continent at the intersection of the shortest routes between Asia, Europe and America. Yakutia is the largest administrative-territorial unit in the world and, concurrently, the largest constituent entity of the Russian Federation (3.1 million km^2). Over 40% of the republic's territory is located beyond the Arctic Circle. The republic accounts for more than 30% of Russia's wildlife, or more than 10% of the entire world.

The population of the republic is about 1 million people (at the beginning of 2019 - 967 thousand people). In terms of population, the Republic of Sakha (Yakutia) takes 5th place in the Far Eastern Federal District and 56th place in Russia as a whole. The population density is one of the lowest in Russia (at the beginning of 2019 - 0.31 people per km^2). At the same time, the average population density in the Arctic Yakutia is 0.04 people per km^2.

Yakutia is known throughout the world as one of the coldest places on earth where people live, as well as diamonds and other reserves of mineral resources. Despite the cold and industrial extraction of raw materials, Yakutia is an agricultural region of Russia. Agriculture plays an important role in the economy of the republic, given that a third of the population lives in rural areas, where it is the main source of income, as well as the basis for ensuring food security.

One of the main sources of restraining the development of the economy of Yakutia is the natural and climatic conditions. Cold and permafrost significantly slow down industrial development, increasing costs due to which there is practically no industrial processing of raw materials in the republic. However, this influence is not only negative. Extreme climatic conditions have contributed to the formation of unique flora and fauna. The low level of industrial development and the lack of industrial processing of raw materials allow Yakutia to remain one of the most unpolluted ecologically clean places on earth.

The Republic of Sakha (Yakutia) has all the necessary prerequisites for the appearance and prospects for the further development of this market. Due to the vast territory and the natural resources located on it, as well as the favorable environmental situation, it has enormous potential in the production of organic products. Unique biodiversity can offer the same unique environmentally friendly products. It is important to note that one of the aspects of organic agriculture is the preservation of a favorable ecological environment, which has become one of the factors in popularizing organic production. Given the fragile ecosystem of Yakutia, organic farming is a great alternative to intensive.

As previously stated, without proper regulation, the formation of an organic market is

Figure 1. Regions (uluses) of the Republic of Sakha (Yakutia) that are part of the Arctic zone of the Russian Federation [15]

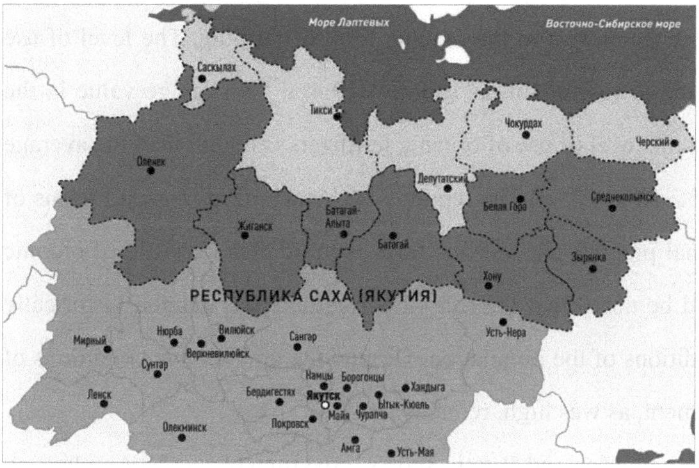

impossible, especially in the Arctic territories. In May 2019, 8 Arctic regions (uluses) of the Republic of Sakha (Yakutia) were included in the Arctic zone of the Russian Federation, so that programs for the development of the Arctic will operate on their territory. Previously, this zone included only 5 regions of the republic, which are located along the coast of the Arctic Ocean. Now 13 of the 34 municipal regions of the republic are officially included in the Arctic zone of the Russian Federation, their total territory is more than half of the territory of Yakutia (1.62 million km^2).

3.2. Agriculture and prospects of organic agriculture in Yakutia

It is well known that organic production, due to its characteristics, requires relatively large areas than traditional (intensive) agriculture. Because of this, it is worth noting separately the vast territory of the republic, which is poorly developed and minimally susceptible to pollution. In general, the environmental situation remains stable, which is confirmed by the annual reports of the Ministry of Ecology, Nature Management and Forestry of the Republic of Sakha (Yakutia). Over the past 5 years, there have been no cases of extremely high (exceeding the maximum one-time maximum permissible concentrations by 50 times) and high air pollution (above 10 MPC).

One of the main factors should be noted the agriculture of Yakutia itself. In the republic, the traditional way of agriculture still prevails, i.e. without the use of external aids (mineral fertilizers, pesticides, etc.), which is the closest to the organic form of farming. The level of use of mineral fertilizers is one of the lowest in Russia (RS(Y) - 29.4%; the average value in the Russian Federation is 53%), and the level of use of organic fertilizers is higher than the average Russian indicator (RS(Y) - 15.9%; RF - 9.3%). The republic is characterized by small forms of management and, as international practice shows, this form is more characteristic of organic production. In general, it should be noted that the role of agriculture was defined historically and is directly related to the traditions of the population. Despite the unfavorable conditions of conduct, the priority of development, as was high, remains so.

As the experience of foreign countries and Russia shows, government regulation plays an important role in the formation and functioning of the market for organic products, without which development proceeds spontaneously and unevenly. For the Republic of Sakha (Yakutia), due to extreme climatic conditions, state regulation is especially important for agriculture, without which development is almost impossible.

The law governing organic agriculture must take into account the characteristics of each territory; therefore, in the world there is no single law and a single logo for organic products. As we found out earlier, the federal law on organic products is of a framework nature. If the adoption of the law is sufficient for regions with developed agriculture, then for the Republic of Sakha (Yakutia), for the effective formation and development of a new sector, the creation of a new system is necessary.

The most appropriate will be the development and adoption of a concept (strategy) for the formation of the organic agricultural sector in the Republic of Sakha (Yakutia). The concept should define goals, priority tasks, basic mechanisms and represent a system of principles and priorities of state policy in the field of agriculture and ecology of the Republic of Sakha (Yakutia). The purpose of the concept is to justify the formation and development of the organic sector of agriculture as one of the priority areas for the development of the agro-industrial complex and rural territories, as well as the preservation of the ecological well-being of the Republic of

Sakha (Yakutia).

An important component of the concept should be the consideration of zonal climatic features of each agricultural region according to the agricultural zoning system of Yakutia.

As part of the concept, it is necessary to provide for the adoption of the republic's law on organic agriculture. Taking into account the analysis of the federal law, the regional law should cover all the main provisions that were not reflected in the federal one, such as the goal, main directions of state policy, rules, methods, etc., according to the recommendations of the FAO. Also based on the principles, rules and regulatory requirements of IFOAM, taking into account regional circumstances. In this case, one should take into account the experience of other constituent entities of the Russian Federation.

Currently, in Yakutia, in addition to the basic law governing agriculture (Law of the Republic of Sakha (Yakutia) dated 04/26/2016 No. 1619-3 No. 791-V "On the Development of Agriculture in the Republic of Sakha (Yakutia)"), laws are dedicated to certain unique branches of agriculture of the republic:

- The Law of the Republic of Sakha (Yakutia) dated June 25, 1997, 3 No. 179-I "On Northern Domestic Reindeer Herding";
- Law of the Republic of Sakha (Yakutia) dated June 7, 2001 No. 3 No. 297-II "On the Protection and Use of the Gene Pool of Yakut Cattle";
- Law of the Republic of Sakha (Yakutia) dated 10.06.2003 No. 53-3 No. 103-III "On herd horse breeding."

These laws can be a good tool for shaping the future legislative framework.

IV. Wild plants as part of the organic products market of the Republic of Sakha (Yakutia)

4.1. Current situation of wild collection in the world, Russia and Yakutia

One of the most promising parts of the organic market of Yakutia is the market of wild plants. Unlike cattle breeding, horse breeding and reindeer husbandry, which are regulated by the basic law on agriculture and their own laws, the collection of wild plants is not regulated in any way, which is why it is the least developed.

The advent of organic agriculture has given a new round to the development of the market of wild plants in the world. The collection of wild plants is defined in IFOAM (The IFOAM Norms for Organic Production and Processing, v. 2014), and is also regulated by the organic laws of the states. According to the Research Institute of Organic Agriculture (FiBL), in 2017 the area of land on which such activities can be carried out reached 40.99 million hectares (including land allocated for beekeeping). The "wild collection" is the most developed in Europe, despite its relatively small territories. The most successful country is Finland, which accounts for almost 30% of the total collection of wild plants (mainly berries) in the world (11.6 million hectares out of 40.99 million hectares) [5].

At present, Russia has important competitive advantages, having the resources to supply significant volumes of various forest products to the world market. Support and development of this direction can become an important component of the whole system of promoting Russian organic products on the world food market.

According to the Research Institute of Organic Agriculture (FiBL) in Russia, the area of organic land used for gathering wild plants (including beekeeping) is more than 30 thousand hectares (2017). Given the territory and estimated reserves of Russia, the country has great potential in the development of harvesting and processing of environmentally friendly wild plants, and also has experience, thanks to farms that are already engaged in this activity.

According to experts, Russia has enormous potential for the development of the wild plant market. According to the Ministry of Agriculture of the Russian Federation, reserves of wild raw materials are estimated at 8.5 million tons per year, but about 6% are used [8]. Every year, according to scientists, in the country harvested wild plants for 50 - 70 billion rubles. However, this is only an insignificant part of what was mined in the forests of the country 20 years ago. Then the harvest of wild plants exceeded the current three to five times [9].

Today in Russia there are three main regions for harvesting and processing wild plants:

the North-Western region (Karelia, Novgorod, Pskov and Arkhangelsk regions), the Central region (Vologda, Vladimir, Ivanovo and Kirov regions) and Siberia (Tomsk region, Altai and Krasnoyarsk Territory) [10].

One of the most promising regions for harvesting wild plants is the Far East, which occupies 41.1% of the territory of the Russian Federation. In the Far East, up to 30% of wild plant resources are concentrated, while the degree of development is not more than 5% of the possible volume of harvesting and sales [11]. About half of the territory of the Far East falls on the largest subject of the country - the Republic of Sakha (Yakutia).

As previously mentioned, the share of Yakutia accounts for more than 30% of Russia's wildlife, or more than 10% of the entire world, thanks to which, the republic has significant reserves of wild plants. According to the Institute of Biological Problems of Cryolithozone SB RAS, the total estimated area of land with the presence of berry-bearing massifs in the North is about 308 million hectares. Estimated berry reserves: lingonberries - 2.1 million tons on an area of 20 million hectares; blueberries - 0.6 million tons on an area of 4.6 million hectares.

There are 11 procurement enterprises in the republic located in 8 regions (uluses). In 2017, according to the Ministry of Agriculture and Food Policy of the Republic of Sakha (Yakutia), 129.6 tons of wild-growing raw materials were collected and about 288.2 tons of products were produced [12]. In previous periods, due to the lack of working capital for the purchase of raw materials (wild berries) in 2015, only 5 out of 11 enterprises worked, and in 2016, 9 enterprises.

Most of the harvesting of wild berries is carried out on the Central and Vilyui group of regions (uluses). This is due to the presence of sales markets (proximity to cities) and affordable transport infrastructure. The existing enterprises of the industry with a total capacity of 1.2 million cans per year are able to procure and process raw materials from wild berries on the territory of Yakutia.

4.2. Problems and prospects of wild collection in Yakutia

The main problems of harvesting and processing of wild plants in the Republic of Sakha (Yakutia), as well as in Russia as a whole, are the lack of working capital from enterprises for the purchase of raw materials, the low attractiveness of harvesting and processing of wild plants to attract credit and other sources of long-term and short-term financing. Also, one of the main problems is the lack of a full ecological and resource assessment of wild plant stocks; existing estimates do not fully reflect reality.

The inherent problems only for the republic are the pronounced seasonality of harvesting of wild plants due to climatic features, the lack of industrial processing of wild plants and the limited material and technical resources for the harvest and processing of wild plants. Separately, it is worth highlighting the problems of territorial fragmentation, including the remoteness from consumption and processing centers, as well as the inaccessibility of wild-growing areas.

Despite the existing problems, in Yakutia they are making a big bet on this area. At the end of October 2018, the Decree of the Head of the Republic of Sakha (Yakutia) "On strategic directions of the socio-economic development of the Republic of Sakha (Yakutia)" was adopted, which defines the priority goals of socio-economic development until 2024. Under the decree, the Government of the Republic of Sakha (Yakutia) was entrusted with the goal of developing non-primary export-oriented industries with high added value to ensure the formation of competitive sectors in the agro-industrial complex, the export share of which will be at least 20% of manufactured products by 2024 [2].

Harvesting and processing of wild plants should become one of such competitive sectors of the agro-industrial complex. This is confirmed by another Decree of the Head of the Republic of Sakha (Yakutia) "On strategic directions for the development of agriculture of the Republic of Sakha (Yakutia)," adopted in December 2018, which defines the priority goals for the development of agriculture in Yakutia until 2024. According to the decree, the Government of the Republic of Sakha (Yakutia) must ensure, by 2024, in addition to increasing the productivity of the main industries, increasing the capacity to produce products from wild raw materials from 180 to 8,000 tons per year with an export orientation [3].

In addition to software aimed at improving the economic and social efficiency of harvesting and processing of wild plants, taking into account export orientation, organic certification can play an important role in development, which will significantly increase the interest of potential subjects and / or countries of consumers.

The Republic of Sakha (Yakutia) has important competitive advantages that may contribute to the emergence of a market for organic products from wild raw materials:

- the presence of a vast territory, including forests, most of which are not affected and not polluted;
- unique biodiversity;
- the presence of unique varieties and species of wild plants;
- favorable environmental conditions;
- high priority for the development of rural areas, environmental protection, public health and future generations on the part of authorities, etc.

To use the existing competitive advantages, it is necessary to legislatively consolidate the production of organic products at the regional level. Especially important for wild plants is the provision on methods and features of organic production in relation to certain types of agricultural products, including products resulting from the collection and (or) processing of wild plants, fruits, berries and mushrooms.

V. Conclusion

In developing the law and for the further development of the market for organic products, it is necessary to attract attention and enlist the support of international and Russian organizations involved in the development and promotion of organic agriculture, emphasizing that the Republic of Sakha (Yakutia) can play an important role in the development and promotion of organic agriculture in the world. After all the preparatory measures, it is necessary to state and prove that the republic is really interested in the development of organic agriculture and can become an example for other countries and regions of Russia. The experience of Yakutia will be able to show that even under extreme climatic conditions, ecological agricultural production is possible.

For the republic, this will have a positive effect in quality:

- providing advisory and informational, including legal, support from leading specialists and industry experts;
- increasing the recognition of products manufactured on its territory in other markets;
- increase the image of the republic.

For organizations, this will have a positive effect in terms of promoting the organic movement, thereby increasing the demand for their services.

In the Republic of Sakha (Yakutia), agricultural exports may become a promising area of economic development, but for access to foreign markets it will be quoted only if it is environmentally friendly, which will be confirmed by appropriate certification. Because of this, the formation of an organic agriculture system becomes necessary in order to develop this direction.

References

1. Федеральный закон от 29.12.2006 №264-ФЗ «О развитии сельского хозяйства» (Federal Law of December 29, 2006 No. 264-FZ "On the Development of Agriculture." ATP "ConsultantPlus." –URL: http://www.consultant.ru/)
2. Федеральный закон от 03.08.2018 №280-ФЗ "Об органической продукции и о внесении изменений в отдельные законодательные акты Российской Федерации" (Federal Law dated 03.08.2018 No. 280-ФЗ "On Organic Products and on Amending Certain Legislative Acts of the Russian Federation." ATP "ConsultantPlus." – URL: http://www.consultant.ru/)
3. Указ Главы Республики Саха (Якутия) от 27.10.2018 №145 «О стратегических направлениях социально-экономического развития Республики Саха (Якутия)» (Decree of the Head of the Republic of Sakha (Yakutia) dated October 27, 2018 No. 145 "On strategic directions of the socio-economic development of the Republic of Sakha

(Yakutia)." URL: https://www.sakha.gov.ru/news/front/view/id/2956141)

4. Указ Главы Республики Саха от 11.12.2018 (Якутия) «О стратегических направлениях развития сельского хозяйства Республики Саха (Якутия)» (Decree of the Head of the Republic of Sakha dated December 12, 2018 (Yakutia) "On strategic directions for the development of agriculture in the Republic of Sakha (Yakutia)." URL: https://www.sakha.gov.ru/news/front/view/id/2973543)
5. Васильев Н.П. Разработка предложений в концепцию формирования органического сектора сельского хозяйства в Республике Саха (Якутия): диссертация магистра государственного и муниципального управления: 38.04.04. – Северо-Восточный федеральный университет, Якутск, 2018 – 104 с. (Научный руководитель – Данилова Л.И.) (Vasiliev N.P. Development of proposals for the concept of the formation of the organic sector of agriculture in the Republic of Sakha (Yakutia): the dissertation of the master of state and municipal administration: 38.04.04. – North Eastern Federal University, Yakutsk, 2018 - 104 p. (Scientific adviser - Danilova L.I.))
6. Elisa Morgera, Carmen Bullón Caro, Gracia Marín Durán. Organic agriculture and law. Food and Agriculture Organization of the United Nations. - Rome, 2015 - 224 p. URL: http://www.fao.org/3/a-i2718r.pdf
7. Willer H. and Lernoud J. (2019): The World of Organic Agriculture. Statistics and Emerging Trends 2019. Research Institute of Organic Agriculture (FIBL), Frick, and IFOAM-Organics International Bonn. URL: http://www.organic-world.net/yearbook/yearbook-2019.html
8. Website of the Food and Agriculture Organization of the United Nations. URL: http://www.fao.org/organicag/oa-faq/oa-faq1/en/
9. A Website of IFOAM - Organics International. URL: https://www.ifoam.bio/
10. Минсельхоз поддержит развитие заготовки и переработки дикоросов. Журнал «Агроинвестор» (The Ministry of Agriculture will support the development of harvesting and processing of wild plants. Magazine "Agroinvestor." URL: https://www.agroinvestor.ru/regions/news/30189-minselkhoz-podderzhit-razvitie-zagotovki-i-pererabotki-dikorosov/)

11. Что мешает жителям Дальнего Востока развивать заготовку дикоросов. ТАСС, информационное агентство (What prevents the inhabitants of the Far East from developing the harvest of wild plants. TASS, newsagency. URL: https://tass.ru/v-strane/5173825)
12. Подножный миллион: как томские предприниматели зарабатывают на дикоросах. РБК (Lifetime million: how Tomsk entrepreneurs earn on wild plants. RBC. URL: https://www.rbc.ru/own_business/03/04/2018/5abcde379a7947f405a5d2ed)
13. Дикоросы на Дальнем Востоке предлагают реализовывать через кооперативы. Рамблер (Wild plants in the Far East are offered to be sold through cooperatives. Rambler. URL: https://news.rambler.ru/other/39923420/?utm_content=rnews&utm_medium=read_more&utm_source=copylink)
14. В Якутии разработают эффективный механизм заготовки и переработки дикоросов. ЯСИА (In Yakutia, they will develop an effective mechanism for harvesting and processing wild plants. YSIA. URL: http://ysia.ru/v-yakutii-razrabotayut-effektivnyj-mehanizm-zagotovki-i-pererabotki-dikorosov/)
15. Site of the Northern Forum. URL: https://www.northernforum.org/en/news-ru/537-arkticheskaya-zona-rossii-popolnilas-vosemyu-rajonami-yakutii

DEVELOPMENT OF TRADITIONAL NATURE MANAGEMENT IN THE CONDITIONS OF INDUSTRIAL DEVELOPMENT OF THE TERRITORIES OF THE OLENEK EVENKIY NATIONAL AREA

Maria Ivanovna Nikolaeva
Bachelor student, Institute of Economics and Finance, NEFU
nicmaiv2010-1@mail.r

Roman Romanovich Nogovytsyn
Doctor of Economics, Professor, Institute of Economics and Finance, NEFU
nogovitsyn50@mail.ru

Abstract.

Traditional nature management in the Far North is a necessary condition for the existence of small indigenous peoples of the North. The life and activity of indigenous peoples is a historical experiencc of a unique ecological culture, which is constantly accumulated and is the development of all mankind. Due to poorly studied, inaccessible areas, harsh climatic conditions and lagging in economic development, the system of traditional environmental management in the Far North of Yakutia requires a detailed study and rethinking of all problems of an economic nature.

This article analyzes the state of traditional nature management (reindeer herding, animal husbandry) on the example of the Olenek Evenk National District, the activities of mining companies and their possible contribution to solving this problem in order to identify prospects for the further development of traditional nature management in the conditions of the Far North of Yakutia.

The peoples of the Far North are the indigenous peoples of the North, which have long since ensured their existence with domestic reindeer herding, hunting for wild deer, giving up furs and catching fish. This tradition has been preserved to this day. The territories where mining companies work - this is primeval nature, flora and fauna, places of migration of wild deer, the life of local residents is unthinkable without all this.

Over the past 10 years, a decrease in the number of domestic reindeer in reindeer herds of the Olenek district of Yakutia has been observed. The current situation is not a reason to leave these territories without attention, but rather requires the involvement of investors to develop and strengthen the material and technical base of traditional environmental facilities.

Considering the present situation of the traditional branches of the region, it is necessary to identify the prospects for the development of traditional environmental management in the territory of the Olenek district of Yakutia in the context of the development of the mining industry. To accomplish this goal it is necessary:

- to study and analyze the state of traditional environmental management activities of industrial companies, their contribution to the socio-economic development of the Olenek region;
- based on the data obtained to identify the prospects and further joint cooperation of industrial companies and the region in the socio-economic development and strengthening the material and technical bases of traditional environmental management.

Keywords: traditional nature management, indigenous peoples, reindeer herding, industry, subsoil users, rare-earth metals.

I. Introduction

Northern domestic reindeer herding is the main traditional economic activity of the region. In the 60–70s of the twentieth century, the area was one of the leading reindeer herding centers in Yakutia, with 10.1% of the deer population of the entire republic. In the 1970s-1980s, the output number of reindeer reached more than 30.0 thousand heads, the net profit from reindeer husbandry amounted to 900.0 thousand rubles, the state surrendered up to 700 tons of meat per year. Since 1991, significant changes have been recorded in the direction of reducing the number of reindeer [2].

Currently, in the Olenyok district there are 4 settlements as part of four rural settlements (see Table 1). The district takes first place in the region.

The basis of the region's economy is agriculture (reindeer herding, livestock breeding) and hunting.

There are 2 agricultural municipal unitary enterprises in the district, the main activity of which is raising domestic deer and hunting. The structure of agricultural production also includes 4 cooperatives, 29 nomadic tribal communities, peasant and personal subsidiary plots.

Table 1. Composition of the MR "Olenek Evenki National District" [3]

№	Rural settlement	Administrative center	Population, number of people	Area, in hectares
1	Olenek National nasleg	Olenek	2139	28737,02
2	Kirbey National nasleg	Kharyyalakh	837	176044,20
3	Zhilindinsky national nasleg	Gilinda	684	89988,44
4	Shologon national nasleg	Eyik	323	23206,40

II. Analysis of financial and economic activities of agricultural enterprises in the Olenek district

2.1. Reindeer herding

Agricultural production currently remains unprofitable. Analysis of the financial and economic activities of agricultural enterprises showed the effect of rising production costs on increasing the cost of production.

The combination of negative factors in agricultural management in the 90s of the last century led to a deterioration in the quality of livestock, horse breeding and reindeer herding. Only in recent years there have been significant changes in the direction of increasing the number of farm animals. This was facilitated by the measures taken to support agricultural enterprises. The collapse of the previously existing system of centralized deliveries of agricultural products and fisheries led to the need to improve the market for local products, to create a flexible procurement and marketing system. In the conditions of a regulated market economy and with effective state support, production and economic activity in agriculture, as well as in the industrial sector, in the future may become one of the locomotives of the region's economy, contribute to the development of the food industry, the creation of new jobs, improving the living standards and welfare of the local population [3].

Currently, there are 4,643 reindeers in the district, which is only 2.7% of the total number of reindeer population in the republic (see Figure 1) [8].

According to the data obtained, it is clear that in recent years there has been a decline in the livestock of deer. I believe that the main reasons for the decrease in the number of deer in the area are:

- Insufficient material and technical equipment of the reindeer herding bases;
- Lack of professional staff caused by the low level and quality of life in rural areas;
- Low level of market infrastructure development;
- Remoteness and inaccessibility of some settlements from the district center;
- Extermination of domestic deer by wolves;

Figure 1. The number of reindeer in the Olenek region from 1991 - 2017 years, the number of heads.

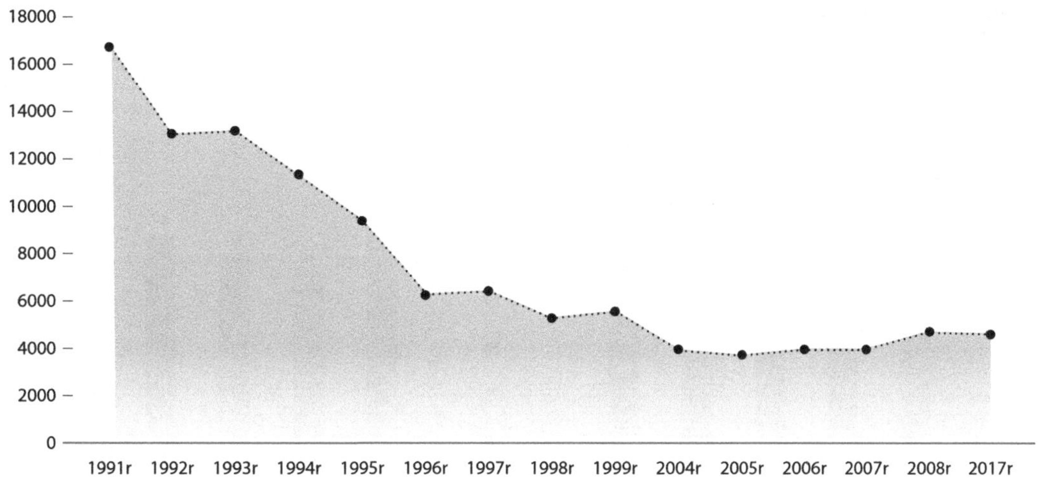

- Wild domesticated deer. In 2008, wild deer took away more than a thousand domestic deer from the municipal unitary enterprise Oleneksky [8].

2.2. Cattle breeding

Cattle breeding is mainly done by central, trans-river and Vilyuisk groups of regions of the republic, which contain 92.0% of the total livestock population.

Cattle breeding on the territory of the Olenek district is practiced only in one nasleg - Shologonsky, the village of Eyyik, which is located 550 kilometers from the district center of the village Olenek and approximately 2,800 kilometers by road from Yakutsk. In the summer time there is no constant air and ground communication with the village, complicating flight absence in Eyike airport.

According to the static data of 2017, 345 people live in [8]. The main areas of economic activity are hunting, livestock and horse breeding. Currently in the village there are about a hundred heads of cattle, horses are much smaller. Since 2004, cattle and horse-breeding farms have been in the balance of the agro-profiled school. On the basis of the farm and horse camp, summer labor camps are held with the involvement of local personnel. Mowing works are

Figure 2. Dynamics of livestock of cattle (Biyan farm) in Shologonsky nasleg of the Olenek region from 2013 to 2017

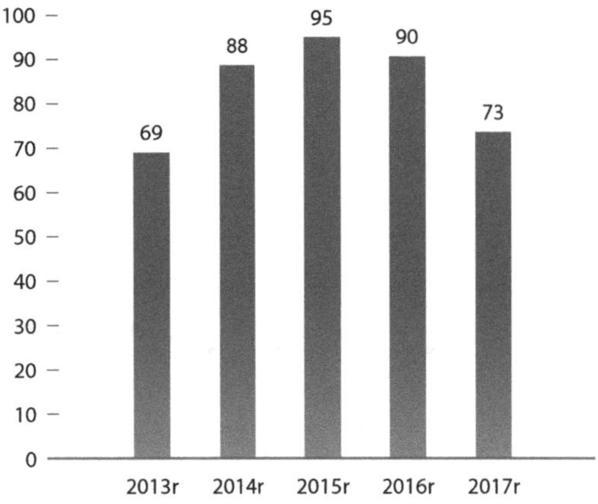

Figure 3. Dynamics of livestock of horses (Sylgysyt horse farm) from 2013 to 2017

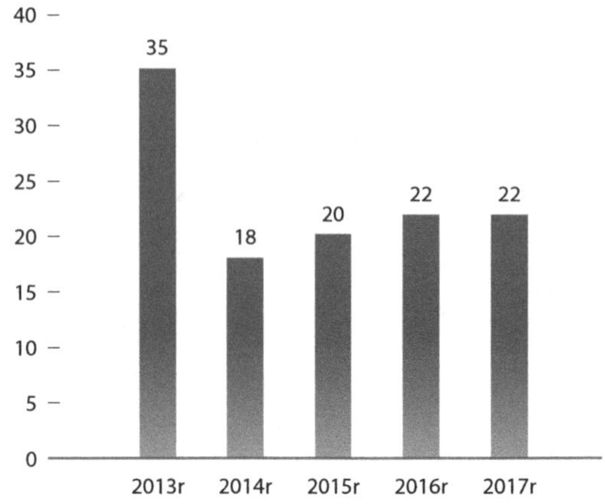

carried out by local residents and school workers (see Figure 2).

The decline in livestock of cattle is mainly influenced by summer harvesting of hay, which is caused by a shortage of workers due to the low population, appropriate machinery and weather conditions.

The number of heads of cattle in the livestock farm "Bolyan" and the horses of the Sylgysyt horse base tend to decrease.

It is possible to list the main problems that still persist and hinder the development of livestock and horse breeding industries:

- lack of pastures, grasslands due to the high water content of the territories;
- low transport availability and isolation of production from sales markets;
- deficiencies in the organization of the procurement system and logistics;
- shortage of labor due to low population (farm workers, brigades for hay work).

III. Agriculture versus Business

3.1. Business and agriculture cooperation

The basis of industry in the territory of the municipal district "Olenek Evenk National District" is determined by the activities of the enterprises of the diamond-mining industry and the extraction of rare-earth metals - the Tomtor deposit.

In 2018, ALROSA company signed an additional agreement on the implementation of a project to support the Far North in agricultural and traditional fishing activities, aimed at reviving national cultures and preserving historical values. In the framework of regional development, the company pays great attention to supporting the tribal communities of reindeer herders and fishermen in the northernmost regions of the Republic of Sakha (Yakutia). The company undertakes to allocate 100 million rubles to the district budget for 5 years. in year.

In the coming years, the development of a unique rare-earth metal deposit in the world will begin on the territory of the district. The auction for the right to use subsoil in 2014 was won by Vostokengineering, a subsidiary of TriArk Mining, a joint venture of the main shareholder of the ICT Group Alexander Nesis and RT-Global Resources of Rostec State Corporation, created to develop the ore mining industry in Russia and the production of oxides of rare-earth metals and niobium, the provision of Russian industry with high-tech materials based on rare-earth metals.

According to forecasts, the company plans to create 500 jobs in the trucking company and about 200 in the service sector. In 2014, the company entered into an agreement with the district - an agreement on social and economic cooperation. It is planned to build a mining plant with a capacity of 200 thousand tons of ore per year, which is approximately 1.8 billion dollars per year. The annual deductions to the local budget under the agreement on joint cooperation between the company and the district are 10%, that is, the company with this forecast volume of production will annually pay about 180 million dollars to the local budget [9].

One should take into account the facts that any industrial development of land has negative environmental consequences for the environment. It is necessary to take into account the

Figure 4. Dividends on shares deducted to the budget of the Oleneksky district, 2015-2018, thousand rubles

factors that influence the lifestyle of local communities:

- the laying of industrial highways, auto winter roads in the region prevents the migration of wild deer, which creates difficulties for local hunters;
- despite the prohibition of the residents of the region to develop alluvial diamond deposits, an auction was held and the deposit would be developed, without taking into account that the river is the only source of drinking water, the object of hunting and fishing;

We consider it an important principle when planning activities of enterprises - subsoil users to include an objective environmental and economic assessment of the natural resource potential of the field, thereby ensuring the implementation of such measures as the introduction of resource-saving and environmental protection technologies, reducing emissions of harmful substances into the environment and so on.

From the above data it can be seen that the contribution to the district budget is significant. There is every reason to believe that the funds allocated to the district budget tend to increase. The high indicator of 2017 indicates that 3 companies LLC Vostokinzhiniring, AK Alrosa, OJSC Nizhne-Lenskoye made payments immediately this year.

3.2. Development of technical base of agriculture

If we take into account the fact that over the past decades, in the regions of the Far North (using the example of the Olenek District), local production in the field of traditional nature has declined, the number of reindeer and cattle is decreasing, I believe that the creation and strengthening of the material and technical base is a necessary condition objects of traditional nature management in the regions of the Far North.

In particular, the problem can be solved through investment programs. Investors can be industrial subsoil companies that master and develop the industrial sector in the territories of the Far North.

For the normal functioning of local traditional environmental facilities, the development and strengthening of the material and technical bases of traditional environmental objects using the example of the Olenek District, I consider it necessary to implement the following measures:

- Conduct a survey on the material security of employees of organizations, for greater reliability of information;
- Strengthen the material and technical base for the activities of reindeer brigades and workers of the clan communities;
- Determine the best routes for the nomadic herding camp;
- Develop a business plan to ensure conditions for improving the quality of life.

The second condition for identifying the prospects for the development of traditional nature management in the Far North, I believe, it is necessary to analyze the allocation of funds, deductions from the budget of industrial companies for the socio-economic development of the region.

For clarity, I have analyzed the amount of funds received on dividends from industrial companies over the past 3 years. (Data taken from information on budget execution of the Olenek Evenki National District budget, link to the site https://mr-olenekskij.sakha.gov.ru).

The total income for 3 years amounted to 315454 thousand rubles. Spent funds in support of agriculture in 2016:

According to the results of 2016, there are 44 enterprises and organizations engaged in

Table 2. Allocation of funds to the local budget, in thousand rubles

2016	
AK Alrosa	49 970,0
Nizhne-Lensk	10000
Vostokengineering	5900
TOTAL	65 870,0
2017	
AK Alrosa	9250
Nizhne-Lensk	4 000,0
Vostokengineering	16600
TOTAL	29 850,0
2018	
AK Alrosa	199351
Nizhne-Lensk	2882,96
Vostokengineering	17500
TOTAL	219734

agriculture in the region, including 31 tribal communities, 5 individual entrepreneurs, 3 LLCs, 3 municipal unitary enterprises and 2 farms involved in poultry farming and cattle breeding.

For reindeer herders of the Municipal Unitary Enterprise "Zhilindinsky" 2 beams on a sleigh of 2.5x5 m were purchased for the amount of 730,000 rubles.

This year, in order to develop agriculture in rural areas, in the village of Eyik, a cow barn for 100 head of cattle for a total amount of 4,949,218 rubles was built at the Eyik Agricultural Production Cooperative.

The created Collective Farm Small Enterprise (owned by Zorkin Afanasy Vitalievich) was given a grant (subsidy) from the budget of the Ministry of Education for the purchase of cattle in the amount of 350 000 rubles. According to the economic method, a barn for 10 heads of cattle was built with a total amount of 290,302 rubles. For household needs A. Zorkin provided by the Xingtai mini tractor.

A towing small boat worth 1 000 000 rubles was purchased. The boat has justified its costs and has been successfully used by the Olenek-Torg MUE for transporting meat from remote hunting areas.

To support agricultural veterans, on the basis of the subprogram "Housing construction for agricultural veterans" of the MCP "Development of Agriculture," Tatyana ProkopyevnaNogovitsyna built a residential building in the amount of 1,136,552 rubles.

Subventions to support reindeer herding - creating working conditions for reindeer herding teams - local budget - 10,364,496.48 rubles.

Support for cattle breeding - 900 000 rubles.

Support for herding horse breeding - 51,200 rubles.

The total amount for supporting agriculture from the local budget in 2016 amounted to 25,295,296.48 rubles, which is 38.4% of the total amount allocated by industrial companies.

For 2017, data on expenditures in support of agriculture were not published. In 2018, funds spent in support of agriculture were spent - 107,440,863.34 rubles, which amounted to 49% of the total amount allocated by industrial companies.

Most of the funds allocated by industrial companies were spent on the construction and repair of residential buildings and infrastructure.

On the other hand, one should take into account the facts that any industrial development of land has negative environmental consequences for the environment. It is necessary to take into account factors that influence the lifestyle of local communities:

- the laying of industrial highways, winter winters in the region prevents the migration of wild deer, which creates difficulties for local hunters;
- Tomtor ores are radioactive. This is due to the fact that they contain radioactive substances such as uranium, thorium, potassium-40.
- despite the ban of the district residents on the development of alluvial diamond deposits, the auction has taken place and the deposit will be developed, while it does not take into account that the river is the only source of drinking water, an object of hunting and fishing;

IV. Conclusion

And thus, we consider it an important principle when planning the activities of enterprises-subsoil users to include an objective environmental and economic assessment of the natural resource potential of the deposit's territory, which will help ensure the implementation of such measures as the introduction of resource-saving and environmental technologies, reduction of harmful substances into the environment, etc.

The most important factor in preserving the originality and survival of the indigenous peoples of the Far North of Yakutia in the modern world is the creation of conditions for the development of their traditional nature management. It is necessary to realize that indigenous minorities live in the north of Western Siberia in the conditions of the Arctic latitudes for more than 4 centuries, while the development and development of mineral resources in these territories does not exceed 20 years.

The right to exist on their ancestral lands and lead a desired lifestyle is as legitimate as the right of other peoples of the state to use the objectively necessary minerals located in the depths of these territories.

References

1. Бартенев, В. На крайнем северо-западе Сибири. / В. Бартенев. - М.: Книга по Требованию, 2011. - 154 с. (Bartenev, V. In the extreme north-west of Siberia. / V. Bartenev. - M .: Book on Demand, 2011. - 154 pages)
2. Все о Севере: Сборник основных нормативных документов с комментариями, регламентирующих жизнь и деятельность в районах Крайнего севера и приравненных к ним местностях: Учебно-практическое пособие: В 2 тт. / Г.В. Груза и др. - Москва: СПб. [и др.] : Питер, 2002. - 310с. (Everything about the North: Collection of the main regulatory documents with comments regulating life and activity in the regions of the Far North and equated localities: Educational and Practical Guide: In 2 vols. / G.V.

Cargo and others - Moscow: SPb. [et al.]: Peter, 2002. - 310 pages)

3. Территории природного природопользования коренных малочисленных народов российского Крайнего Севера (проблемы и перспективы). - М., ИГП РАН. (Монография) / А.А. Транин. (Territories of nature management of indigenous peoples of the Russian Far North (problems and prospects). - M., IHP RAS. (Monograph) / A.A. Tranin).
4. Санникова Я. М. Развитие оленеводства на Севере Якутии в 1990-х годах: количественные показатели / Я. М. Санникова // Научный диалог. — 2017. — № 11. — С. 425—437. (SannikovaYa. M. The development of reindeer husbandry in the North of Yakutia in the 1990s: quantitative indicators / Ya. M. Sannikova // Scientific dialogue. - 2017. - № 11. - pages 425-437).
5. Протасов, В.Ф. Экономика природопользования: Учебное пособие / В.Ф. Протасов. — М.: КУРС, НИЦ ИНФРА-М, 2013. — 304 с. (Protasov, V.F. Environmental Economics: Tutorial / V.F. Protasov. - M .: KURS, SIC INFRA-M, 2013. - 304 p).
6. Постановление Правительства Республики Саха (Якутия) от 4 сентября 2017 г. http://sakha.gov.ru/ (Resolution of the Government of the Republic of Sakha (Yakutia) of September 4, 2017 http://sakha.gov.ru/)
7. Якут. ведомости (прил. к газ. «Якутия») от 08.09.2015, N32; (Yakut. statements (supplement to the newspaper "Yakutia") of 09.09.2015, N32)
8. Сайт Оленекского эвенкийского национального района //https://республика-саха-якутия.рф/stati/jakutija/olenyokskii-ulus-raion.html (The site of the Olenek Evenk National District //https://respay-sakhaakautiya.rf/stati/jakutija/olenyokskii-ulus-raion.html);
9. Развитие скотоводства в Якутии http://geolike.ru/page/gl_4669.htm (The development of cattle breeding in Yakutia http://geolike.ru/page/gl_4669.htm);
10. Сайт АО «Нижнеленское» - http://nlykt.ru/; (Website of JSC Nizhnelenskoye - http://nlykt.ru/);
11. Годовые отчеты ОАО «Алмазы Анабара» за 2008–2016 гг. – //http://alanab.ykt. ru/; (Annual reports of OAO AlmazyAnabara for 2008–2016. - // http: // alanab. ykt. ru /);
12. Годовые отчеты ОАО «Нижне-Ленское» за 2008–2016 гг. – //http://www. nlykt. ru/;

(Annual reports of OAO Nizhne-Lenskoye for 2008–2016 - // http: // www. nlykt. ru /);

13. Годовые отчеты ОАО АК «АЛРОСА» за 2008–2016 гг. – //http://www. alrosa. ru/. (Annual reports of OJSC AK ALROSA for 2008–2016. - // http: // www. alrosa. ru /).

14. О деятельности компании ООО «ТриАркМайнинг» //http://threearc.rumining // http://threearc.ru (About the activities of the company "TriArkMining" //http://threearc. rumining //http://threearc.ru)

ESTABLISHMENT OF NEW TRADE LAW SYSTEM: TO PROMOTE SUSTAINABILITY BETWEEN KOREA AND THE RUSSIAN ARCTIC

Bongchul Kim
Ph.D in Law and Associate Professor, Division of International Studies,
Hankuk University of Foreign Studies, Seoul
bong625@hufs.ac.kr

Sunghwah Ko
Ph.D Candidate of International Politics, Hankuk University of Foreign Studies
sko2392@ hufs.ac.kr

Abstract.

Korea and Russia are actualizing the cooperation in the Arctic area. Korean companies have begun to bring the real economic benefits. However, since there are some according troublesome aspects, measures that can lead to sustainable development through the supplementation of relevant norms are critical. Russia is also aware of these problems in obtaining economic benefits in the future; cooperation between the two countries should be extended to sufficiently cover this point. The laws related to the region are vague and does not encompass every field. In addition, when it comes to the national interests, many situations rise from areas where international and national laws are not clearly harmonized. Therefore, efforts should be made to reflect the interests of both sides and to maintain economic benefits, in case Korea participates in Russia's development of the area, as well as for the legal foundation to reduce negative issues. The Korea-Russia FTA negotiation is on the track for the purpose.

The two governments should consider various tasks, such as harmonizing with the former FTAs and dealing with the domestic law in accordance with the new FTA. The two countries also have to conduct researches on the efficient use of the FTA and for the 'Sustainable Arctic Development.'

Keywords: Sustainable Arctic Development, Korea-Russia FTA, Korea-EAEU FTA, Economic Development of Far East, Northern Sea Route

I. Introduction

Russia is actively delivering a number of projects to develop new shipping routes as well as natural resources in the Arctic region. The country still continues to take aggressive measures, including the plan to set up the "Ministry for the Development of the Russian Far East and Arctic" as in the federal level. (Staalesen, A., 2019) This situation is affected by the globalization of the international economy, and the communities are also connected to many variables. The international community is seeking for sustainable development methods that involve considerable attention and effort to preserve the Arctic area. (Zadorin, M., Klisheva, O., Vezhlivtseva, K. & Antufieva, D., 2017)

Korea and Russia are constantly diversifying cooperation methods. In particular, as Russian government imply economic significance to Far East-Siberian region and the possibility of developing Arctic shipping routes is becoming realistic as glaciers in this area have gone smaller. Researches regarding utilization of the Russian Arctic and its resources, and expansion of Arctic routes are already underway in Korea. This trend is accelerating, especially in conjunction with Korean government's 'New Northern Policy.' Nevertheless, so far most of the domestic research achievements are short-term proposals, taking into account policies and political situations of the countries.

International legislation related to the development of the Arctic region has steadily expanded its scope of discipline. Russia has a duty to respect and abide by the law and the government is showing signs of strengthening domestic legal discipline based on the standards of international law. However, the country still sometimes offers different opinions from the international community's concern related to the development of the region after the economic sanctions and fails to avoid conflicts with other countries in terms of policies and institutions.

In this context, in order to expand exchanges between Korea and Russia in related to the sustainable development of the area, it is essential to look at the conflict of the system from a legal point of view. It is of interest to establish a new bilateral normative system to avoid confrontations, which are specified to this issue. This paper looks at international and domestic legal discourses that may be relevant to the development of the Arctic area and seeks to derive legal challenges that could be discussed in the future, such as in the Korea-Russia FTA.

II. Developments in the Arctic

2.1. Development of the Arctic Region by Russia

From Russia's point of view, the economic value of this particular region is enormous, that the Arctic can be considered as the stepping stone to overcome difficulties, such as international economic sanctions. (Kim, S. W., 2017) Furthermore, this area can provide Russia benefits in many aspects, including its national security, politics, military, technology, and environment, beyond the mere economic perspective of the region as a hub of resources. The Russian government is making great efforts for economic development while securing security awareness of the area. (Seidler, C., 2010)

The potential for development in Arctic area ranges widely from the tourism industry to the large-scale resource exploitation. As each of these possibilities are closely linked to one another, Russia is keen on locating areas where its potential synergies lie in. In this sense, Russia is showing high interest in developing resources that are not in the economic sanction list. Moreover, the exploration and utilization of the route across the regional ocean is recently receiving massive attention along with the climate change. Russia is being active in improving the innovative systems regarding the development and preservation of the Arctic area. This country has steadily tried to forge partnerships with foreign companies and to implement advanced technologies with the aim of the sustainable development of the region.

With regard to the development of the Arctic region, the global interest in the Northern Sea Route (NSR) that runs through the Arctic sea, is also growing significantly. The NSR can be distinguished into the northwest one in the Canadian waters, linking North America and Europe, and the northeast one in Russian waters which links Asia and Europe. (Yun, Y. M., 2009) The Northeast route, especially, has the advantage that is geographically shorter than the generally used current route, which connects East Asia and Europe through the Suez Canal, and accordingly, it is able to greatly reduce the sailing days and logistics costs. (Humpert, M. & Raspotnik, A., 2012)

This route is expected to expand largely as the climate change affected glaciers are shrinking and ice-breaking technology is developing. Therefore, many countries are using the route in a dramatic manner. (Park, J. K., 2016) In Korea's context, it is also possible that the route will revolutionize the global logistics system if it is well settled, where it is able to cut the operating hours by up to half from Busan to Europe. Korea explored the Arctic route as well with the research purpose icebreaker Araon and now continues to build foundation for its commercial use.

Liquefied Natural Gas (LNG) has emerged as a theme that is now discussed at the highest levels of Russian politics. (Henderson, J. & Yermakov, V., 2019) A case in point related to the development of Arctic area is the 'Yamal LNG Project' invested by France and China for a further step in Yamal Peninsula, Russia. The region has reserves of about 2.5 billion tons of oil and 3.5 billion tons of gas. The core of the project is to build logistic bases to transport the exploited resources to Europe and Far East Asia region. The copper mines in the Chukotka area and the construction of the Kamchatka LNG transshipment terminal are also linked to such projects. (Hodges, J., Shiryaevskaya, A. & Khrennikova, D., 2018)

2.2. Potential for Growth of the Arctic Development related Industries

The development of the Arctic region will provide opportunities for related industries to grow together. For example, resource exploitation remains as a highly anticipated field and the plant market with direct links to the exploitation is growing rapidly. The Russian plant market, which stood at around $8.2 billion in 2000, had grown up to $15.8 billion in 2010, nearly double the figure in a decade. The attraction power of the Russian market comes from the possibility of combining the orders for plants with Korea's resource development.

Samsung Heavy Industry has supplied Sakhalin with the world's largest 33 story ocean platform "Runsko-A," and has won orders for three 70 million tons of icebreaker for the Arctic shipping line from Russia's largest state-run shipping company Sovcomflot. Daewoo Shipbuilding & Marine Engineering also participated in a project to modernize 'Zvezda dockyard,' which is under Russia's state-run shipbuilding group 'United Shipbuilding Co.,' located in the Bolshoi Kamen area near Vladivostok. Daewoo Shipbuilding & Marine Engineering is co-participating in the process of manufacturing LNG tankers, floating plants, and drilling vessels. The company won all 15 orders for the first "Yamal Project" in 2014, which is worth a total of $4.8 billion.

This basically means that Korea's technology has opened the era of full-fledged LNG transportation to the Arctic and touched off for energy development in the region. For Russia, it has also been a trigger to have confidence in the development of Arctic energy and transport through the route. It is meaningful that the Yamal LNG project is carried out with the participation and support from foreign countries not only with Russia's own labor force, but also sustainably maintained under the economic sanctions. The project created momentum for Russia's development of the area, and gave Korea the motivation to participate in. (Kim, S. W., 2017)

However, there are major limitations for companies to operate finances through foreign exchange control in the Far East Russia region, which includes the friction between the central and local governments, excessive tax investigations, environmental regulations, and control of remittance to overseas. Furthermore, the society has several challenges on the development of the region. For example, in the area there are indigenous minorities who have long lived on the ground, where the jurisdiction of the Russian government could not reach deep enough. These people are considerably vulnerable to changes in the environment and society following regional development.

In terms of cooperation with the international community, sometimes the appropriate cooperation with the third countries, such as Korea, provides a clue to solving these complex internal problems. Of course, for now, the idea that Russia will solve its own problems in cooperation with the outside world might sound a bit infeasible, and that such efforts could also be an ambiguous or abstract in long-term perspective. Nevertheless, in the process of establishing Korea-Russia economic cooperation and the excavation of new industries, there will be the possibility of bilateral policy cooperation, or at least to extract the momentum of new industries.

2.3. Cooperation Possibility between Korea and Russia on the Arctic Route

As the development of the region goes active in the close future, it will ratchet the demand for ships and equipment up, which are needed for exploration and navigation of the route and mining, transport and storage of resources. Therefore, while investing in the development of related new materials and core technologies, Korea should attempt to hold joint research with Russian institutes and sustain the exchange. The climate change in the area and the deteriorated facilities are putting Russia's port infrastructure in urgent need. Approaching from the other side, it can be an opportunity for the Northeast Asian country to eagerly participate in modernizing the ports, reflecting the its own port development technology. (Jeh, S. H., & Min, J. Y., 2014)

The NSR has been commercially used in near 2010, which steadily increased the frequency from 41 times in 2011, 46 times in 2012, to 71 times in 2013. In 2017, 10.7 million tons of cargo were transported via the route, and even the 2018, the summer ship Maersk succeeded in navigating the first container ship, Venta Maersk, through the sea route without the assist of an icebreaker. Based on this route, Maersk has been considering to utilize this route through cooperating with an icebreaker, however, it is still on the examination process of possible sailing days and the rising costs for breaking additional ice. (Baker, J., 2019)

Bulk cargo is likely to be used early in the use of Arctic shipping routes, as long as the transport conditions are simple and the demands for specific goods are adequate. In the future, a direct transport demand for the routes to Northeast Asia will be generated in accordance with the exploitation of resources in the region. The container transport can only be carried out if it is maintained sustainably and the global container shipping market is forming an economy of scale due to the growing size of ships. However, in the case of Arctic shipping routes, it is difficult to actually realize the economy of scale, because of the limited number of ships. Furthermore, as there is still a high risk, the economic feasibility is low due to the high insurance premium and navigation fee. (Park, J. H. & Lee, M. G., 2015)

In 2010, the Korean government launched 'Eurasia Initiative Project,' which encompasses Russia and Central Asia, as a way to unite the Eurasian continent into a single economic community and to build peace on the Korean Peninsula by inducing openness to North Korea. The Korea's domestic interest in Arctic region and Arctic routes has also increased in the context of this project. The Korean government is paying attention on linking the ports in Russia's Far East area. It aims to connect Korean ports to the Arctic routes, continental railways, and Russia's Far East ports in a bid to strengthen its logistics and energy network. The government prepared the basis for reducing fees for using port facilities from January 2014 and attempted to expand infrastructure, including the personnel trainings for sailing in polar areas.

III. Law of the Arctic for Korea-Russia Cooperation

3.1. Law for the Northern Sea Route

The legal issues in traditional aspect, the Arctic region was mainly put on the table for the sake of sovereignty, rights, and jurisdiction of coastal countries. For example, there are various types of laws applicable to the issues in the Arctic sea like: (1) treaty law, such as United Nations Convention on the Law of the Sea (UNCLOS), the International Convention for the Safety of Life at Sea (SOLAS), and the 1973 International Convention for the Prevention of Pollution from Ships (MARPOL 1973) as modified by the Protocol 1978 thereto (MARPOL 73/78); (2) customary law; (3) 'soft law' such as the guidelines of the International Maritime Organization (IMO); and (4) domestic laws and regulations of the coastal states of the sea. (Østreng, W. et al., 2013) Then, the international laws have affected the enactment and application of domestic laws in the related countries. For example, the UNCLOS does not have specific provisions for the Arctic sea itself, but the provisions of Article 234 on 'Ice-covered areas' provide the basic principles for environmental protection and conservation applicable to the sea. (Solski, J. J., 2013)

The legal status of the NSR is closely intertwined with the legal status of the Arctic Sea. Russia has prepared and enforced domestic laws based on such international laws. (Rho, Y. D. & Park, W., 2011) The 2012 Federal Law of Shipping on the Water Area of the NSR (Federal Law 132-FZ) amended in certain respects the 1998 Federal Act on Coastal Waters as well as the 1999 Marchant Shipping Code of the Russian Federation. (Bobrova, J., 2016) Russian domestic law subtly shifted from claiming sovereignty in the Arctic sea, to a more functional role enabling safe navigation in the NSR. (Okochi, M., 2020)

Article 14 of the federal law describes the NSR as 'historically developed national transport communication of the Russian Federation.' Any navigation by vessels in the Russian route is to be organized on an approval and remuneration basis, subject to compliance with specific rules for such navigation. Then, Rules of Navigation in the Water Area of the NSR was approved by the order of the Ministry of Transport of Russia in 2013. Based on the domestic laws, 'The Northern Sea Route Administration' was established as a federal state institution. According to the government, the main targets of the institution are ensuring safe navigation and protection of marine environment from the pollution in the water area of the NSR.

The laws cover all vessels that pass through the Russian Arctic routes and the vessels are subject to the application regardless of their country. The laws allow the Russian government to adjust the shipping operations in consideration of weather conditions on the routes. The ship operators or captains who wish to pass through the Russian NSR must notify the type and duration of operation to the maritime operations headquarters and apply to use the respective route. Russia also prohibited ships that did not carry the 'letter of financial ship-owner's guarantee' on board, as part of its civil liability for environmental pollution in the Arctic coast and the vicinity of the sea.

Under the laws, the ships that use the area must meet the requirements and the captain and his agent must also have experience in operating ships in the ice zone. The authorities may conduct a crackdown inspection in the event that ships operating on the route are brining risk for sea or for pollution. Furthermore, it is mandatory to carry the 'Ice pilot' in certain waters. For a foreign warship to operate the route, a sailing plan, including the name of the warship and the captain, the purpose of the operation and the expected route and timing, must be submitted to the government 45 days in advance.

If Korea and Russia sustainably cooperate on the Arctic development, both might be able to make legal co-suggestions to the international society in case of necessity. For example, there is no general international law yet to discipline the responsibility for pollution or damage, even though the marine plants for resource exploitation, like ships, are at risk of leakage accidents and pollution. These problems are simply being solved only by the voluntary agreement between the domestic laws of respective countries, regional cooperative arrangements, or the operators of offshore plants. Seoul and Moscow could consider proposing general norms to the international community, along with signing a bilateral agreement between the two.

3.2. Necessity of New Bilateral Law for the Sustainable Arctic Development

Korea and Russia have often joined together in expanding multilateral treaties on the international stage while continuing their efforts on economic cooperation since the establishment of diplomatic ties. At the same time, the two partners signed bilateral treaties for continuing their direct cooperation. These treaties are mainly for investment, resource exploitation, transport, and etc., but also include promises of military and security issues. The bilateral treaties have largely provided disciplines on the cooperation.

Among the treaties, the 'Agreement between the Government of the Republic of Korea and the Government of Russian Federation on Economic Cooperation in the Republic of Sakha (Yakutia) 1995' covers the Northeast Asian (the Russian Far East) area. The treaty also creates new usability with the recent Arctic region issues. The legal infrastructure for realizing a new level of cooperation is also necessary to consolidate and harmonize various bilateral agreements that have been signed so far to discipline various areas of the cooperation. (Kim, B. C., 2015)

Now we need to pay attention to the previous Free Trade Agreements (FTA) that are signed between Korea and many other countries. The FTA promises to remove trade barriers, including tariffs on trade between signatories, while the latest deal calls for the removal of passive trade barriers, as well as providing special trade benefits to the partner. In the end, the FTA has become the most leveraged legal base among various international economic treaties, which most WTO member countries also are using as well. FTA signatories are now fully committed to its original purpose – to provide special trade benefits for the economic sake of the partner, however, they are also used for non-economic purposes. (Kim, B. C., 2018)

Korea is focusing more on multilateral economic cooperation such as WTO, and also trying to establish bilateral preferential trade relations through FTAs. The Korean government pursues diversification of trade and economic cooperation in international community while anticipating the improvement of trade environment by signing FTAs. Russia has maintained its long-standing economic dependence with the Commonwealth of Independent States (CIS) while providing special trade benefits through the FTAs, as well as strengthening its political influence based on this point. Furthermore, Russia has recently signed strategic FTAs with countries that do not belong to the CIS members, including Vietnam, to pursue diverse trade relations, economic benefits, and non-economic objectives. (Kim, B. C., 2013)

Korea and Russia agreed to initiate the negotiations at the Korea-Russia summit in 2018 and the governments of the two countries initiated the two sides' FTA negotiations in service and investment in Moscow on June 2019. The FTA talks in the service and investment sectors are expected to help Korean companies increase their presence in Russia's medical, logistics, product distribution and tourism markets. In addition, transparency and predictability are expected to be improved with regard to investment in Russia.

3.3. Challenges to the Cooperation including the Korea-Russia FTA

The more Korea continues to put in efforts to expand efficient economic cooperation and market openness by signing FTAs with major global countries, the more essential it becomes to settle a stable legal foundation. Furthermore, in the recent international community, such legal bases usually start from signing FTAs; Korea has signed numerous FTAs to expand trade and economic cooperation with various countries so far. As Russia also moves forward from emphasizing only the economic ties with the CIS countries, the possibility of an FTA with Korea has increased. The two partners already started the official talk on the FTA relation mainly in the investment area.

However, even if these two sides have the will to sign for the FTA, it cannot be actualized right away; in order to conclude the treaty, various procedures such as investigation and negotiation are necessary. In particular, efforts are needed to build up the environment for the Korea-Russia FTA, while addressing various domestic and international legal challenges. To this end, there should be legal discussions on a different level, more than simply securing the possibility and necessity of cooperation between Korea and Russia, and a cautious consideration of the FTA itself.

The Eurasian Economic Union (EAEU), a customs union that has Belarus, Kazakhstan, and Kyrgyzstan, was founded in responds to EU which is more focused on the Western Europe. According to this economic community's agreement on the establishment, all the member states must be included in the treaty, so long as one of the member states is willing to sign any economic agreements, such as FTAs, with third countries. In the end, the 'Korea-Russia FTA' will be expanded to 'Korea-EAEU FTA' negotiations under the regulation. Korea has already experienced similar situation while pushing for the FTAs with EU and ASEAN. The question is whether the economic effectiveness of the FTA with EAEU members, not Russia, is sufficient to cover up the potential adverse effects.

The FTA can also contribute on the security issues regarding the Korean peninsula. Inter-Korean economic exchanges have a specialty which is somewhat different from transactions with other countries or within the domestic. It is suggested that the specialty of the inter-Korea exchange, which implies that Korea and Russia's cooperation can have impact on peace for the Korean Peninsula. Furthermore, it is also necessary for Korea to come up with a legal mechanism to recognize the granting preferential treatment through the FTA, considering its exchanges with the North as a special transaction within the nation – which is an exception to the principle of Most-Favored-Nation treatment in the WTO system. (Kim, B. C., 2018)

Recently, North Korea has been making moves to be considered as 'a country of legal-conformity' in the international community despite the international economic sanctions. For example, North Korea is trying to be incorporated into the international trade environment and trade rules in a long-term perspective, including joining the CISG, which is a general treaty on international trade. Given that these images were hard to expect in the past, North Korea's such effort is certainly meaningful that it is preparing to facilitate economic exchanges within the entire Korean Peninsula in a long-term perspective. This is what needs to be considered in the process of signing the Korea-Russia FTA.

IV. Conclusion

Korea and Russia have expanded various areas of economic cooperation since they established diplomatic ties in the 1990s. Investment and commodity trade between the two have grown significantly, that seeing Korean products in the Russian market became a more common daily thing. Now that the two countries are looking for a new model of cooperation, to achieve further development of the Arctic region, the source of new marketability. Both Korea and Russia will be able to share the goals of regional development and transportation efficiency and create new markets through the development of the area.

As seen above, the two countries are already actualizing cooperation in broad spectrum for the region. With the rapid exploitation of resources due to climate change and technological development, Korean companies have begun to bring the real economic benefits, having positive effects on related industries such as the construction of transport and special ships. However, since there are some according troublesome aspects, measures that can lead to sustainable development through the supplementation of relevant norms are critical. Russia is also aware of these problems in obtaining economic benefits in the future; cooperation between the two countries should be extended to sufficiently cover this point.

The provisions of international law related to the Arctic region are vague and does not encompass every area. In addition, when it comes to the national interests, many situations rise from areas where international and national laws are not clearly harmonized. This is why international community's cooperation is essential; for example, there is a possibility of conflict between the international law regarding the Arctic shipping and domestic law of Russia. Therefore, efforts should be made to reflect the interests of both sides and to maintain economic benefits, in case Korea participates in Russia's development of the area, as well as for the legal foundation to reduce negative issues.

The official negotiation for the Korea-Russia FTA launched in 2019. In the process of the negotiation, the Korean governments should consider various tasks, such as harmonizing with the FTAs Korea has been signing, and dealing with the domestic law in accordance with the new FTA, based on the previous experiences. From Russia's point of view, special circumstances such as the EAEU should be taken in consideration. The process of signing the FTA, which will serve as the international legal basis for cooperation between the partners, should be clearly marked for the purpose of 'Sustainable Arctic Development.' In Korea's perspective, it should consider the possibility that the FTA could be used in non-economic areas such as on the Korean Peninsula issue.

Reference

1. Baker, J. (2019, June 14). Maersk considers northern sea route service. Lloyd's List. from https://lloydslist.maritimeintelligence.informa.com/LL1127916/Maersk-considers-northern-sea-route-service
2. Bobrova, Julia. (2016). The Northern Sea Route: National Regime in the Changing International Context. Policy Brief No. 9, Russian International Affairs Council, November 2016, 4-5.
3. Henderson, J., & Yermakov, V. (2019). Russian LNG: Becoming a global force. November 2019, Oxford Institute for Energy Studies. 1.
4. Hodges, J., Shiryaevskaya, A. & Khrennikova, D. (2018, August 28) Melting Ice in the Arctic Is Opening a New Energy Trade Route, Bloomberg. from https://www.bloombergquint.com/business/arctic-ice-melt-opens-lng-energy-trade-route-near-north-pole.
5. Humpert, M. & Raspotnik, A. (2012). The future of Arctic shipping along the transpolar sea route. Arctic Yearbook, 2012(1), 281-283
6. Jeh, S. H. & Min, J. (2014). Russian Arctic Development Strategy and New Possibility for Korea-Russia Cooperation. KIEP Research Paper No. World Economic Update, 1-6.
7. Kim, B. C. (2013). Regional Trade Agreements of Korea and Russia-The Possibility of the Korea-Russia FTA. The Korean Journal of Slavic Studies. 29(1), 12.
8. Kim, B. C. (2015). The changes of Korean Domestic Laws with the FTA system. Chonbuk Law Review, 44. 421.
9. Kim, B. C. (2018). The Evolution of Korean FTAs and Rediscovery of the Legal Function. The International Commerce & Law Review, 79. 179-182.
10. Kim, S. W. (2017). Western Economic Sanctions and Russian Arctic Development: Focusing on Natural Gas. Slav newspaper, 32(4). 51-52.
11. Okochi, M. (2020) The Northern Sea Route: International Law and Russian Regulations. Briefing Paper. 2020(4). European Institute for Asian Studies. 4.
12. Ostreng, W., Eger, K. M., Fløistad, B., Jørgensen-Dahl, A., Lothe, L., Mejlænder-

Larsen, M., & Wergeland, T. (2013). Shipping in Arctic waters: a comparison of the Northeast, Northwest and trans polar passages. Springer Science & Business Media. 241-250.

13. Rho, Y. D. & Park, W. (2011). An Analysis of the Russia's Bill of the Federal Law on the Water Areas of Northern Sea Route. Seoul International Law Journal, 18(2). 97-121.
14. Park, J. K. (2016). Russian Transport Logistics Development Strategy: Focusing on the 'Arctic Region,' Slav newspaper, 30(1). 29-30.
15. Park, J. H., & Lee, M. G. (2015). A study on competitiveness and effect analysis for developing a port specialized in Northern Sea Route. Journal of Navigation and Port Research, 39(3), 244.
16. Seidler, C. (2009). Arktisches Monopoly. Der Kampf um die Rohstoffe der Polarregion, München. (translated by Mihwa Park, Seoul: The soup, 2010). 258.
17. Solski, J. J. (2013). New Developments in Russian Regulation of Navigation on the Northern Sea Route. Arctic Review on Law and Politics. 4(1). 95-98.
18. Staalesen, A. (2019, January 21). Russia's Far East Ministry to Get Powers over Arctic policy. Eye on the Arctic. from https://www.rcinet.ca/eye-on-the-arctic/2019/01/21/russia-arctic-development-policy-far-east-ministry-administration-politics/
19. Yun, Y. M. (2009). Strategy of Russian Marine Security over the North Pole Region: Focusing on the development of the Arctic Ocean and the Marine Cooperation between Korea and Russia on the North Pole, East and West Studies, 21(2). 55.
20. Zadorin, M., Klisheva, O., Vezhlivtseva, K. & Antufieva, D. (2017) Russian Laws on Indigenous Issues. Guarantees, Communities, Territories of Traditional Land Use: Translated and Commented. Rovaniemi: University of Lapland. 4-5.

* This work was based on the Article from Bongchul Kim, Journal of Contemporary Eastern Asia, 2020, Vol. 19 No. 1: 84-96.

DEVELOPMENT OF THE DIGITAL ECONOMY IN THE ARCTIC REGIONS OF RUSSIA: RESOURCE POTENTIAL OF THE REPUBLIC OF SAKHA (YAKUTIA)

Galina Ratz
Head of the Economics and Finance Department of the Institute of Finance and Economics, Doctor of Economics, professor, M.K. Ammosov North-Eastern Federal University Yakutsk, Russia
galina-ratz@mail.ru

Sardana Gavrileva
International Relations Office, Leading Specialist
Doctoral student of the Institute of Finance and Economics,
M.K. Ammosov North-Eastern Federal University Yakutsk, Russia
sa.gavrilieva@s-vfu.ru

Liudmila Gavrilieva
Associate Professor of the Department of Foreign Languages for Technical and Natural Sciences, Institute of Foreign Languages and Regional Studies
M.K. Ammosov North-Eastern Federal University Yakutsk, Russia
lgavrilieva@mail.ru

Abstract.

Digital technology area is the most rapidly developing area in the world. Russian Federation is also involved in this trend. During the last few years in Russia were accepted the number of regulatory acts in this field. Of course there is still where to grow, but the Republic of Sakha (Yakutia) also support digitalization and use digital technologies in many aspects of its' population lives. For the further development of the republic it is necessary to provide qualified personnel not only in IT but also in the economy sphere. Specialists in interdisciplinary areas of IT and Economics are highly competitive in the labor market of Yakutia and Russia. The article is devoted to the main elements of the digital economy development in the Republic of Sakha (Yakutia).

Keywords: The digital economy, the Republic of Sakha (Yakutia), digital technologies, North-Eastern Federal University, IT sphere.

I. Introduction

One of the priorities of economic policy in Russia has been the development of the digital economy. The digitalization of the economy began to actively develop from January 2015 after the Davos Forum, which focused on the development of the digital economy in Eastern Europe. After this, the World Economic Forum's Russia Council launched the development of the Digital Russia project. The goal of this project was the idea of changing Russian society with the help of digital technologies.

Russian Presidential Address to the Federal Assembly of December 1, 2016 gives the following definition: digital economy is "not a separate industry, but a way of life, a new basis for the development of the system of government, economy, business, social sphere, the issue of national security and independence" The transition to a digital economy implies "an unprecedented scale transformation, encompassing all spheres of society, without exception, affecting every citizen."

In the Russia digital economy report of 2018 it is written that "the ongoing Russian government commitment to digital transformation as a national priority, if complemented by effective policies across key economic sectors and a results-oriented focus on implementation, will enable the country to join the world's digital transformation leaders and position it for a technological breakthrough and the achievement of the economic and social benefits it implies."

II. Russia's digital economy program

The potential of digitalization creates the prerequisites for the competitive advantages of states and businesses both nationally and globally. By 2045, more than 100 billion devices will be connected to the Internet around the world. These will be mobile and portable devices, medical devices, industrial sensors, cars, clothes, etc.

July 28, 2017 by order of the Government of the Russian Federation No. 1632-r, the Digital Economy of the Russian Federation program was adopted, which is aimed at creating conditions for the development of a knowledge society in the Russian Federation, improving the welfare and quality of life of citizens of our country by increasing the availability and quality of goods and services produced in the digital economy using modern digital technologies, raising awareness and digital literacy, improving the availability and quality of public services for citizens, as well as security both domestically and abroad.

The objectives of the program are:

- creating an ecosystem of the digital economy of the Russian Federation, in which data in digital form is a key factor in production in all areas of socio-economic activity;
- creating conditions for the development of high-tech businesses;
- increasing competitiveness in the global market of the economy of the Russian Federation.

The digital economy is represented by 3 levels that affect the lives of citizens and society:

- markets and sectors of the economy where interact suppliers and consumers of goods, works and services;
- platforms and technologies where competencies for areas of activity are formed;
- an environment that creates the conditions for the development of platforms and technologies and the effective interaction of market entities and economic sectors and covers regulation, information infrastructure, human resources and information security.

The main digital technologies included in the Project are:

- Big data;
- Neurotechnologies and artificial intelligence;

- Distributed ledger systems;
- Quantum technologies;
- New production technologies;
- Industrial Internet;
- Components of robotics;
- Wireless technologies;
- Technologies of virtual and additional realities.

On July 28, 2017, the Digital Economy of the Russian Federation Program was adopted. The direction of "Digital Economy" involves the development of high-tech businesses in 5 areas:

1) Personnel and Education

Improvement of the education system, which should provide the digital economy with competent personnel. Transformation of the labor market.

2) Information Infrastructure

The development of communication networks, the development of a system of Russian data centers, the introduction of digital data processing platforms to meet the needs of citizens, business and government.

3) Information Security

Providing protection of the individual, society and the state from internal and external information threats, which ensures the realization of constitutional rights and freedoms of man and citizen, decent quality and standard of living, sovereignty and sustainable socio-economic development of the Russian Federation.

4) Formation of research competencies and technological background

Creation of a support system for search and applied research in the field of digital economy (research infrastructure of digital platforms), ensuring technological independence and national security in each of the areas of cross-cutting digital technologies that are globally competitive.

5) Regulation

Formation of a new regular environment, providing a favorable legal regime for the emergence and development of modern technologies, as well as for the implementation of economic security associated with their use.

Full digitization of the economy means:

- High-speed Internet networks connection for everyone;
- Digital platforms: state digital platforms are a digital ecosystem, a technological environment with an API that provides services that managing life situations of citizens, as well as a platform where government contracts are formed with steak holders receiving government services;
- Platform companies are one of the basic elements of the new economy.

A significant part of the document is the roadmap for the implementation of the Program. For each sphere there are goals, deadlines for the periods for 2018, 2020 and 2024. Each direction has a list of expected results.

In the area of "Regulation," it is planned to form a center of competencies that will provide monitoring and legal regulation of the digital economy.

Competency models will be developed in the area of "Personnel and Education," which contribute to the effective work of society, the labor market, business and education in the digital economy. Specialized venture fund will be created to support promising educational projects. Also financial support will be provided for teachers and organizations that work with talented youth. Educational organizations should use distance technologies and various forms and types of e-learning.

In the area of "Formation of research competencies and technological background" in the field of modern technologies, it is planned to create mechanisms to support the training of specialists capable of conducting world-class research. This refers to the provision of research leave, compensation of salaries, education abroad. By 2024, at least 500 specialists must undergo such training and return to Russia.

In the area of "Information Security," special attention is paid to information sovereignty (control over the Russian segment of the Internet), the fight against unlawful actions and import substitution. At all facilities of the information infrastructure, by 2024, the use of domestic equipment should be ensured. The share of domestic enterprises using the Russian payment system should be 90%, against 25% at present.

Digital economy offers great opportunities for the development of public administration system:

- minimization of the corruption;
- tax optimization;
- provision of public services through a united digital platform.

The state should strive to create favorable conditions for increasing the competitiveness of the national digital environment with the aim of attracting foreign entrepreneurs to the Russian digital economy through the provision of preferential financing conditions, assistance in introducing innovative developments, and providing grants for talented entrepreneurs.

III. Digital economy in Republic of Sakha (Yakutia)

3.1. Yakutia's efforts

Republic of Sakha (Yakutia) is actively involving into Russian digital transformation. 6 years ago Yakutsk (the capital of Yakutia) among the first cities in Russia started to implement "Smart city" projects. As a result of national project "Digital Economy" infrastructure of the Yakutsk must be combined into united system and the city must become comfortable and safe for all the citizens. Currently, the Republic of Sakha (Yakutia) has all the prerequisites for the development of the digital economy. First of all, one of the most important factors in the implementation of the project is human potential. The republic is characterized by a high proportion of young specialists who are able to quickly integrate and master new technologies.

In 2019, Yakutia was among the five regions of Russia for the pilot launch of the educational digital certificate system along with Bashkortostan, Tatarstan, Rostov and Tula regions. In five regions of the country, the first results of testing the model for providing personal digital certificates as part of the federal project "Personnel for the Digital Economy" of the national program "Digital Economy of the Russian Federation" were summed up. According to the results of the first stage of the project, 1000 residents of Yakutia with secondary or higher professional education became the owners of personal digital certificates.

Today, Yakutia has a full range of development institutions: Advanced Development Zone, Technopark, Venture Capital Fund, Investment Development Agency, Yakutia Development Corporation, IT-park and many others. There are proper conditions for training specialists in the field of IT-technologies in Yakutia.

The digital economy is used in the Republic of Sakha (Yakutia) in the following areas: medicine, education, connections, banking. One of the problems is the limited infrastructure in the northern regions.

Currently, in Yakutia, for the development of the digital economy, it is necessary to prepare a regulatory framework, systematize directions, develop and approve a roadmap. Great attention is attached to the preparation of the legal framework for 2018-2019. In 2017, 27 bills were decided at the federal level. And in 2019 - 26 bills will be decided. This work will be carried out in all regions of the Russian Federation.

In Yakutia is built the infrastructure for the provision of services and the execution of state and municipal functions in electronic form (total of 456 services are provided in electronic form). The proportion of citizens who use public and municipal services is 46.2% of the republic's population older than 14 years, while in Russia it is 64.3%. Among the regions of the Russian Federation, Yakutia ranks 38th place.

There is confidence that the Internet will develop with new megaprojects. The Internet is tied to large energy sites. All fiber lines go along the largest power lines, gas pipeline or oil pipeline. At the end of 2017, 5583 km of fiber-optic communication lines were built in Yakutia. 93 localities connected to the fiber-optic communication link, which is 69% of the population.

At the same time in Yakutia there are areas where fiber optic communication link (FOCL) coverage is 100%. For example, during 2015-2017 FOCL are connected to 23 settlements of the Megino-Kangalassky district. In 2019-2020 FOCL will be connected to settlements of Verkhnevilyuisky, Vilyuisky, Gorny districts, which lie along the federal highway "Vilyui."

During 2019, more than 1,600 km of fiber-optic lines were built in the republic; more than 50 settlements were connected; 318 social objects were connected to the Internet in all regions of the republic, of which 218 were connected via fiber optic. According to the latest news FOCL will cover the Arctic zone of Yakutia, particularly the area of Udachniy – Kharyyalah – Olenek by the end of 2020.

Experts believe that the rate of advent of innovative technologies in the economy and the growth of "creative industries" depend on the level of digital literacy of the population.

In the Russian Federation from October 1 to October 27, 2018 a trial population census was conducted, in which every citizen of the country who received an account on the state services portal (Gosuslugi) could take part. In the Republic of Sakha (Yakutia), a trial population census was conducted on the territory of the Khangalassky municipal district. The census was carried out via the Internet or on paper or electronic questionnaires on tablet computers or smartphones. Such census made it possible to determine the population's need for kindergartens, schools, housing, to determine the age and occupational structure of the population, the level of migration, etc., which makes it possible to refine the work of municipal and city authorities.

From October 1 to October 25, 2020, will be conducted the All-Russian Population Census. Innovation of upcoming Population Census - citizens of the Russian Federation will be able to independently pass it by filling out census forms on the State service portal "Gosuslugi." This kind of census will be applied for the first time in Russia. In addition, the census can be taken at special stationary sites, which will be open at the multifunctional centers (MFC).

3.2. Structures supporting the work of the digital economy in Yakutia

1) Brain - DPC - Data Processing Center, part of the state institution "Information Center." Here are the servers that store the information of all government sites. The data center is a strategic object.

2) Cerebral vessels - RCIT, or the Republican Center for Information and Communication Technologies. Here are combined all the "wires" for the state authorities, municipalities and budgetary processes of the Ministry of Finance of Yakutia. In contrast to the Data Processing

Center (sites for users), RCIT provides internal servers for state bodies: salary payments to public sector employee, unemployment benefits and social benefits, provision of Far Eastern hectare, the work of the MFC, Registry Office, Justices of the Peace, and the very important – State Automated System "Vybory," the work of election campaigns.

3) Eyes and ears - TCTRB or State Unitary Enterprise "Technical Center for Television and Radio Broadcasting." In addition to radio and television, provides the Internet (wired and via satellite). Internet for private houses and by the federal program - free Wi-Fi in public places to enter the portal of public services (in hospitals, administrations of districts).

4) Hands - IT park. Creating a digital economy itself will be a new pro-state structure - IT-park. Residents of the IT-park will create computer programs, applications for mobile devices and software, which in the future will be in use not only in the markets of the Far East and Central Russia, but also will have access to foreign markets.

Digital economy is developing in Yakutia in the sphere of training of specialists. Schools of Yakutia are switching to electronic educational literature, increasing informational and communicative competence of teachers, testing the educational portal "Russian Electronic School." In 2018-2022 schools of the republic will work on the concept of e-education development in Yakutia, in the system of secondary vocational education, the implementation of the Russian priority project "Modern Digital Educational Environment" will start.

Higher education in Yakutia should also be connected to the training of specialists in IT sphere. North-Eastern Federal University is planning to increase target reception of the students majoring in IT in 2020. Right now there are studying mostly students from Yakutia, but new rector Anatoly Nikolaev suppose that increase in IT majors will attract students from other cities of Far North of the Russian Federation.

Specialists in IT sphere are highly demanded in Russia and particularly in Yakutia. There are a lot of opportunities for the students majoring in IT, including internships in IT companies and foreign universities of Asia and Europe. The Institute of Mathematics and Informatics of the North-Eastern Federal University provide wide range of programs for future programmers and information scientists. Along with that there is also program that educates future IT-economists. In Yakutia there are a lot of job offers for the specialists in this area and according to the Minister of Innovations, Digital development and Info-communicational technologies Anatoly Semenov by 2032 there will be 10 000 high-paying jobs in Yakutia. Today Yakutian companies generate 70% of IT service export in Far North area of Russia.

In addition to IT sphere it is necessary to provide the region with specialists in the digital economy, first of all, the Institute of Finance and Economics of the M.K. Ammosov North-Eastern Federal University has proposed training of professionals who meet the requirements of the digital work environment and the modern knowledge society, as well as the global digital space. This is the inclusion of disciplines in electronic business in all bachelor degree programs of the Institute Finance and Economics:

- Network Economy;
- The Basics of Electronic Business;
- Internet Marketing;
- E-Commerce;
- International Economic Relations;
- International Business.

It is necessary to open educational program "Trading," with major "Electronic Commerce," to open the undergraduate program "Internet (digital) marketing." And consider the possibility of opening such new of undergraduate programs as "Business analytics and statistics," "Stock markets and technologies."

Today, technical or economic knowledge alone is not enough. A promising and highly demanded on the market direction of training specialists is the bachelor's and master's degree programs "Business Informatics," the "Electronic Business" profile. The program is supposed to implement in conjunction with the Institute of Mathematics and Informatics.

Since 2019 in our University is implementing master programs in convergent sciences. The initiator of the project was the NEFU former rector Evgenia Mikhailova. This project includes three areas of training: Physics, Economics, and Cultural Studies.

Upcoming specialists will have to work to bridge the gap between academic research, practice and business, because some of classes will be common for all students. At present, the period from the idea to its entry into the market in Russia is longer than in other countries. Therefore, the soonest implementation and use of ideas will help to improve the quality of life. This project also includes several disciplines in the digital economy: International Digital Law, Digital Marketing.

The goal of the program "Convergence: Business Management in the Digital Economy" is to deepen students' understanding of the features of the functioning of economic entities in a digital economy; to introduce them new trends in the field of IT technologies; to instill the skills of making sound economic decisions in the conditions of digital transformation. The training is based on a project-oriented approach using the methods of mathematical modeling, analysis and visualization of big data, case studies, and group work. The program includes relevant disciplines such as: "Digital Transformation of Organization," "Digital Marketing," "IT Law," "Intellectual Property," "Internet Entrepreneurship," "Consumer Psychology," "International Digital Law," etc.

In a highly competitive and cross-border digital economy a key success factor is not a technology, but new models for managing technology and data, allowing rapid respond and modeling of future challenges and problems for states, business and civil society.

IV. Conclusion

As a result of the introduction of new technologies, transaction costs are expected to decrease for individual economic units and, in general, for the entire economic system. Experts believe that the development of the digital economy in Russia will increase GDP by 19-34%, in China - by 22% by 2025. If we recall the thesis of Kenneth Joseph Arrow that "transaction costs are the costs of managing the economic system," then saving these costs takes up a significant part of the growth due to the introduction of new technologies. Thus, the digital economy today covers almost all countries. The countries of the European Union most advanced in this direction: Great Britain, Germany, Denmark, France, and Sweden.

Over the next five years, it is planned to cover the entire educational system of Yakutia with a digital economy. Digitalization will cover not only the web-sites of all schools, but also the training of directors and employees of educational departments. Three centers of digital education should be opened (in the format of an IT club) with coverage for 1.2 thousand children. Although many areas are characterized by low speed Internet in 2019 the digitalization process has begun in 15 schools and 2 colleges of the republic, which have fiber optics.

In the Republic of Sakha (Yakutia) we have the "Network City" system, modules with which pupils can study during days off due to cold weather. Through the state services portal "Gosuslugi" the population can choose a school for their children and register them in it, as well as in kindergartens and summer camps. Further development in the republic is associated with competitive selection for subsidies for the work of digital education centers, which will be held from July 1 to August 1 annually. Great expectations are associated with the launch on of the federal information service platform, which will determine the work and its final results. For its successful operation, it is necessary to connect the Internet at a speed of 100 megabits per second in cities and 50 megabits per second in rural areas.

In the Republic of Sakha (Yakutia), it is planned to train foreign citizens in secondary and higher education programs. This is the International Summer and Winter Schools of Creative Industries (IT, design, art, etc.) in collaboration with the British School of Design, where the digital economy will find its application.

References

1. The program "Digital Economy of the Russian Federation." URL: http://d-russia.ru/wp-content/uploads/2017/05/programmaCE.pdf.
2. "Russia Digital Economy Report" September 2018 by World Bank Group URL:http://documents.worldbank.org/curated/en/860291539115402187/pdf/Competing-in-the-Digital-Age-Policy-Implications-for-the-Russian-Federation-Russia-Digital-Economy-

Report.pdf

3. The state program of the Russian Federation "Information Society (2011-2020)": Decree of the Government of the Russian Federation of April 15, 2014 No. 313
4. Veduta E.N., Dzhakubova T.N. Big Data and Economic Cybernetics // Public Administration. Electronic Bulletin. 2017. №63 P.43-66. : http: //http//e-joournal.spa.msu.ru/vestnik/item/63_2017veduta_dzhakubova.htm.
5. Castells, M. The Information Age: Economy, Society and Culture: Translated from English by O.I. Shkaratan M .: SU-HSE, 2000.
6. Brendeleva E.A., Goncharov Yu.A., Kolomeytseva A.A., Maksakova M.A., Mukhamadieva D.N., Safronchuk M.V., Stolbov M.I., Strelets I.A. The basis of the digital economy: schoolbook / team of authors; under the editorship of M.I. Stolbova, E.A. Brendeleva.-Moscow.: SCIENTIFIC LIBRARY Publishing House, 2018.-238c.
7. Review of regional periodicals.

RUSSIAN EAST ARCTIC STUDIES

Proceedings of the International Scientific and Practice Conference

Prof. Bongchul Kim at HUFS
Prof. Larisa Pisareva at NEFU

First Printed	8 January, 2021
First Published	15 January, 2021
Director	Seongwoo Yun
Executive Contents Creator	Sunho Shin
Contents Creator	Keunyoung Lee
Designer	Seunghyeon Ko
Published by	HANKUK UNIVERSITY OF FOREIGN STUDIES KNOWLEDGE CONTENTS & PRESS 107, Imun-ro, Dongdaemun-gu, Seoul 02450, Korea Tel.) 82-2-2173-2497 Fax.) 82-2-2173-3363 E-mail) press@hufs.ac.kr Online) http://press.hufs.ac.kr
Printed by	Twinbell Media Tel.) 82-2-2088-1810
ISBN	979-11-5901-838-1 [93960]
Price	20,000 Won